D0801786

An Invisible Country

An Invisible Country

STEPHAN WACKWITZ

Translated by Stephen Lehmann

Foreword by Wendy Lesser

PAUL DRY BOOKS
Philadelphia 2005

First Paul Dry Books Edition, 2005

Paul Dry Books, Inc.
Philadelphia, Pennsylvania
www.pauldrybooks.com

Translation copyright © 2005 Paul Dry Books, Inc.
Foreword copyright © 2005 Wendy Lesser
Copyright © 2003 S. Fischer Verlag GmbH, Frankfurt am Main

The publication of this work was supported by a grant from the Goethe-Institut.

Text type: Meridien
Display type: Novarese
Composed by P. M. Gordon Associates, Inc.
Designed by Adrianne Onderdonk Dudden

1 3 5 7 9 8 6 4 2
Printed in the United States of America

Library of Congress Cataloging-in-Publication Data
Wackwitz, Stephan.
  [Unsichtbares Land. English]
  An invisible country / Stephan Wackwitz ; translated by Stephen Lehmann.
—1st Paul Dry Books ed.
        p. cm.
  ISBN 1-58988-022-6 (alk. paper)
  1. Wackwitz, Stephan. 2. Authors, German—20th century—Biography.
3. Wackwitz, Andreas. 4. Wackwitz family. 5. Germany—History—
20th century—Biography. I. Lehmann, Stephen. II. Title.
  PT2685.A373Z4713 2005
  834'.92—dc22

                                                    2005003542

ISBN 1-58988-022-6

Contents

Foreword

I first heard of Stephan Wackwitz in the fall of 1989, when John Berger—a longtime consulting editor to *The Threepenny Review*, but better known to the wider world as an eminent writer, art critic, and filmmaker—told me about an article Wackwitz had written in German on the musician Tom Waits. At the time I knew no German, and very little about Germany: if you had asked me to free-associate on the subject, I would have come up with Adolf Hitler first and possibly Rainer Werner Fassbinder as a distant second. I suspect that most Americans of my age (born in 1952), ethnicity (Jewish), and education (good) would have had similarly limited associations. My trust in John Berger, however, trumped my ignorance about modern German culture, and I agreed to look at the piece.

It arrived in a rough English translation, accompanied by its German original, but even the roughness could not disguise the virtues of the essay—as a piece of criticism that was also social commentary, and as a piece of writing that effectively conveyed the personality of its author as well as its subject. I can still, to this day, remember the enormously satisfying process of editing that essay for its English-language debut. For the whole of one evening, extending late into the night, I sat at my dining-room table, a German-English dictionary by my side, and gradually smoothed out every sentence. Years later, when I was to find myself in Berlin, surrounded by and infatuated with German, I traced my instantaneous love for the language back to that singular experience of grappling with Wackwitz's sentences.

Now that I have read Stephen Lehmann's elegant translation of *An Invisible Country*, I understand that this was no mere coincidence. It turns out that, of all possible guides to the contemporary German sensibility, Wackwitz is probably the best qualified to be mine.

We are, in some ways, mirror images of each other, exactly the same age, postwar babies from opposite sides of the unspeakable event that binds our two cultures together. (For the Holocaust has joined the Germans to the Jews as permanently as its perpetrators once hoped to keep them apart: you cannot be a thinking German these days without defining yourself in relation to the Jews, and vice versa.) Wackwitz left Germany at the age of thirty and has since then lived almost permanently abroad—first in England, later in Japan, now in Poland—whereas I stuck close to my native California ground and only visited Germany for the first time at the age of fifty-one. Our lives are curiously interconnected nonetheless. Reading this strange, complicated memoir of his, I was startled to learn that he has an aunt on Euclid Avenue, a few short blocks away from my Berkeley house. Even that American aunt, however, though she has been here for decades, turns out to be in many ways a citizen of the "invisible country" inhabited by the German Wackwitzes; the fate is apparently not one that can be escaped just by emigrating.

An Invisible Country is actually three or four books folded into one—not folded neatly like paper or cloth, but folded as a marble cake batter is, with wide swaths of chocolate meandering here and there through the vanilla. There is the story of Stephan Wackwitz's own life, and then there is the parallel but in some ways opposite story of his grandfather's life, rendered through the memoir that Pastor Wackwitz wrote in the 1950s, 60s, and 70s after he had returned from his mission to Africa, and long after he had left his parish in Poland, just outside Auschwitz. And then (as this last-mentioned name will suggest to even the most casual reader) there is that other history, not just familial and personal, but national and infamous.

Germans are a history-minded people. They love to keep track of how far back their family goes in a single location, who inhabited what house for centuries, things like that. When I visited Lübeck, the hometown Thomas Mann immortalized in *Buddenbrooks,* I ate in a restaurant that had once been a private house, and the menu came with a list of all the people who had occupied that house from 1284 up to the present. Wackwitz himself can trace his own family back to 1402. This kind of unbroken record is virtually unheard-of among Americans. For us, time is a series of unconnected plateaus, brief historical high points that are surrounded on either side by unfathomable abysses. We cannot help but admire a culture that keeps such a close watch on its past; we also cannot help fearing it. Both responses are reasonable.

Early on in *An Invisible Country,* Stephan Wackwitz brings up a "famous story" by Johann Peter Hebel, about an eighteenth-century man who dies in a mining accident just before his marriage, is mummified by the surrounding chemicals, and then gets unearthed fifty years later, still youthful-looking and fully preserved. A strikingly similar image ends the first of the four tales in W. G. Sebald's *The Emigrants,* only this time the young man falls into an alpine glacier in the summer of 1914 and reappears, externally unchanged, after seventy-two years have passed. "And so they are ever returning to us, the dead," says Sebald, whose book—in this respect very much like Wackwitz's—is an oblique commentary on Germany's relationship to the Holocaust. For both writers, the story of the well-preserved young man has a poignance that we who are not German can only begin to imagine. To cheat time by embracing death is a Faustian bargain of the first order. But also, for a culture that so values historical continuity, there is the fearfulness of that gap in time (a gap not unlike the period 1933 to 1945, which is represented in at least one piece of German public art simply by a blank, black rectangle). The standard American analogy is the tale of Rip Van Winkel, who slept through the major events of his lifetime, only to come back and find everything altered. But the characters in Wackwitz's and Sebald's tales do not wake up; they remain oblivious to the changes that have occurred, and instead it is their own inalterability which strikes bystanders as ghostlike. These *revenants* pointedly recall, through their artificially preserved innocence, everything that has been lost in the meantime.

Wackwitz is both sharp and tender as an observer, both analytic and emotional. He understands how to use family stories in ways that will both move and horrify us, and he understands how to use himself as an element in those stories. He gives us his grandfather's writing, and then he gives us his own perspective on that writing—most notably in the fascinating episode of the African cobra, a story that I do not want to give away, and that in any case I could not render with the utter delicacy, the Freudian-tinged but completely undogmatic intelligence, with which Wackwitz handles it. He also conveys, with the intensity of a dream (and often, in fact, *through* dreams, which he introduces quite skillfully), the uncanny power that certain places can hold over us. He makes us understand why the English word *wanderlust* harks immediately back to its German roots, and why the German word *Heimat* suggests more than either "home" or "home-land." Most of all, he allows us to experience—vicariously, imperfectly, but nonetheless deeply—the strange situation of the contemporary German.

Even the impulsive decision to leave Germany and seek out a new life turns out, at the end, to be Wackwitz's way of acting out his German destiny. Or, as he puts it:

> When a person leaves the life he knows and sets out for the unknown—which has to be better than death, what-ever happens—it may be the right decision, or one that is pleasurable, or even the only decision possible. This was the tradition of my ancestors, and it was completely consistent with, and perhaps even secretly waiting for, the ideology and the actions of the Nazis. The dreams and fantasies so violently released during Hitler's climb to power became stronger than caution, reason, a sense of responsibility, or conscience. . . . Perhaps one has to imag-ine them as a state-sanctioned and state-protected dream afflicting 60 million people simultaneously: the castle park of Laskowitz joining with millions of other childhood memories of infinity, and suddenly stretching from the

Atlantic to the Urals. Once exposed, such megalomanic fantasies are buried in the shame they have left in their wake.

Stephan Wackwitz may be writing primarily about his culture, but we are free to glean our own meanings from what he has to say. That is, the Germans are not the only people about whom one might observe that their most appealing traits are also their most dangerous ones. What would we Americans be, for instance, without our unquenchable optimism, our boundless energy? And yet where are these qualities leading us at the moment? As in the dark Germanic fairy-tales with which it has affinities, *An Invisible Country* holds up a tarnished, shadowy, ghost-ridden mirror into which, if we are wise, we might well be afraid to look.

Wendy Lesser

TRANSLATOR'S NOTE: My thanks go to Paul Farber and Elizabeth Lewis for their invaluable help in improving the manuscript on its way to publication. I would also like to thank Stephan Wackwitz for his patient participation in what became a collaborative effort—for good-naturedly answering endless questions, as well as adding some sentences that were not in the original and authorizing the deletion of occasional passages for the sake of a clearer translation.

Stephen Lehmann

An Invisible Country

1 Ghosts

Throughout the nineteenth and well into the twentieth century, ghosts abounded in the area around the old Galician capital of Auschwitz. It was as if the demons who were to be granted their historic opportunity in that remote corner of the former Dual Monarchy had been lying in wait since the end of the Middle Ages, lurking in the trees, ponds, villages, and parsonages of the Duchy and the surrounding estates. For centuries Poles, Germans, and Jews came from all over, bringing their tales and their ghosts to the marshy, birch-covered hill country at the upper reaches of the Vistula River. In the period between the two world wars, the dread of doubles, specters, and poltergeists was still as alive and commonplace in the Austrian-Prussian-Polish province as were the tales of the Mongolian invasion of the thirteenth century and the Swedish atrocities of the seventeenth.

As late as the 1930s, people talked of weird creatures that appeared during the nights of Advent on the so-called "Jews Meadows" of nearby Lobnitz, or of spectral mountains and forests near Bielitz into which people were lured by will-o'-

the-wisps, never to emerge again. Locals spoke to one another of ghostly winds, night hunters, bush women, sprites, and noontime spirits, or of spooky candles in Old-Bielitz that "came slowly down the path through the field toward the house and into the room through locked windows. My grandmother and great-grandmother saw them with their own eyes. And when all the many lights had entered the room, the lamp went out. Then the candles suddenly disappeared, and the room was dark. Both women were afraid and knew: This means something. And, indeed, my great-grandfather died soon afterwards."

It is clear that for my father, who was born in 1922 in an area that was still semi-medieval—a few kilometers further north, it was already highly industrialized—some of these ghosts were part of the family. "Late in the evening, the maids from the Anhalt parsonage would see a pastor in his cassock—he had died long before—sitting in front of the house, reading a big book. At midnight there would often be a sound of something creeping through the house, and unseen hands would turn the handle of the clothes wringer in the vestibule. Who did it and who the pastor was . . . no one knew." My grandfather had described the parsonage ghost of Anhalt in his contribution to Alfred Karasek-Langer and Elfriede Strzygowski's *The Tales of the Beskid-Germans* (published in 1931 in Plauen in a mustard-yellow binding with clumsy, ghoulish ink drawings). My grandfather served as pastor of the German congregation in the village of Anhalt, barely ten kilometers north of Auschwitz, from 1921— by then it was part of Poland—until 1933. I never asked my grandfather whether he had ever heard the clothes wringer in the vestibule, or whether he, himself, had seen the ghostly pastor sitting in front of the parsonage. But my father, his oldest son, assures me in all seriousness that as a child he used to hear mysterious steps and a ghostly breathing at night in the large, late-baroque house—up through the interwar years the highest and most imposing house in that part of the country. There the nights of the 1920s must have been as still as they were in 1770, the year the colony of Anhalt was founded at the southern edge of Frederick II's Prussian empire.

Today, the parsonage of Anhalt is situated on a busy road that connects the Teschen-Kattowitz highway to the Auschwitz memorials. When my father was young, months would go by without a car passing through the area. To the north, the Upper Silesian industrial zone had pushed its last outposts to the far side of the nearby hills. And to the south lay a sleepy, largely Jewish Galician country town which a few years later would become a symbol of the twentieth century. When the camps were in operation, one would be able to see the factories of Auschwitz and Monowitz from the hill of the neighboring town. But above all, when the wind blew from that direction, one smelled them.

During his childhood here, he said, it stank everywhere, sometimes almost unbearably, of burnt hair. And if the weather was right and you forgot to close the windows, a kind of fatty-slimy soot settled on the furniture, the dishes, and the floor, and got stuck in your hair. This is what the caretaker of the Protestant church of Anhalt/Holdunów told me on a spring day in 1999, when he showed me the Anhalt parsonage and drove with me to Pless and then the few kilometers to Auschwitz. When they were children, he said, they climbed the nearby hill and saw the smoke rising in the distance. I asked him what they made of it. "It was people being burnt," said the old man in the passenger seat, watching my reaction from the corner of his eyes.

My grandmother spoke again and again of family life in Anhalt. She told of the garden, in which my father and his siblings once dug a deep hole trying to reach the burning core of the earth. Of skating in the hard winters. And sometimes, when we asked her, of that ghost in the parsonage. But only when I came to Anhalt myself did I understand where this place actually was. As if they were ghosts themselves, my grandparents, my aunts, my uncle, and my father had gone down a narrow corridor through a time and a place that meant something entirely different to them than to almost every other person on earth. When they arrived, nothing remarkable had yet happened there. And when the heart of darkness opened, they had already left. They never spoke about the fact that the scene of their childhood and the site of the century's greatest crime were separated by nothing more than a longish walk and barely a decade. Perhaps they refused to think about it. Everyone is entitled to a childhood free of history. But standing in the overgrown garden behind the former parsonage of Holdunów, the son and nephew of those children photographed so long ago in their high boots, lace-trimmed clothes, and short trousers, I knew that the ghost of the parsonage of Anhalt lived on in my life, even if I had never seen it, just as the clothes wringer in the vestibule was turned by unseen hands. "Who did it, and who the pastor was . . . no one knew."

2 *An Unexpected Reappearance*

It was a strange letter that my father received by registered
mail on a spring day in 1993 at the door of his house on Lake
Constance. The return address was an office that, as I later
discovered, owed its founding to a most serious and reasonable international agreement. At first, however, and more
so as I continued to think about the peculiar story that my
father had told me on the phone that same day, the existence of this agency struck me as fictional, almost like a fairy
tale. As if Jorge Luis Borges or Danilo Kiš had invented the
"Berlin Office for Notification of the Relatives of Former Soldiers of the German Army"—an office that on official sta-
tionery matter-of-factly informed my father that in the
course of the decades-long processing of the erstwhile belongings of German ex-prisoners of war they had come upon
an object that was his. And this object, in compliance with
the applicable rules and regulations, was now to be returned
to him. The object in question was a camera; inside it was
film that apparently had been exposed.

September 1939—the German army had just marched into Poland—found my seventeen-year-old father, his parents, and four siblings aboard the steamer *Adolph Woermann* on their way from the territory that had been German Southwest Africa to Bremerhaven. The decrepit steamer was soon captured by a British cruiser, and my father was then interned for six years in Canada, sparing him the Russian campaign and probably his life. That he had been carrying a camera which was confiscated by the Royal Navy was a detail he had long since forgotten. For decades, it lay waiting in a brown cardboard box at the office in Berlin, in a brick and limestone building that had once been a factory. Its rooms were piled to the ceiling with cardboard boxes of this type, containing rings, letters, medals, photos, diaries, children's drawings, and garters owned by the dead. My father had been given the camera in Windhoek for his seventeenth birthday, and on a November day in 1939 on the high seas, more or less at the latitude of Saint Helena, he had handed it over to the authorities of the Royal Navy in exchange for a receipt now long lost. A lifetime had passed since that moment, and he had reached retirement without ever thinking of the camera again.

Fifty million people failed to return from World War II. But in 1993, the camera confiscated half a century earlier by a British naval officer, from a boy who thirteen years later was to become my father, was restored from the death-depot in Berlin to its elderly, gray-haired owner. "In the meantime, the city of Lisbon in Portugal was destroyed by an earthquake," wrote Johann Peter Hebel in his famous story about a man who was killed in an accident on the eve of his wedding to a young Swedish woman. Mummified in the vitriol of the Falun mines for fifty years, he remained young, "and the Seven Years War was fought, and the Emperor Francis I died, and the Order of the Jesuits was banned and Poland was divided, and the Empress Maria Theresa died, and Struensee was executed, America became independent, and the united powers of France and Spain failed to conquer Gibraltar. The Turks held General Stein captive in Hungary's Veteran Caves, and the Emperor Joseph died, too. King Gustav of Sweden conquered Russian Finland, and the French Revolution and the long war began, and the Emperor Leopold II went to his grave as well. Napoleon conquered Prussia, and the English bombed Copenhagen, and the farmers sowed and reaped. The miller milled, the smiths hammered, and the miners dug for veins of metal in their subterranean workshop. In 1809 (shortly before or after Midsummer's Day), as the miners of Falun were connecting two shafts a good 300 cubits beneath the earth, out of the debris and iron vitriol they dug the body of the young man. His corpse, having been completely saturated in the ferrous sulfate, was perfectly preserved. The features of his face and his age were still utterly identifiable, as if he had died only an hour ago or had taken a short nap at work."

My father, availing himself of the opportunity presented by this peculiar occurrence and of his senior-citizen discount, decided to take a quick trip to Berlin. There he showed his passport, filled out the necessary forms, and was handed the camera. The woman responsible for this particular job said that she systematically processed each object entrusted to her—often they had some importance in relation to an inheritance or a pension or insurance: yellowed military or worker passbooks and the like. She followed the trail of its owner, she said, as long as there was any hope of returning it to the family of the deceased—or sometimes, as in this instance, to a prisoner of war who was still living. My father's camera had presented no difficulties. To locate the camera's owner, she had only to investigate the inscription "Wackwitz Windhuk" that had been cut with a knife into the glued-on piece of cardboard on the back of the camera case, look up our name in the Berlin phonebook, and call my uncle who was listed there. It wasn't, she said, always that easy.

The young miner in Hebel's story lay "undecayed and unchanged" in the dark earth while wars, revolutions, notorious fatalities and earthquakes, the seasons, and humanity's daily labors orbited around his immutability. And when the old woman who had once been engaged to the dead man recognized his youthful form ("more with delight and joy than pain," writes Hebel), all who were standing around them were gripped by sadness, and wept. With this camera that he was once again holding, my father had taken pictures in the final days before his departure from the Mandate of Southwest Africa, where his father, in the years after his time in Polish Upper Silesia, was once again pastor in a foreign country.

My father and I felt strangely moved as we talked on the phone, imagining how the film from 1939—perhaps it could still be developed—might have preserved a last glimpse, now fifty years old, of the monument of the "Rider of Southwest"; the picture of Christ Church and the parsonage in Windhoek; the faces of my father's fellow Boy Scouts, who had prepared a touching farewell at the train station for their seventeen-year-old leader, about to return forever to the mother country; the steel walls of the *Adolph Woermann,* high as a house, lying at the dock in Walvis Bay; the scenes of confusion and despair that followed soon afterwards, as the crew and passengers in lifeboats drifted on the high seas before the steamer sank. My father and I assumed that the man who was now in his eighth decade would be able to recognize the seventeen-year-old boy he once was. In the darkroom (we thought vaguely), he might discover a meaning that would be revealed to his old eyes after half a century: the first contours of those houses, monuments, and landscapes re-emerging in the weak red light. Without quite admitting it, for a moment we secretly hoped for illumination. Or at least for the appearance of a ghost.

The camera to which we rather unrealistically entrusted all this was a No. 1A Pocket Kodak, an extendable "spool-film folding camera" that was readily available from 1926 into the 1930s and was "made in USA by Eastman Kodak Company Rochester N.Y." This information was to be found on a small tin plate underneath the lens at the head of the accordion-like bellows made of a leathery elastic cardboard that could be extended on a rail inside the tin flap. One looked down into the viewfinder, adjusted the shutter speed and the aperture, and triggered the peculiarly final-sounding click with a little tin lever. Half a century ago these movements had preserved a few fractions of a second of the year war broke out. In fact, one can make these same motions to this day, since my father's camera survived the war and the decades afterwards without incurring the slightest damage.

Of course, the No. 1A Pocket Kodak cannot perform magic. In fact, it is not the least bit special. The Eastman Kodak Company manufactured and sold more than two hundred thousand of them, a success story from the early days of mass photography. It is now worth less than a hundred euros in an antique store or flea market. And when my father opened his rediscovered camera in the darkroom, he found that in the course of the darkness of that half-century in Berlin the film had decomposed, revealing only blackness such as reigns at the bottom of the sea. Unlike tragedies and novels, the film provided no dramatic moment of recognition, no photo in which the angel of history—invisible to the contemporaries of 1939—stands somewhere in the background on the deck of the *Adolph Woermann*. The silver-halogen on the gelatin film of the 1930s could not make time stand still. Unlike the iron vitriol of Falun, it could not effect a surprising historical twist of the kind recounted in Hebel's "calendar" story. Nevertheless, if in time I were to find meaning, then it would be in a manner much more complicated and problematic: not like the punch line of a classic anecdote, but as the invisible center of the confusing, hidden, and entwined entanglements of a *family romance*.

3 *Silence*

To the best of my recollection, my grandfather didn't speak to me more than two dozen times in his life, at least about anything more serious than "Would you pass the salt," or "The bathroom is free," or "Hey, pipe down." Outside the family, he was known as a man with something to say, known even for his charm and quick wit. But in his grand-children's presence he became mute—something I never un-derstood when I was a child. At the time, I told myself that since we were, after all, a family, the moment would come when somehow we would have to interact—perhaps at breakfast or after lunch or while drinking our afternoon cof-fee. We would do something in which even my father and my uncle and, of course, my grandfather would simply have to participate. Surely, I felt, it should be possible for them— for once—to say something. My grandmother, my mother, and my aunts seemed to have gotten used to the obdurate silence of the men of the family when in the company of their wives, children, and grandchildren, and they viewed it with amused indulgence. I could only react with something like panic. At an age at which children want nothing more fervently than to be completely normal, I felt it was not normal that the men never said anything. When I later began to sense the comical side of our family life, my grandfather's jittery desperation on our account had intensified into a kind of muteness. I was repeatedly shocked to discover that the man who spoke with such eloquence and vitality to random neighbors completely lost these qualities at breakfast or at the dinner table. I had to acknowledge that the man sitting across from me was not merely morose, he was barely able, in his role as head of the family, to summon the breath and vocal energy necessary to make himself understood.

When my grandfather spoke in the presence of us children—and strangely, also when he talked to my grandmother—he affected a pained squeak, as if pleading for mercy. As I grew into adulthood, I found this behavior not only increasingly irritating but truly unnerving. It's not supposed to be this way between close relatives, let alone between husband and wife, I thought. When I became interested in trying to speak to girls myself, my grandfather's tone with women seemed especially ridiculous to me. When we challenged him to communicate with us in a way that he interpreted as unreasonable (which didn't take much), he would sigh from the depths of his familial feebleness, "Please, just leave me alone." But even then, it dawned on me why it was only in the presence of the children that my grandfather became so irritated and flaccid. The more I thought about the despair that my sister, my cousins, and I provoked in him, the more clearly I understood that my grandfather's silence—like his occasional outbursts of anger toward us— was an accusation against the women. Without them, after all, we would not have been there. For some reason, my grandfather, unlike other adults, was not able to find it a good thing that we were so much younger than he. We promised him no future. We only depressed him. And if I was never really close enough to him to be lastingly worried about his nervous coldness and hardness, his rejection of us did sometimes preoccupy me. The sadness he expressed in the presence of his family was, I felt, a peculiar deviation that turned the natural order of things between children and adults on its head.

A few years later, I stood on the threshold of adulthood and had lost all interest in my grandfather's familial rigidity-attacks. I could not have cared less about his suffering on our account. Whatever he had to say, had he ever said anything, I no longer cared to know. I had gotten used to the idea that children and men apparently belong to different tribes that happen to inhabit the same territory; though not especially hostile, they regard each other watchfully and with a certain mutual mistrust. (The women formed a different group, also closed to us, but in a different way.) Not until the 1970s, when my older cousins became parents and their husbands would go on about their babies, playing with them, occasionally even changing their diapers and bathing them (at the time that seemed to me indescribably silly, but it also filled me with a diffused sense of envy)—only then did I realize that things could have been otherwise. (It was just such trivialities that signaled the end of the postwar period in Germany: families sometimes having Sunday lunch at a restaurant, women wearing skirts so short they might have been little girls, and men playing with children.) But my grandfather wanted nothing to do with me. Thus I was able to observe him, and I observed him closely and heartlessly. He

was, I finally decided when I was fourteen or fifteen, funny—
involuntarily funny.

I seized the opportunity to express this new awareness in
what turned out to be my first experience of literary success,
a school essay on "a description of a person." My topic was
my grandfather. I can remember I wrote that when he was
on holiday, "wearing a Hawaiian shirt on which all the won-
ders and horrors of the jungle are depicted" (a formulation
of which I was especially proud and that I remember to this
day), he demanded the same respect from the railroad official as he would have had he been clothed in his clerical garb
down to the cassock and Geneva bands. But then, there he
would be again, sitting helplessly at breakfast. He would
stretch his hand toward a desired dish, faintly shake a clump
of weakly drooping fingers, and emit a kind of whimper that
the initiated knew to interpret as "May I have some, too?"

When I was sixteen or seventeen and no longer really
needed or wanted to know, I finally figured out that my
grandfather was capable of more than silence and whimpering. I discovered that men's lives begin when the children
are in bed, just as dark creatures of legend doze through the
day's business in some remote place, coming to life only at
night. The nightly awakening followed a ritual. The table
was cleared, the women took the children away, the pleading whimpering ceased. Suffering modulated into good-
natured grunts: the moment of comfort had arrived. Still
sighing, but only for appearances, just (so to speak) for de-
cency's sake, my grandfather stood up, almost cheerfully. He
looked around at his sons. (I was now accepted into their
company, though only probationally, without the status of
full membership.) "How about it?" he asked in roguish col-
lusion. "Maybe a *vino* after all?"

Then, while complaining ironically about his sons having emptied his supply (inevitably mentioning the legend of the pelican who ripped open its own breast with its beak in order to feed its young), my grandfather, after another long and comfortably ritualized discussion about the selection he was going to make, brought the bottles in from the kitchen. And some of them were of extraordinary quality, though at the time, of course, it was wasted on me. Nevertheless, their content, together with the aroma of the cigars that everyone lit up, quickly transported me into a pleasant state of wooziness and heightened spirits. So this was what it was like to be an adult.

I no longer know the details of what actually happened in the course of those evenings. No doubt, given my status as apprentice, they sent me to bed after the first glass. All I remember is my grandfather's irritated weepiness quickly mutating into a kind of ironically simulated grumpiness. If we younger ones did everything right, he would move on to another phase, telling long stories and holding forth on world affairs and his earlier life, with monologues about Africa, Anhalt, Breslau, about the climbing of the Matterhorn and mountain hiking in the High Tatras—descriptions and observations that one was allowed to interrupt, if at all, only on cue or with helpful and encouraging questions. If my grandfather sensed a lack of enthusiasm on his listeners' part or if someone expressed a reservation that gave the slightest hint of incredulity, let alone criticism, he would quickly lapse into sullen silence and revert to his slack moodiness. The spell was broken, and his sons, as well as grandsons, had to go to bed.

The further we got into the 1960s and the more adult I became, the more often did such disruptions and interruptions occur. As time passed, it became ever clearer that it was his oldest grandson, especially, who increasingly troubled my grandfather—not only because of remarks I sometimes made, but mainly, I think, for the simple reason that my growing up went hand in hand with an insidious but unmistakable change in his sons and, above all, in the world beyond the family. My growing up spoiled his good mood and the fun he had gotten out of being in the company of other men. Most of his contemporaries had died long before, or he had lost touch with them (men with whom he could communicate without having to explain himself, wordlessly, or with a quotation, an allusion, a sarcastic or knowing glance, as my father and uncle—as my friends and I—spoke with one another). My grandfather came to need historical explanation in his own lifetime, while still, so to speak, alive and kicking. That he defended himself against his loneliness during these years by describing and explaining himself in detail to his family (and probably to himself) was only logical. Given our slow wits and recalcitrance, however, he did this not orally, but by means of an expansive, written, literary undertaking.

From the 1950s almost until his death, in the overbearing and depressed atmosphere of his dark study—redolent of cigars, books, and dust, on its floor the preserved leopard's pelt with wide-open jaws and brown glass eyes that had frightened me as a child—he wrote his memoirs for his children and grandchildren. No family gathering, no lavish family celebration, would pass without my grandfather's presenting another volume of this serialized autobiography. Typically it contained two to three hundred densely typed onionskin pages. Each of his five children received one copy. In almost a quarter of a century, a pile containing many hundreds of thousands of words accumulated in this manner. At the time, I regarded this as an eccentricity of my grandfather's as peculiar and embarrassing as his fits of nervous exhaustion at breakfast or his brightened loquaciousness over wine at night. Since then, I've come to understand that these writings were a belated example of the countless memoirs written and published in ridiculous (or uncanny) profusion for a time after the First World War. Not only Kaiser Wilhelm II himself, and his aides, but less eminent or indeed completely unknown Wilhelminians capped and recapitulated their lives in this fashion. My grandfather's densely typed pages tell the story of a life and a country that disappeared forever with the German army's invasion of Poland and the distant but nonetheless causally related sinking of the steamer *Adolph Woermann* in the South Atlantic. It is the story of a man who in 1939 was shipwrecked for the rest of his life, a man who had as little use for the country in which he lived as he had for his grandson.

After that first phone call from my father when I learned the history of the rediscovered camera, I wondered—in the office, under the shower, on my way to work, on my bicycle over the weekend—what the long-forgotten film in a No. 1A Pocket Kodak purchased around 1935 in the British Mandate of Southwest Africa might have shown, had the last pictures been preserved in this camera that had escaped the destruction of an entire country. Thinking about my father's Pocket Kodak hardened into an idée fixe, as if, on the solid ground of my own country and my own life, I could never tire of the sinking of the *Adolph Woermann* as I saw and painted it in my imagination. It was as if a secret about me had sunk, together with my grandparents' household goods, in the South Atlantic on that morning at the beginning of the Second World War. So one evening in 1999, I took the marbled green volume containing my grandfather's memories of South Africa from the little-used corner of the library where it had stood unread for decades. I found the passage quickly.

Our train left Windhoek at 1, on Sunday, the 20th of August. Many friends had come to shake our hands one more time. It was a classic train station farewell. They slipped us chocolate, cookies, cigars, fruit, a bottle of red wine from B., and other light refreshments for the journey. Holding their pennants, the Boy Scout troop "Captain von Erckert" and Gutschu's German youth group stood in formation beside the train, and the girls' friends, too, came in their scout uniforms. The children had also had their own goodbye-parties at school and in their scouting groups. As the train began to move, Gutschu clenched his teeth, Elisabeth threw herself onto her seat, crying aloud from the sorrow of parting, Beate sobbed along with her, tears ran down Mother's cheeks, and I wavered between laughter and tears.—Gutschu had recently become "completely scoutified," as I wrote home in June '39. "He is one of the seven group leaders in the Windhoek Squad and would rather stay here." And, indeed, possibly more than the other children, he left the best part of his childhood here in Southwest. Providing us with an honor guard, his friends drove in a car to the next station, Brakwater, which was a surprise even to him. We saw the car overtake the train on the Okahandja Road. When the train arrived in Brakwater, they were all standing in formation on the station platform, calling to us and singing. We had just enough time to give them some of our chocolate when the train began to pull out of the station. Once we were on board in Walvis Bay, just before our departure, Gutschu received a telegram from them.

When small, I often imagined how all the furniture, clothes, and books, the hunting trophies and toys from "Southwest," the dishes that my grandmother and the household help had taken so much time and trouble to wrap in newspaper and pack in wooden crates were lying at that moment in deep darkness on the cold sea bottom off the African coast. Everything would still be there, carefully stowed in the storeroom of the sunken *Adolph Woermann*. In the world we now inhabited, in which everything would proceed without these objects, we would never see any of them again. Yet they were as close to my grandparents and to my father as our breakfast dishes, the kitchen cupboard, and my toys were to me, as close as the framed print of the Annunciation from the Dahlem Art Museum that hung over my bed and that I looked at before going to sleep. At home, when my grandfather or an uncle or an aunt would find themselves looking in a distracted moment for a particular book or piece of furniture, we would be told that it had "gone down with the rest." It was as if, in those unconsidered moments, the adults secretly lived on the ocean floor.

But it wasn't only because my parents' earlier life lay in a time deep under the sea or under the rubble of bombed-out cities that the country in which I grew up seemed spectral. Children, for example, want to know dependably, to learn in school, how big their country is. But ours didn't seem to have proper borders like other countries. It ended in dotted, strangely unstable lines, in stretches of land to which one couldn't drive and which no one could really picture, despite the instructional films in geography—for example, the one about the Curonian Spit—that we were sometimes allowed to watch in school. (Pine trees in the ocean breeze; sand dunes; sunsets in black and white, over which showers of spots would rustle and crackle before the film ran out and the front spool was suddenly empty, spinning away. The curtains had to be opened, and despair sat like a guest of stone on the wooden bench next to me as class resumed.) Much of the dramatic loss of authority that school and country were to suffer in 1968 can be traced, it seems to me in retrospect, to just such screenings. It wasn't only that they never said anything at the breakfast table. They couldn't even give us reliable information about the size of our country.

Being searched for weapons, we were docked at Lobito for two days. Shortly before 7, I was on board again, and at 8 the boat was secretly unmoored. With soundless engines and very slowly, the maneuvering of the rudder difficult but masterfully done, we set off from the wharf. The Portuguese customs guard didn't want to leave, but was finally persuaded to get into a boat and was rowed back, while the soldiers guarding the shore ran back and forth in alarm. The Windhuk sailed with us—it, too, completely darkened. When we had left the bay behind us and made our way around the lighthouse, the Windhuk passed us at a distance of one or two nautical miles; we saw only the sea-lights on its wake. It sailed twice as fast as we did, and arrived happily in South America and later, if I remember correctly, in Murmansk. We looked back for a long time at the lights of Lobito and at the street lights on the long dune on which cars chased back and forth like a farewell illumination. We remained on deck far into the night engaged in very lively conversation. In the morning after breakfast, Captain Burfeind gave us more information: in the long run, the situation in Lobito would have become untenable, the provision of food increasingly difficult, the harbor offi-

cials less and less cooperative, so that in the end, unavoidably, we would have been interned in Angola, with its unhealthy climate. We had just enough fuel oil left to get us to South America, but a stationary boat consumes increasingly large quantities of fuel, and we had no prospect of its being replenished. And since the political conditions were more favorable in South America than in Angola, Burfeind decided to risk the journey. If it went well—and our prospects weren't entirely bad—we might be able to reach Germany by taking a northern route in the winter weather past Iceland and Norway. Fuel oil was obtainable in South America. But just in case, we should put our most essential belongings in order and get them packed, because if the enemy were to discover the ship, it would go down, and we would all have to get into the lifeboats.

Reading my grandfather's memoirs, I could never really understand why the Germans on the *Adolph Woermann* were so eager to get to Germany—and then to Stalingrad. In my father's place, I thought, I would rather have stayed in Lobito, in spite of the heat. Or I would have sought training in some sensible line of work in Buenos Aires, probably becoming a businessman. After the war, I would have returned occasionally to West Germany on business trips. I would have been a man of substance, perhaps shaking hands a few times with Borges or Gombrowicz at cocktail receptions, a man whose house would be graced in front by blossoming jacarandas, under foreign clouds, by the sea. But in 1939, my father knew nothing of Stalingrad and nothing of West Germany. He had imagined his future as an adult, heroic version of Boy Scout life and the country to which he was returning as a territory characterized by a still-undetermined expanse and magnificence, and with a firm grounding in reality. That's not the way things worked out. Boy and camera were lost in a limbo as opaque as an undeveloped film, like the span of time in which the face of a dead miner remains fixed in ferrous vitriol, like the eastern border of our country when I was a child.

The moon was waxing and the weather, as always in this part of the world, was beautiful. On November 21, soon after daybreak, a ship was sighted ahead of us. When we came on deck, we heard that our ship had reversed direction. The foreign ship was approaching us quickly, and by 9 or 10 it had caught up with us. It was the English steamer Weimarana.

The *Adolph Woermann* had been camouflaged as a Portuguese ship. But the English quickly realized what the foreign flag concealed.

When we first encountered the Weimarana, our luggage—three small suitcases, a laundry bag, a violin case—was ready, and the maneuvering of the lifeboats had been practiced ahead of time. The ocean was rougher than in the previous days, windforce 4, but otherwise the weather was good. No one among us panicked, none of the children cried.

The captain of the *Adolph Woermann*, Otto Burfeind, had already opened the bulkheads. Slowly the huge steamer, with its load of copper and vanadium (important for the war), together with the household goods of my grandparents (the furniture and the books, the clothes and the pictures, the kudu antlers, the preserved lion pelts, the toys), began to sink into the Atlantic.

It was November 22, this year's Day of Prayer and Repentance. When the lifeboats were in the water, we saw the English cruiser *Neptune* racing toward us at full speed. Appearing suddenly before us, it looked magnificent, and after almost thirty years I still remember that the sight of the sleek gray ship speeding toward us with the British battle flag waving—a red cross on a white field and the Union Jack canton—gave me a pleasure that was almost aesthetic. Our ship was flying the German flag again. To the English captain's demand: "Stop immediately!" we answered: "Ship sinking, we're getting into the lifeboats." In our boats lying next to the ship, we discussed the situation and awaited our orders. There was no surplus of seafaring expertise in our lifeboat; except for one or two sailors, we had but a few stewards and two musicians from the ship's band, one of whom was so seasick he couldn't move. The wind pushed the boats against the side of the ship where they were lifted and lowered by the waves. What would happen to us now? Then Dr. Lehfeld, a high-school teacher returning home from Sumatra, carefully opened his cigar case and offered me one of his cigars. I said, "Egad, Lehfeld, I will never forget you for this!" Calmly we lit our stogies and smoked at leisure. After some time, we were told to row our boats to the Weimarana. This was by no means easy, as our boat lacked a proper nautical command. Lehfeld and I rowed as best we could, and over valleys and ridges of waves we reached the Weimarana, which, however, contrary to all expectations, was in no way prepared to receive us on board.

Instead the cruiser *Neptune* delivered the German ship's crew to Plymouth and imprisonment. For seven years, until his twenty-fourth birthday, my father was kept alive and out of battle, first in the south of England, and then in Canada (". . . and the farmers sowed and reaped. The miller milled, and the smiths hammered, and the miners dug for veins of metal in their subterranean workshop").

I so wished that the seventeen-year-old Boy Scout with the camera in the lifeboat next to the sinking *Adolph Woermann* had taken a picture of the teacher Dr. Lehfeld and my grandfather smoking their Sumatras as they rocked on the Atlantic waves. A cigar on the high seas. These steely Wilhelminian nerves, this officer's stoicism, this Epicureanism shaped by the First World War—it would have been a souvenir of my grandfather that I gladly would have held onto. There is no picture I would rather place on my desk next to the one of my son than that of the two men—presumably Dr. Lehfeld, too, had been an officer in the First World War—watching their own shipwreck as smoking observers.

But there is no photo of this moment, no proof that it even happened. And perhaps it doesn't really matter, as my father and I decided when he phoned to tell me of the failed attempt to develop the 1939 roll of film. Nevertheless, since the return of the camera, I suddenly see with greater clarity the dead old man whom I've remembered for decades only as a whimper and a finger-shake. Now, for the first time, I can imagine something that had to do with his life: the bottle of red wine that his friend gave him for the journey; the sea-lanterns along the bow of the dark and silent sister-ship as it overtook the *Adolph Woermann;* the laughing and waving of the Boy Scouts in their car, passing the train on the Okahandja Road from Windhoek to Walvis Bay; the violin case on the deck next to the packed suitcases; and even the jacaranda bushes in front of my father's house in Buenos Aires—which, after all, existed only in my dreams.

From beginning to end, I have read the closely typed pages on onion-skin paper about our family's African history, just as I read the other volumes of my grandfather's memoirs: half a dozen notebooks in A4 format. Some are bound in marbled cardboard covers of various colors, others in the design of 1950s-style kitchen curtains. They accompanied me when I left Germany in the dismal winter days of 1999 to work for a few years about an hour's drive from the ghostly landscape—so well known to world history—where my father grew up. In my first months there, I read little else: one volume after the next, as if, after decades of silence and nervous indifference, a note left for me in a bottle in the South Atlantic in 1939 had, defying all probability, finally reached its goal.

What I learned in this way about my grandfather's own *family romance* surprised me and made me uneasy—especially because my life, in the meantime, has turned out much like that of a man whom (when he was still alive and I was young) I had wanted to avoid resembling as much as possible. There are more, and more important, parallels than that we both like smoking cigars and that grandson, like grandfather, practices his profession out of the country. The small, seemingly coincidental similarities, as well as the important ones that could not be mere coincidence, have come to pass despite my intentions. Sometimes during my reading, it seemed to me that over the past decades my life and the life of my grandfather had come to an understanding behind my back. Looking up from the yellowing onion-skin paper, I realize that it has taken almost half a century to figure this out. It was a moving, but ambiguous reunion. After decades, much of what my grandfather told of himself shocked and disgusted me, while some things filled me with a kind of despairing pride in him. Above all, however, one image has not left me: two men watching the disappearance of the lives they knew (and the disappearance of a world in which they required no explanation), not whimpering, but serene, almost cheerful, observing and smoking. It is as if my imagination and memory developed the photographs left for half a century in a cardboard box in Berlin. ("The features of his face and his age were still utterly identifiable, as if he had died only an hour ago or had taken a short nap at work.")

"A dream?" Vronsky repeated, and he suddenly remembered the peasant whom he'd seen in his dream. "Yes, a dream," she said. "I dreamt that I ran into my bedroom to get something, or to look for something. You know how dreams so often are," she said, "and there I saw something standing in the corner of the room . . ." "Oh, what nonsense! How can you believe in such a thing?" But she would not be interrupted. What she wanted to say was too important to her. "And this something turned around, and I saw that it was a small, gaunt peasant with a scraggly beard. I wanted to run away, but he bent over a sack and dug around in it with his hands." Her face expressed horror, and Vronsky, too, remembered his own dream with horror.   —Tolstoy, *Anna Karenina*

4 *Chameleon Years*

At no later than forty (so it is said), men and women become responsible for the way they look. As I study the pictures in our family album, it strikes me that even at seventy, my grandfather had the good looks of a man who for all his life never fundamentally doubted himself. Though he had lived through quite a bit, he behaved as if nothing had happened. He bore no scars and was comfortable with the features of his face, as he was with the inelegant, self-righteous, and slightly shabby propriety with which people in the early 1960s dressed (and led their lives). The stories and memories that his three daughters have of him—they, too, are now old, but to this day they see themselves, above all, as his daughters—derive from an enthusiasm that, even as a child, I knew to be a kind of infatuation: something, I should think, that cannot always have been good for their marriages.

He was a large man with white hair and an equally white moustache that, looking back, I somehow associate with Errol Flynn. In his study with the leopard pelt on the floor— it was at the taxidermist's when he left southern Africa, and had escaped the sinking of the *Adolph Woermann*—a bushman's bow hung over his desk, together with three arrows in a quiver. His ballpoint pens, pencils, and note cards carefully cut from used envelopes and other scraps of paper lay in a silver writing set adorned with small molded deer antlers on which one could place a pencil or skewer notes.

The memories of my grandfather's appearance that have stayed with me are for the most part of trivialities, and not particularly appealing: the old man's very large ears; the slightly muffled clattering noise of his dentures when he ate; his morose tonelessness and faked helplessness at breakfast; a smell of aftershave; the way his moustache sometimes bristled when he spoke; the complicated hanging of the watchchain in the buttonhole of his vest (into which the button also had to fit), often causing me to consider how much trouble it must be to put everything on in the morning only to have to take it all off again in the evening; the noise the iron tip of his walking stick made on our occasional walks through field and forest; a desk that he gave me when I was twelve (the moss-green, washable Formica surface, thin, round legs, and drawers made of particleboard and cardboard); his old raincoat.

And yet had he allowed it, I could easily have admired him. My reasons might have been different from those of my aunts, but I, too, would have admired him, and gladly. For example, that it was actually he who had shot the leopard whose pelt lay in front of the desk with the leather-covered armchair would have been a wonderful thing for a small boy to imagine.

The dog continued to bark at it, and P. threw some stones into the crown of the tree. It tore after the dog again, with a hissing that was both gruesome and beautiful, and as it momentarily lowered its head and made to strike at the dog with its paws, I shot it through the neck from a distance of 15 to 20 meters. It shuddered, and after a few minutes it was dead. Trying to kill a leopard that is caught in an iron trap is not undangerous. Often its leg has been cut through to what's left of the tendon, which it then tears when it lunges. More than a few hunters have had very unpleasant encounters of this kind. That I faced a challenge greater than simply shooting at a leopard in an iron trap gave me special satisfaction. It was a midsize leopardess, 1.65 meters long from her nose to the tip of her tail. I, of course, got the pelt. I sent it to Leipzig to be prepared, and, later, more than one of my grandchildren had to be taken by the hand before they dared approach the gaping jaws and the predator's glowing eyes.

He was almost as tall as I am, and we were the same age when our hair turned white. As an old man, he lost the potbelly that in midlife almost invariably distorts the figure of married men with his build (and mine); his face and erect posture took on something of the look of a retired soldier honorably discharged after several campaigns, or of a scientist who in the course of his research had just crossed an unexplored continent. But as long as he was alive, I was separated from him and his adventures by an ever-widening zone of mutual irritation. At the time, I hardly understood the estrangement, but I know today that it was a reflection of the distance between the cities and landscapes in which we lived (and which, the older he became, he grew to despise as mine alone) and that invisible country of which he still felt himself to be a citizen. In order to admire him, I would not only have had to surrender myself, but also my country. Sometimes I think he saw me as a kind of enemy of the state.

My grandfather, Andreas Wackwitz, was born in 1893 in Primkenau, a little country town now called Przemków, in Lower Silesia. The last German empress grew up in its castle. For generations, the heads of the Wackwitz family belonged to its elite—they were tile manufacturers, master coopers, town fathers. My grandfather's grandmother was descended from an impoverished family of the region's Polish nobility. In 1909 her son, my great-grandfather, became the Laskowitz forest warden, responsible for seven thousand acres of woods thirty kilometers southeast of Breslau. Since the sixteenth-century, village and castle had been property of the counts of Saurma-Jeltsch. The memories of the man who was walking beside me in the 1960s, making that noise with the iron tip of his walking stick, provide insights into a corporate-feudal self-confidence that at the time would also have given a young boy a sense of security and freedom. Having once encountered it, perhaps one really would no longer wish to live without it, like the French nobleman who said that the person who had not lived during the time before the Revolution did not know what life was.

My grandfather volunteered for and survived the First World War. He served on the Galician front and later in the trenches and fields of Flanders, a soldier from the first day to the last. The war seems to have been more important to him than his studies, more than any intellectual or artistic experience. Nonetheless, although he never made much of it, he was very musical, as befitted a Protestant theologian of the time. Music was the only art that ever meant anything to him. And having studied the Protestant discipline of homiletics, he had learned to express his thoughts and feelings clearly, appropriately, and often very beautifully. But that the life of an intellectual or an artist, with its own specific triumphs and defeats, could give someone as much self-confidence, happiness, and substance as a military or administrative career is an idea he could never have understood. Nor could he comprehend that his younger son, later a Professor of Organ in Berlin, wished to see himself as an artist, a desire that probably was a source of deep shame to my uncle his entire life. My grandfather could never have given this his approval; playing the piano and the organ was a skill one simply possessed. You just picked it up somehow. In his mind, it was something you just did—perhaps this was why I never wished to study it, and didn't.

After high school, he toyed with the idea of working for a newspaper but instead went into law. In the last semester before the war started, against his father's express but clearly not-very-persistent opposition, he switched from law to theology. As he himself admits, he changed course not so much because of some kind of sudden conversion, but because he foresaw that a career in law would be neither secure nor satisfying. In his description of his native Laskowitz, my grandfather mentions, in passing and with pride, that *a head royal forester would hardly have traded places with a royal district officer.* Andreas Wackwitz's true ambition, though he never attained it, was to be a Prussian district officer. It was a profession that is extinct today, and it carried a prestige one can no longer imagine. But at the time, the position of Prussian district officer shone with a glory that emanates today, perhaps, from the career of a successful artist or entrepreneur. To find out what a district officer in Prussia actually did, one has to consult old encyclopedias, for example Meyers *Lexikon* of 1927: "District Officer, in Prussia the highest office in the state administration (District Office), appointed by the Ministry of State, which is not bound by the legally sanctioned recommendations of the local legislature. The D.O. is in charge of the activities of the District Administration, notably the supervision of the Police Administration; he is Chairman of the local legislature and local council." My grandfather did not become Prussian district officer, nor would he become a judge or a lawyer. He became a pastor. In 1956, remembering the young man he once was, he understood without quite realizing it that he had thereby become something like a Prussian district officer, after all.

Trying to summarize the expectations I had of my life, that is, my thoughts about what I wanted to accomplish in and with my life, this is what I would say: wherever I happened to be, I wanted to create order. Somehow, I wanted to help make things better and to stem decline. There was no arguing with the fact that the rule of law in its various manifestations is of great importance—all the way up to the police and carrying out of punishment. But I decided that it was, after all, better to deal with that large area of normal life that takes place within the law than with all those who fight among themselves over the law or who come into conflict with it. Thus I saw in the administrative activity of a Prussian district officer, for example, a high and very noble ideal, but for me, of course, this was not an option.

In no way could his father have financed the more or less unpaid lean years of the preparatory and early stages of this career—an expense that effectively barred the middle class. The financial stress was exacerbated by an older brother who wanted to become a forester and could continue the family tradition only by the rather costly route of reserve officer in a hunting battalion. Before embarking on a career, my grandfather found himself in a paradox: the state to which he longed to dedicate himself excluded him at the outset from the position that embodied its authority most brilliantly, depriving him even of the chance to test or prove himself.

By the end of the Great War, the profession that my grandfather had wanted to pursue no longer existed. As the following decades would reveal, the order that he had wanted to help maintain—as pastor, if not as district officer—had collapsed completely and forever. But for the rest of his life, my grandfather could never quite admit it. During his last semesters (from 1918 to 1920), the self-confidence of the Head Forester's son had grown both rancid and militant. (At the time, he was studying in Breslau, an hour's train ride from the forester's lodge and from his fiancée, whom he had met during his leaves from the front when she was working as household help for his parents.) The student Andreas Gustav Wackwitz, who had gone so far as to fight in the Kapp Putsch in a short civil war against the government of the Republic, was penalized neither by a *Berufsverbot*—the civil service blacklist—nor in any other way. He found employment with a small German village congregation in Anhalt, in the partitioned area of Upper Silesia occupied by Poland in accordance with the Treaty of Versailles. Thanks to a quick and leniently conducted examination and a series of casually-made decisions, the young war veteran slipped imperceptibly into the role and routine of a German representative of those colonial professions, attitudes, and careers that from the nineteenth into the middle decades of the twentieth century were to offer astonishing, if somewhat unorthodox, career opportunities to so many courageous and ambitious young middle-class men in England, France, and Belgium. In Poland, Andreas Wackwitz became an *Auslandsdeutscher,* a German living outside the country. It was not only a thirst for adventure that determined this career choice. A Protestant pastor in Polish Upper Silesia, even after 1918, was much more than an official in the administration of the church. He was the actual head of the congregation in their ongoing struggle with the German *Volk* against Catholic authorities and the detested Polish Republic. The Protestant pastor of Anhalt was a kind of Prussian district officer in his resistance to the postwar order of Versailles.

"Expatriates"—the adventurers, the colonial soldiers, the administrative heroes of the Indian empire—have their natural place in England's cultural and literary history. Until the 1930s, life abroad offered a realistic and readily available career opportunity for enterprising young Britons without means. Men who were not afraid of the heat, the responsibility, and the toil, who took upon themselves the loneliness of the first tour of duty (which in India, for example, usually lasted four years and longer), did not need inherited capital to make their fortunes abroad. The imperial propaganda exemplified in the works of Rudyard Kipling and Joseph Conrad, sweetened and enhanced the colonizer's second-class status. These enterprising young people could tell themselves that although they owned nothing as yet, they had taken upon themselves the weight of the civilizing mission. They carried the *White Man's Burden*.

In Germany, such pioneers of globalization remained rare and rather obscure figures. German colonial policy was not idealized by the great writers of the day, but by the likes of Karl May and Hans Grimm. Our colonial empire was too small and too recent for a career in Togo or Nauru to have been a respectable or even a realistic option for gentlemen. He who ventured there never really lost the whiff of the outsider, one who had failed at home. If my grandfather had been born in Wales or Essex instead of Silesia, he could have gone to India as a matter of course and to great social acclaim, even in 1933. But after 1918, Germany no longer had colonies. My grandfather's posting to Windhoek in former German Southwest Africa (the country was a British Mandate in 1933 and remained so until the end of the war) was in a sense a fallback solution for a forty-year-old who had proven himself politically reliable in his devotion to the *Volk* but who, after twelve years in Poland, had probably outlived his usefulness to his country.

In his early years in Anhalt, Andreas Wackwitz surely had not come to terms with the fact that, living outside Germany, he had a clearly defined role with a particular place in the world and in history. Polish since 1921, the village was still only a few kilometers and hardly half an hour train ride from the nearest mid-size German city. No one at the time could have believed that Anhalt/Holdunów would still be Polish seventy years later. In no way did Andreas Wackwitz anticipate bequeathing the life of an expatriate not only to his son but even to his grandson—who, in his summer vacations in the 1960s sat next to him at breakfast, uncommunicative and vaguely rebellious, casting impertinent glances.

Going through the volumes of his memoir, thinking about him and digging through my memories, I became aware of a feature in my grandfather's life that I found disturbing. It was his peculiar gift for turning up in the background of various historical places of the last century and at different historical moments of his era, without being really involved in these places and moments, without his presence at just this place and time having any consequences, or without his even being aware of the strangeness of it all. In this rather dubious manner, I gradually acquired a familial relationship to some of the central events of the last century.

In his pseudo-documentary *Zelig*, Woody Allen plays a kind of historical confidence man. In "documentary" scenes he appears in the background or on the periphery of episodes with Nazi luminaries or famous jazz musicians or even cardinals (where, if I remember the movie correctly, Pope Pius VI discovers him among his entourage and drives him away, beating at him with his staff). In the 1930s, the "chameleon man," Leonard Zelig, becomes a celebrity, a social lion, the subject of hit songs in the style of the times ("Chameleon Days"), and a highly paid endorser of products ("When I'm through changing into people, I like to change into Pendleton underwear"). Saul Bellow, Susan Sontag, and Bruno Bettelheim appear as talking heads in the movie and expound on Leonard Zelig's cultural and historical significance.

My grandfather turns up, Zelig-like, somewhere in the background of so many historic photographs and documentary film clips that sometimes I would ask myself whether the obscure but unavoidable ubiquity of his *curriculum vitae* in the history of the last century did not suggest a noteworthy, albeit questionable, capacity to empathize and adapt— a pathological malleability. It was only after 1945—after the defeat of the Kaiser's last, catastrophically perverted successor—that this changed into the rigidity that gave his grandson so much trouble. Was it only then, I wondered, when he had lost his center of gravity, that he began to manifest that cast-iron fixity?

That Andreas Wackwitz participated in World War I from beginning to end, as well as in the Kapp Putsch, is not really all that troubling. Nor that he lived in the immediate vicinity of Auschwitz from 1921 to 1933 (moreover, in the same late baroque parsonage where Friedrich Schleiermacher had lived as a child in the late eighteenth century, perhaps seeing the same ghostly figures as did my father, a century later). And that Adolf Hitler came twice within his view and earshot is nothing more than an interesting coincidence, the sort of thing that can and does happen in the course of other lives, too. That he was to spend time in German Southwest Africa —such a notorious flash point for the struggles and fantasies of my generation (the "Third World" of disappearing colonialism)—even this could still be acceptable from the point of view of probability. Nevertheless, since I began to concern myself with my grandfather's memoirs and papers, the circumstances of his return to Germany have given me more to think about than is perhaps healthy. They have put my grandfather in that ghostly, meaningful light that has no place in real life, but exists legitimately only in fiction.

It is very strange indeed, even incredible, that—after his return from Africa, after shipwreck and imprisonment, ten years before he was to be expelled by the Communists from their territory and taken in by the Church of the State of Hamburg—my grandfather settled in Luckenwalde (in Brandenburg), of all places. Because as the highest local religious authority, he became responsible for a pious and athletic teenager whose name was Alfred Willi Rudolf Dutschke, but who, twenty years later, after he had long since been famous and until he was shot in the head, insisted with childlike obstinacy on the first name of Rudi. His notoriety in Germany was a byproduct of the student rebellion. He was our "Danny Le Rouge," our Malcolm X, leader of a children's crusade that shook Germany and made it the country I live in. Small, almost dwarfish, long-haired, bookish to the point of absurdity, always in the same sweater he had knit himself, always in a good mood, always in the first row of the innumerable, long-forgotten demonstrations for and against God knows what. An unemployed young clerk shot him in the head on Berlin's Kurfürstendamm in April 1968. He survived: He learned to walk, speak, and write again. He spent some time in Britain and Denmark. He co-founded the Green Party. Time moved on. He never really recovered; he never regained his former radiance or prominence. He died in 1979 (an epileptic seizure in the bathtub, his wife in the other room, at Christmas). In the end, I think, he shared my grandfather's fate of needing historical explanation while still alive. True, the athletic and pious Dutschke boys lived with their mother on the other side of the tracks in one of Luckenwalde's housing developments. And it is also true that they did not go to the main church on the market square (except for special occasions), but to Saint Peter's. Nonetheless it is unlikely that my grandfather had not occasionally noticed young Rudi in the long decade from 1940 to 1950, and that he hadn't at least heard the odd remark about the youngest and most eager of the four Dutschke sons. In the small town, particularly during the godless Nazi years, one would have known of the congregation's especially reliable "pillars" and about the family's "circumstances." Anyway, my aunt in Berlin, who went to school with Rudi, remembers him fairly well.

Yet in his memoirs, Andreas Wackwitz fails to write so much as a word about the person who was far and away the most famous member of the Luckenwalde congregation. I, in whose life Rudi Dutschke played no minor role (although I never met him personally), am perhaps not the only person who finds weird the subterranean encounter of my

grandfather with the most charismatic man of my generation. In a novel, such a turn of events would be criticized as
too "meaningful" and would probably succeed only as a
comedic, or at least grotesquely overdetermined, plot element—such as only a figure like Woody Allen's Leonard Zelig
could bring off credibly and get away with. But perhaps every
life, if it lasts long enough and exposes one sufficiently to the
world, takes on such exemplary, parodistic, and significant
features, and maybe all lives spent in times of turmoil are
"chameleon years."

It has fallen to me, however, the oldest grandson of this
many-sided man, to look behind and between the factual,
tangible, and historically accountable events of my grandfather's life as told in his memoirs, in order to see its dream
figures and phantoms, who have in turn haunted my own
life. On closer inspection, they always appear both frightful
and a bit ridiculous. A small, muscular, almost dwarf-like
young man in a turtleneck pullover with unkempt hair
(Dutschke); a thin young man with his hair properly parted,
listening on August 2, 1914, in Munich's Odeon Square to
the proclamation of war and looking, at last, completely
happy and free (Hitler); the bushman's bow and three arrows in a leather quiver, from which long black hair hangs
down; the leopard's pelt, smelling of dust, with its stuffed
head, its mouth wide open, flashing teeth smooth as porcelain; a Bantu, lost and stumbling about in the South African
desert, searching for my grandfather's horse.

The past is a foreign country: they do things differently there.

—L. P. Hartley, *The Go-Between*

5 Anomie

Not until the end of the century did I understand how much my grandfather and I could have meant to each other. According to a 1927 encyclopedia, for example, the Namib is "a coastal desert in former German Southwest Africa, up to 100 kilometers across, with almost no vegetation . . . The region with the world's lowest precipitation (14 mm annually), it is important for diamonds discovered near Lüderitz Bay." But my grandfather was not after diamonds on his 1935 "Hunt on Horseback in the Namib Desert"—the title of a long essay he wrote for the magazine *Welt und Haus*. It seems to me, rather, that on this journey he was searching for happiness, and it is happiness that he found.

The small, green parrots were cavorting about in the tree above us with a ceaseless, shrill shrieking and chattering. Two oryx approaching the water were evidently surprised to find us already there, and after staring at us for a long time with stupid faces they cantered off. P. complained about the heat and urged us to get going. I insisted that we reach water by evening. He growled something like: There are times when you have to be able to go without water! and gave me a lecture on the perseverance and toughness that a real African has to show. So we rode on through endless herds of oryx and zebra, mountain ranges to the left and right. Quietly, I reminded P. about the water as the sun began to set. He said: It's not much further. We rode another hour. I reminded him again. P. said: We'll be there soon. It's there, behind the bluff. We rode an hour to the bluff. The moon rose; the air grew cool. A broad plateau opened up on the top of the bluff, at whose edge the moonlight revealed a rugged mountain range. That's where the water was supposed to be. How far until we're there? I asked. P. said: It's not far. We rode for over an hour, through valleys and ravines. We came upon a dry creek and found holes scraped out by zebras, three-quarters of a meter deep, but they, too, were dry. We proceeded in silence, and I began to grow sullen. The heat of the day had caused my body to become a dry sponge. I said that I didn't want to be measured against the same standard as the old colonial troops, that I wasn't used to this kind of desert ride. P. said nothing. Suddenly he said: Now that we've come this far, we might as well ride on to the watering hole that I'd intended to reach tomorrow. I asked: How far is it? He said: Maybe a kilometer. Let's go! I said with a last burst of energy. We continued in the moonlight, going up and down, the saddles crunching, the hoofs smacking on the stones. There were stretches where we walked the horses. Instead of one kilometer, it became four or five; it took over an hour. Only P.'s promise, given on his word of honor, that there was sure to be a lot of water, and even running water, reconciled me to my fate. When we finally did come to a gap in the mountains, we could make out large trees in the moonlight below, and the sound of croaking frogs. I drank the last gulp from the canteen, for we were finally at our goal. Except for two cups of tea, P. had drunk nothing the entire day! We led the horses down and pitched camp under a huge wild fig tree. In the blink of an eye *a big fire was blazing, a real captain's fire boiling and roasting our dinner. P. had shot a springbok on the way. Fried in fat with salt, pepper, and onions, its liver is a delicacy, and after the exertions of the day, it was a very special delicacy indeed. Twice we cooked up a large, 2-liter pot of tea, and for a first course we had pea meal sausage with meat and rice, with the liver as the main course. At the end, tea and more tea, and cigars. Then we lay for a long time in front of the fire and exchanged war stories. It was a wonderful evening, doubly so because we knew that we were beside the most glorious water and that the frogs would be croaking us to sleep. The nearest person was 100 kilometers away!*

Some parts of my grandfather's account feel to me as if I had dreamt them myself—most vividly the hours-long ride through herds of zebra and oryx. When I'm happy, I sometimes dream of eternal, carefree Saturday afternoons in infinite landscapes or parks. And in the dream I know that I have died and have entered the eternal hunting grounds of paradise. Why didn't my grandfather leave me a more substantial idea of happiness than these dreams of infinity? Maybe another passage can shed some light here.

After waiting for several days in vain for a leopard, we decided to ride to the plains to hunt for springbok. We wanted to get an early start, but in the course of the night the horses had run away! P. showered curses on the kaffir Isaak for not having tied them securely enough, but what was the point?—they were gone. Isaak rushed off to begin his search. One hour passed, then two, and then Isaak, too, was missing, leaving us with no choice but to search ourselves. We climbed the face of the cliff and found a suitable vantage point. Fortunately, with our binoculars we were able to see the runaway horses four to five kilometers away. We also spotted Isaak, who was wandering about aimlessly. By waving we were able to signal the direction in which he was to go; from where he was, he couldn't see the horses.

Remembering my childhood, I have a pretty good idea of how Isaak felt as he wandered aimlessly about in the coastal desert. In the face of my grandfather and his expectations, I myself was regularly overcome by the anomie that held poor Isaak "aimlessly wandering about" in the Namib—a peculiarly embarrassing and unpleasant condition that manages to combine feelings of inadequacy and shame, passivity and dreaminess, resigned submissiveness, but also a suppressed rebelliousness that only makes things worse. It would start with my not speaking clearly enough for my grandfather, who, when I was brought into the patriarchal presence by my parents, grandmother, or aunts and had to account for myself, would scold me, half humorously, half really ill-tempered: "Don't mumble!"

One particularly painful conversation took place when I was in my mid-twenties, relatively mature, and preparing for my qualifying exams to become a teacher. It was about Wilhelm Busch's humorous *Jobsiade,* a topic that my grandfather chose because he was in good spirits and disposed to make concessions to my inferior intellectual capacity. I had not read a word of the *Jobsiade* (and have not read it to this day), though I didn't dare admit it, as we would otherwise have had nothing whatsoever to talk about. In the course of this conversation, which, of course, was conducted almost exclusively by my grandfather, he and I were so absolutely and indescribably at a loss with each other that he gave up on me, perhaps forever. For the rest of the visit he barely spoke to me. It seems to me now that our colossal non-relationship, so evident that day in his study, had existed along with the leopard's pelt (by now somewhat scurfy) all our lives. It existed then and always. In fact, it persists to this day.

I also remember earlier episodes of awkwardness, inadequacy, and irresponsibility, and moods of irremediable and fathomless lassitude that permanently determined my nonrelationship to my grandfather. Under different political circumstances, his practical matter-of-factness, his adventurousness, his instinct for freedom, his feel for nature, his courage and self-confidence, and that stony fixedness of opinions and actions could have served as a model that I desperately needed. But as matters stood, I reacted in horror and disgust, and became sluggish.

A brilliant October morning in the Kaiserstuhl, for example, in the early 1970s. One of those family gatherings that took place every few years while my grandparents were still alive. The agenda: parading of the troops, family sociability, and of course, the presentation of the latest installment of my grandfather's memoirs. Although this was the last place I wanted to be, I had no choice. I had graduated from high school a few months earlier and my university years lay before me as open, promising, and warmed by the hazy autumn sun as were the morning vineyards and valleys into which we were walking. My grandfather poked the iron tip of his walking stick into the gravel of the path. I was wearing a dark gray cashmere turtleneck pullover that was a gift from an American uncle and on that morning represented in some vague way the sophistication and freedom that were awaiting me in my immediate future. But on our walk into the vineyards of the Kaiserstuhl, I became filled with dark forebodings: on this autumn morning of my future we would—I was quite sure of it—fall into some sort of unavoidable, male conversation that would hurl me irresistibly into a state of deep anomie.

And that is just what happened. While we were walking, my grandfather tried to persuade me to join a dueling fraternity—in all seriousness, as my cautious sideway glances confirmed—and if possible one that was also nationalist. It slipped out as hesitantly and mysteriously as had my mother's imparting of the facts of life several years earlier. It could only help my career, he said; fraternities made a man of you. My grandfather did not know who I was and never would know: familial loneliness and lassitude sat like sad harpies on my shoulders. Nonetheless, little though I knew it on that October morning, all my attempts to live my life differently from my grandfather would be in vain. I was to waste a large part of my precious student years in one of those carnivalesque-communist brigades—a voluntary slavery that I took upon myself, casting sophistication and freedom to the winds. Half a decade lost at an age in which a single year is longer and more important than five years at my present age. But that is another story.

Freedom seemed to be mine, but it was, in fact, out of my reach. Stunned, I eyed my grandfather with disgust on that autumn morning in the beginning of the 1970s, parrying his suggestions and warnings as he walked energetically next to me, swinging his walking stick, trapped in his past. Yet in my fashion, I held to his advice fairly closely, though I made sure that if I were indeed to fulfill my grandfather's wishes, it would be in such a way as to afford him the greatest possible irritation.

But the secret of my futurelessness at the beginning of the 1970s was, it seems to me now after thinking so long about my grandfather's futurelessness, not buried in the southern African Namib, but in that invisible country between the Vistula and the Sola rivers, between the Carpathian Mountains and the swamp, between Kattowitz and Auschwitz. And I began to explore the history of our *family romance* knowing that in my search for this secret I would have to venture into very strange regions, into more than one invisible country, and into frighteningly alien times. I would go where my grandfather had worked before he went to Africa, and where my father was born, the landscape to which for half a century not only my family, but all of Germany has been silently and strangely bound. And I would also have to lose myself in the history of the world war that we call the "First," though for the English—with a greater and more fitting respect for its significance—it remains "The Great War." Led by my grandfather's notes, I would have to seek out the Laskowitz castle and park, the forester's house in which the old man had lived as a child. I would be the first of us to walk there since 1945. I would have to traverse many countries, cities, and eras—and three years would pass until I finally returned to my own.

6 *Invented Story*

Driving or biking the sixty kilometers between Kraków and Auschwitz on an early summer day, one enters a landscape that looks as if it had been copied from a 1930s children's book. For miles on end, tree-lined roads follow the gentle curves of the Vistula River into a hot, burned, Tuscan landscape, past baroque monasteries and estates as big as magic castles. Their verandas and battlements loom over forests, river, and hills as if in one of Eichendorff's romantic novels. Travelers have to dodge the village dogs chasing after them and brake for flocks of geese on the wide market roads. The neo-baroque town halls were built—as the inscriptions on the gables testify—by the provincial administration of the Austrian-Hungarian Dual Monarchy in the nineteenth century, while the absurdly oversize churches with their stage-set facades date from two centuries before that. Side streets lead down to the Vistula, which, hardly more substantial than a brook, can be crossed only on an old-fashioned ferry. A bored eighteen-year-old is on duty, enjoying the companionship of his girlfriend, who is dressed in her Sunday best (stiletto heels and swept-up hair, the little Fiat next to the concrete landing). When the weather is good, the snow-covered Carpathian Mountains are visible in the distance. This magical, strangely beautiful hill country stretches in all directions toward the horizon.

For centuries, people moved here from all over Europe. In the Middle Ages and into the Renaissance, Kraków was a kind of New York or nineteenth-century Buenos Aires: a multi-cultural city of German, Flemish, and Italian merchants, Spanish Jews, and Polish noble families, more benevolently watched over than actually ruled by artistically-inclined and somewhat detached kings from a hilltop Florentine court overlooking the river. Following the King's example, these noblemen brought colonists to their endless, thinly settled estates. Here—having been granted fruitful soil, freedom from taxation, a well-ordered infrastructure, and protection from political and religious persecution— young Bohemian, Silesian, Saxon, Thuringian, Swabian, and Bavarian peasants created something that had existed nowhere before. This part of central Europe was once a utopia, the Old World's only counterpart to the freedom and entrepreneurial independence of the American West.

True to type, the settlers were self-confident, even centuries after the Golden Age of the Polish Renaissance state. By around 1770, at the time of the American Revolution, peasants and burghers from the Ukraine to the Languedoc were seized by a vague nervousness. The German literary movement known as *Sturm und Drang* ("Storm and Stress") and the first great works of Goethe and Schiller (*Werther*, *The Robbers*) were as much echoes of this subterranean, rumbling rebelliousness as were the founding of the Illuminati and the Enlightenment's other secret societies; as was the dramatic spread of poaching and the stealing of timber in the most disparate regions of Europe; as was the popularity of all manner of Robin Hood-like robber-heroes (the *Schinderhannes*, the Bavarian *Hiesel*); as were the Bohemian peasant rebellions of 1775, the village riots in Silesia in 1765, and between 1759 and 1768, the unrest among Augsburg's weavers.

The pre-storm atmosphere of this decade was also apparent in the Beskid piedmont, that happily remote region between the Vistula River and the Carpathian Mountains. The settlers had been brought there as free peasants by the Polish Piast princes in the late fourteenth century, but had long since become weak and oppressed. In the sixteenth century, many became Hussites; later, Lutherans or Calvinists. The supporters of the Counter Reformation, however, whether ecclesiastical or secular, no longer regarded them as mere heretics; victorious Catholicism had absorbed the spirit and values of early nationalism. By the early modern period, the medieval colonists, still speaking German and maintaining their cultural distinctiveness and above all their Protestant faith, had themselves become something like political pariahs, *Volksfeinde*, public enemies.

Close to Bielsko-Biała, the first foothills of the Beskids slope up from near the old country highway. What look from the hills around Kraków to be gently rising foothills of distant snow-capped mountains are in fact steep and dark cliffs. In the winter, storms plunge to the plains below. In the early summer and late autumn, poisonously warm and dry *föhn* winds pull at trees and houses, inflict headaches and racing hearts and, upon souls, a poetic confusion; the air as clear as if one could see from here to the end of the world. The Beskid foothills suffered a Mongol invasion in about 1370. In the same decade, their ruler, Tamerlane (at the eastern edge of Asia—in Korea, ten thousand kilometers away), ordered a naval invasion of Japan, which was repulsed by Zen-trained Samurai archers and by a typhoon that men later called *Kamikaze*—holy wind.

A few kilometers east of Bielsko-Biała the road goes through a village called Kozy. The automobile traffic pokes its way into the village center, past a neo-classical manor house and a park that has seen better days; it passes a small concrete monument with the obligatory benches, a jungle gym for kids, and piles of dog poop. The traffic causes tremors in the roadside supermarkets and hamburger joints and the stately nineteenth-century houses that now serve as kindergartens or offices of the district administration. *Kozy* means "goats." According to folk wisdom, the village took the name to commemorate the two goats that had survived the Mongols. When the Polish rulers repopulated the devastated land with colonists, the village was founded anew by enterprising young peasants, probably from Thuringia, and was given the name Seibersdorf.

To understand the unique history of Seibersdorf/Kozy, one must recall what Protestantism meant in early modern times. "Seibersdorf and Alzen—in Polish, Kozy and Halsnow—are villages on the Polish-Silesian border, almost a mile from Biała, the nearest Silesian town," according to the *Miscellanea Groningana,* a seven-volume Latin history of the Reformation printed in Groningen and Bremen in 1762. "The owner of the former has long been the noble family von Rusocki; of the latter, the noble family von Zydowski. At the end of the century, after God's grace revealed the light of the Reformation, the Rusockis were among the many families of the nobility who followed the light of Truth and joined the purified religion. Not satisfied with their own, personal conversion, they also enjoined their subjects in Seibersdorf to accept the new faith." In this, Herr von Rusocki was no exception: numerous noblemen in sixteenth-century southern Poland engaged in pious correspondence with no less a figure than Calvin himself. It is not difficult to understand how Rusocki's serfs would have followed him in his conversion as in everything else.

Certain historical events have become such an integral part of our inner lives that historians have to conjure them consciously before their eyes. The primal experience of the Protestant revolution—the certainty that the soul has direct and absolutely autonomous access to God and to one's own moral vision—is an event of this type. It is a certainty that derives from the mentality of the upper classes of late Antiquity, was passed from the Stoa to the early Christians, and then apparently forgotten for centuries. Without it there would be no modernity, no consumer society, no democracy. It is limitless and invisible, powerful and consoling. We come closest to perceiving it, or grasping it, when we hear certain arias or chorales by Bach: passages for brass, the beating of timpani, and melodies that had been invented for kings and then were suddenly there for God—which meant for everyone. What occurred in Seibersdorf and in countless other villages and manors toward the middle of the sixteenth century can rightly be called a revolution.

In the sixteenth century, men and women throughout Europe lived in filth and cold. They hungered and labored for others from dawn to dusk. They said to themselves: We are not scum. We are God's children, and what we transact with Him is no one's business but our own. The Protestants of early modern Europe declared a state of emergency that stopped at the frontiers of their soul but unleashed a power that broke dynasties and ended eras. The religious revolutions of the early modern age created an inner space where Bohemian and southern Polish peasants could look in the eye not only their liege lords, but also the Roman emperor Marcus Aurelius and the American revolutionary Thomas Jefferson. God became a part of their souls that came into existence only through a kind of conversation with Him. No matter what happened, the Protestant burghers, laborers, and peasants of the sixteenth and seventeenth centuries would no longer be scum.

A hundred years later, in about 1650, when "the heirs of the ruling family led dissolute lives and fell into old errors" (according to the *Miscellanea Groningana*), Seibersdorf's German inhabitants, the co-religionists of old Rusocki, held to the true teaching with stoic and proto-democratic stubbornness. Their church taken from them, they gathered for worship in the forest, where the Catholic masters left them in peace, knowing that the Protestant blockheads "were well armed and would not easily tolerate injustice." Religious and political tensions persisted, it seems, in a precarious and poisoned equilibrium, an anti-Catholic (and anti-Polish) peasant rebellion put on ice, a religious war in aspic. It is probably not entirely inaccurate to compare the situation in Seibersdorf at that time to the Bosnian and Herzegovian villages that became *killing fields* before the eyes of a stunned and paralyzed world in the early 1990s, and one can imagine the enslaved, hate-filled, and strangely calm stupor that spread through much of central Europe in the centuries after the medieval colonization of the east as being something like rural Yugoslavia.

Nevertheless, it is difficult for a modern observer not to feel a bit of admiration for the Seibersdorf Protestants, who on a Sunday morning left the Catholic church behind them and proceeded to the forest armed with scythes, cudgels, and knives, seeking salvation in their own manner. Perhaps the wayward and dissolute Rusocki great-grandson, who for decades, Sunday after Sunday, did not dare interfere with his serfs' rebellion against him, could hear "A Mighty Fortress Is Our God" and other hymns behind the walls of his manor house. When these forest services ceased, it "wasn't so much because of the resistance of their enemies," as the *Miscellanea Groningana* explicitly states, but "partly because of the discord that had developed among the villagers themselves, partly due to the weakening of their original zeal, and mainly because Reverend Milecki had become too old to make the journey to Seibersdorf and was no longer able to exhort and strengthen them in their faith." The congregation, robbed of its spiritual nourishment, went into a state of decline. It was but a symptom of its inner collapse that a servant girl betrayed the site where the chalice and other church implements were buried, "so that the congregants finally began to disperse, as they were oppressed by many acts of injustice and the still harder yoke of servitude."

Those who remained loyal Protestants walked the forty kilometers to Teschen or north to Pless—to weddings or baptisms, and, once a year, to communion. There, the scattered sheep, who for generations had had to suffer the harassment that a closed village community is capable of meting toward outsiders, were given shelter. According to the sources (all, of course, partisan toward the Protestants), they were burned alive, their land was taken from them, as were their children, who were raised in distant villages. The dead were buried outside the cemetery walls. The Catholic priest was said to have called his two dogs Luther and Calvin. The ostracized Protestants sought shelter in the desolate forests, where "they held their services and conducted Holy Communion at night, the pastor having come in disguise from Poland or Silesia," as a congregational letter later laments.

Such was the situation in which the Protestant community of Seibersdorf found itself after the Thirty Years' War, and presumably it would have continued in this manner indefinitely. But then something unexpected happened. For a historic moment, the remote Beskid village won the attention and solidarity of its co-religionists throughout Protestant Europe, as well as the grace of the Prussian king Frederick II (Frederick the Great), and above all the interest of the enlightened-pietistic circles of intellectuals that had linked the disparate parts of Europe from university metropolises to the smallest village congregations through an extensive network of correspondence, mutual help, and prayer. During the years 1740–42, Frederick annexed Silesia, ended the Counter Reformation, issued edicts of tolerance and extended his enlightened-mercantile programs of economic stimulation, development of infrastructure, and internal colonization of the new province, whose border ran along the Vistula, twenty kilometers north of Kozy/Seibersdorf.

Legend ascribes what happened after that to a supernatural vision. Seibersdorf's Joan of Arc was Eva Mandzla, of whom we know little more than her name. Local birth registers do not even show that she really existed. But "one day while at prayer she had a strange vision. She saw the Gospels in her room, open to a passage in Matthew—*Come to me, all who labor and are heavy laden, and I will give you rest*—with the name *Urban* shining brightly above it. Joyous at this sign from heaven, she described it to her co-religionists at a secret gathering in the forest. Like Eva Mandzla, they took

courage and waited for Saint Urban's Day with great anticipation, but it passed, and nothing changed. This repeated
itself year after year, and it became increasingly difficult for
the villagers of Seibersdorf to believe that help would ever
come. Even after thirty years, however, Eva Mandzla did not
lose hope. In the meantime, she had married and borne a
son, and when the Catholic priest gave him the name Urban without any prompting, she believed with new conviction that this name would bring happiness to the people of
Seibersdorf. Her son was confirmed on Saint Urban's Day
in Pless in Prussia, where the Protestants had to go for a pastor of their faith. And from Prussia would come their rescue." (Again, from the mustard-yellow volume by Alfred
Karasek-Langer and Elfriede Strzygowski, *The Tales of the
Beskid-Germans*, Plauen, 1931.)

The former capital Pless is now known as Pszczyna. A neo-
baroque palace with a clock on its façade dominates the market square, where hungry-looking sixteen-year-old boys with
bottles of beer and cigarettes sit around on benches, spitting
the pavement wet. Behind the square, a park merges into
the Beskid forests, as if, after each turn, the path extends further yet, and thus to the end of the world. In 1770, the city
belonged to the Thuringian Counts of Coethen-Anhalt, who
had moved their court to Upper Silesia in 1765. The large
Protestant congregation of court officials, military men, and
craftsmen was under the care of the Protestant military chaplain Johann Gottlieb Adolph Schleyermacher, who visited
the scattered congregations on extensive official journeys
from his headquarters in Breslau. It was in Breslau that
Friedrich Daniel Ernst Schleyermacher was born in 1768.
Johann Gottlieb Adolph's oldest son (his name modernized
to Friedrich Schleiermacher) would become one of the most

important philosophers of the nineteenth century, "a hero," according to Karl Barth, "as theology is rarely given." It is hardly possible to overestimate Friedrich Schleiermacher's influence on German liberalism. Not only was he opposed to traditional Lutheran orthodoxy and its rigors. He also proposed a theological and philosophical alternative to the German "philosophy of consciousness"—a friendly, liberal aberration from Fichte's endless, futile, fundamentalist, and infinitely influential quest for ever more basic certainties. Schleiermacher placed solidarity over objectivity, according to the American liberal philosopher Richard Rorty. And if there is a strong streak of liberalism, individualism, and free thought in German Protestantism, it was planted there by Schleiermacher, a man who two hundred years ago wrote, "All human beings are artists," and who grew up in the same Anhalt parsonage as my father.

Johann Gottlieb Adolph, the great man's father, descended from a family of excitable, unstable, and altogether problematic sectarians. In 1740—the year in which *Urban* came in a vision to Eva Mandzla—Schleiermacher's grandfather was serving as pastor to a kind of pietistic theocracy in Wuppertal. In 1751, falling victim to ongoing epiphanies, visitations, and prophecies, he was forced to flee his congregation and sought sanctuary in Arnheim in Holland. His son, the father of the theologian, was also to spend his life on the edge of religious madness—an aspect of the intellectual landscape of German idealism necessary for understanding the young Goethe, Hölderlin, Hegel, and yes, Friedrich Schleiermacher. Johann Gottlieb Adolph seems to have found a certain peace in Moravian pietism. But his letters to his young, intellectually rebellious, guilt-ridden son, with their fearful, verbose lack of understanding (to say nothing of their teary formulas, metaphors, and ecstatic clichés) make for painful reading even today.

In Pless, Johann Gottlieb Adolph Schleyermacher got to know the Beskid peasants who had been inspired by the vision of Saint Urban. When the chaplain came to town, they made the journey from Seibersdorf: infants were baptized, couples married, he who suffered from fears, sins, and quarrels received support both temporal and spiritual. Schleyermacher wrote to his Zurich friend Johann Kaspar Lavater, "I was, myself, often in tears, seeing them long for a better understanding, something I satisfied only very incompletely, since they could be away from their village but briefly." But it was not only the signs and miracles the confused Protestant reported so faithfully and longingly that would have been familiar to Johann Gottlieb Adolph. His tearful account of the peasants' emotional needs also evokes a political-sentimental ideal of the *Storm and Stress* period; one thinks, for example, of Johann Kaspar Hirzel's image of the peasant in *The Economy of the Philosophical Peasant* who pulls himself up by his own bootstraps—a plebian ally invented by the intellectuals of the time in order to advance their ideology of education and perfectibility.

We don't know whether such "philosophical peasants" ever really existed. The forgotten ideal they represented, however, is as present in Schiller's and Lenz's early "self-helper" dramas, as it is in Herder's fantasies about how a country pastor "can best spread culture and reason among that honorable part of humankind known as 'the people.'" Instructed by the enlightened young theologians who, fresh from university, had been banished to unthinkably remote country congregations (at least this is how their rebellious contemporaries of the *Storm and Stress* imagined it), country people—so it was imagined—would learn to help themselves: they would try new methods of cultivation, learn to read and write and refuse henceforth to simply endure whatever was dished out to them. The alliance that was to be forged between the military chaplain Schleyermacher and the peasants of Seibersdorf emerged from the spirit of reform that is one of the fundamental experiences of classical German philosophy and literature. It became the focus of the aging pastor's life and ultimately resulted in the deliverance of the congregation.

As the years passed, Johann Gottlieb Adolph Schleyermacher became *spiritus rector* of a daring and, at first glance, seemingly unworkable project. For centuries, the Seibersdorf Protestants were not only farmers but also weavers, working at home and with their families. The growth of Prussian military power after the Peace of Hubertusburg resulted in a steady demand for cloth for uniforms, and on January 5, 1770, Frederick the Great promulgated an edict on broadsheets throughout Poland that promised liberties and privileges to foreign craftsmen, especially to weavers, if they would emigrate to Silesia. As a consequence, the Beskid piedmont experienced a revival of the utopian emigration that in the late Middle Ages had brought Jews from all over Europe, as well as peasants from rural Germany, merchants from Italy, and cloth dealers from Flanders. Signaled by the mysterious writing that was revealed to the Virgin of Seibersdorf over her Bible, the tradition of the village's ancestors seemed to come alive again among its peasants and weavers, who apparently understood that traditions exist only to be relinquished at the proper moment, and that something better than death can be found everywhere.

On April 15, 1770, the District Officer of Pless reported to the Berlin court via Minister Schlabrendorf in Breslau that a deputation of the Seibersdorf Protestants had presented themselves and had offered the Prussian king nothing less that an exodus of the entire village in order to resettle north of the Vistula. The self-help program of the chaplain Schleyermacher and his philanthropic allies in Zurich, Riga, Nantes, and Holland seems to have borne fruit among the self-confident and savvy peasants of Seibersdorf. Politely but firmly, they stated their demands and conditions: "Ten years exemption from taxation; exemption from conscription for themselves and their children; exemption from duty on goods brought with them; horses and wagons for their household goods, since otherwise they would not be able to transport everything at the same time; and adequate military protection upon departure and en route. These privileges corresponded in their essentials to the edict of January 5, 1770. But beyond this, the villagers demanded that funds be collected in all Prussian lands, both privately and from churches, to finance the building of houses; that they be given permission to build a Protestant church, for which a second fund would be created, and that they receive, as well, an advance of four hundred to five hundred talers on the first fund so that the poorer ones among them could immediately begin building their houses." (Andreas Wackwitz, *The Historic Development of the German Enclave Anhalt-Gatsch in Upper Silesia,* Plauen, 1932.) The peasants and weavers of Seibersdorf understood, finally, that they were not scum.

The rest of their story reminds one of a film by John Ford, of *Red River* ("Take 'em to Missouri, Matt") or *She Wore a Yellow Ribbon.* But probably no film is more illuminating about what was to be the heroic climax in the subsequent history of Protestant émigré communities than the Mormon epic *Wagon Master.* With the help of this history, one can understand that the heroic American story of departure and new beginning, determination and solidarity, God-fearingness and contempt of death rests on a European experience. Across the sea, this epic was not invented, but repeated.

At the end of April 1770, a letter from the Prussian king reached his future subjects in Pless. A month later, Lieutenant Georg von Woyrsch crossed the border river, Vistula, at the village Miedzna with two squadrons of seventy men each and two hundred covered wagons. There, at night, he left one of these squadrons behind to secure the retreat. On the evening of the next day the peasants of Seibersdorf reached the Miedzna ford with their wives, children, animals, household goods, scythes, Bibles, hymnals, and their communion chalice. They successfully crossed the river with covered wagons, animals, and people ("Away/We're bound away/'Cross the wide Missouri"), and on May 25, 1770, they stood on Prussian ground, in the promised land of religious freedom.

We cannot determine whether the chaplain Schleyermacher or the Seibersdorf village mayor had arranged for the exodus to take place on the eve of Saint Urban's Day, thus fulfilling the prophecy of Eva Mandzla, or whether the Breslau Board for War and Domain had a hand in it. We do know that the alliance between philosopher and peasant that was called for at the same time in Herder's pamphlets—a peculiar and touching friendship between Friedrich Schleiermacher's father and the Protestant settlers from Kozy—was to be realized in the following decades.

After their new liege, Count Erdmann von Anhalt-Coethen, presented the courageous and pious men and women of Seibersdorf with lumber for construction and uncultivated land behind a mountain ridge ten kilometers north of Auschwitz, they erected a farm village in the same style as that of their late-medieval ancestors five hundred years earlier in the Beskid piedmont to the south. The Protestant *Internationale* from Prussia to Holland, alerted by broadsheets and letters in Zurich, Hamburg, Stargard, and Basel, provided them with money, Bibles, and open letters meant to edify and encourage. In 1778, Johann Gottlieb Adolph Schleyermacher gave up his position in the city of Breslau and moved to join the colonists, who were slowly and laboriously building their village in an area between forest and swamp. They gave it the name Anhalt—according to legend because one couldn't go further than this spot (the literal meaning of "Anhalt" being "stop" or "halt") but more probably to honor the ancestral homeland of their new liege.

When my grandfather, Schleyermacher's penultimate German successor, assumed his pastoral duties just after Anhalt became Polish in 1921, the pastor's garden that had been planted by his famous predecessor stretched a good distance behind the late-baroque prayer house, schoolhouse, and parsonage. "Behind the parsonage, he transformed a two-acre piece of land into a garden. Probably it was still covered with bushes, and it must have taken a lot of work to clear. Even thirty years later, Schleyermacher's son, at the time a professor in Halle, remembers working in the garden at his father's side. It must have given them both pleasure, since it had been created from scratch and was manifestly successful. In 1806, Friedrich Schleiermacher wrote from Halle expressing regret at not having seen the village of his childhood during his recent visit to Silesia. He writes that since his parents lived in rented apartments in Breslau he had no memories of the city, but he would have gladly gone to see Anhalt once again. 'A house is there that was first occupied by my father, a garden that was first planted by him and in which I helped him. There I had my first experience of piety, and it is the furthest point to which I can trace back my inner life.' Some of the old lindens in the parsonage garden as well as in the cemetery may have been planted by Schleiermacher." (Andreas Wackwitz, *Historic Development . . .*)

On an early summer day in 1999, I stood behind the parsonage of Anhalt. Even now, it is the largest building on the street that passes through the village of Holdunów, and one can still enjoy its baroque proportions visible beneath sheets of tin and plastic. Its façade will resurface when Holdunów—like country towns in Germany fifteen years ago—rediscovers its past and is restored. But the parsonage garden has disappeared forever. Behind the house there is an extensive piece of fallow land on which plots for single-family homes have been marked off with little wooden stakes. In the distance, a train line crosses through birches and pines. I stood in the spring wind. Behind me, separated from Schleiermacher's pastoral garden by only a ridge of hills, lay the industrial district of Auschwitz. I thought of Friedrich Schleiermacher's testimony to his "inner life" (uncited by my grandfather), which saw its beginning two hundred years ago on this plot of earth now being prepared for construction. It is a testimony to his "own inner torment," the kind that sometimes befalls thirteen-year-olds. It concerns "a wonderful skepticism: it occurred to me that all old writers, and with them history as we knew it, had been invented. I had no reason for thinking this other than that I knew of no proof for their authenticity and that everything that I knew of them seemed fictional and disconnected. I became withdrawn and kept this strange, tormenting thought to myself, because I still had a reputation for intelligence and didn't want to ruin it because of my—as I thought—unique ignorance and ineptitude. I decided to wait to see what time would disclose—confirmation or refutation." (Schleiermacher, *Autobiography*, 1794.)

In the Anhalt parsonage garden, while memories, emotions, and specters gathered around me, I thought: Now we can understand the idée fixe with which the philosopher tormented himself as a child better than could his parents and his teachers, better than he understood it himself. His obsessive thoughts about antiquity, about all of history, as something that in all likelihood had been invented; his doubts about whether the famous battles and negotiations had really taken place, whether the great men had really lived—this child of the eighteenth century could talk to us without losing his reputation of "intelligence." We know that not only America continually reinvents itself—every few decades a few hundred kilometers further westwards—but that Europe, too, has disappeared more than once and has had to reconstruct its history from "fictional" and "disconnected" pieces. Then it was time for me to walk a bit farther up the slope to the house of the Holdunów Protestant churchwarden and his wife for coffee, some crumb cake, and an afternoon's conversation—in German, by the way.

7 Four Wars

Those who study the past—writers, historians, and the like—share one wish: to distance themselves from it. They transform corpses into figures of bronze or stone, stories into printed books, the everyday objects of great and holy men into relics and museum pieces. Writers, historians, and theologians work ceaselessly to reshape life's residue into something that reminds them less of life. At work is a mix of shame, disgust, and fear, as if the scraps of paper, locks of hair, letters, and other little piles left over from the past emit a peculiar radiation with a foul smell and the power to discomfort. As if they had been soaked in ptomaine. As if the dead could return and get us.

Above the maid's room of my aunt's apartment in Berlin, between the kitchen and the long corridor that leads to the bedrooms in the back, there is a roomy crawlspace where among unused suitcases and broken appliances nests a cardboard box measuring fifty centimeters by thirty centimeters. It bears the reddish-brown imprint of *Uncle Tuca* (after *Chiq-*

uita, the second company to market bananas as a brand name item) and the image of a man's head—wide and silly, but also smiling as if he were the owner of an estate or a hacienda, resplendent in a checkered shirt and peculiarly white sideburns, healthy and dumb as life itself.

"On shipboard one comes across many stupid depictions, but this is one of the stupidest of all," says the resigned and melancholy Gracchus, whose bark is blown by "the wind that blows in the lowest regions of death" in Kafka's tale "The Hunter Gracchus." He is speaking to the mayor of Riva, who is respectfully moved, but also of course somewhat taken aback. Gracchus points to the small picture on the wall across from his pallet: "A Bushman, apparently, who is aiming his spear at me and taking cover as best he can behind a magnificently painted shield." I don't know if my grandfather packed the box adorned with the picture of the foolish-looking, Bushman-like Uncle Tuca—a bark blown through time by a wind from death's nether regions—or whether it was my aunt who put these papers and notebooks there after my grandfather's death, when she cleared out her parents' apartment.

For example, the hunting log of the Laskowitz Head Forester:

No. 97. Number of kills: 1; Species: wildcat; Date: 19 April 1911. Note: Near Klein Dupine. Black, evening, chased by Treu onto the tree.

No. 98. 1 cuckoo; 6 June; probably a sparrow-hawk; shot in flight with my triple-barreled gun

No. 99. 1 shrike; 16 June; near Anschwitz with triple-barreled gun; sat on a wire; blown into 1000 pieces.

And so on, through the years. Or the diary kept by Gustav Wackwitz, my grandfather's brother, a pilot in Artillery Air Division 235—a diary kept until a hot July day in 1918 when, age twenty-three, he fell with his airplane from the sky. ("It is my hope that this book and those that follow will record many successful flights to the front. May it be the will of God that I am spared a cruel fate at the beginning of my career as a pilot and that I make a real contribution to the success of our efforts in the air. *Heil und Sieg!* Wackwitz.")

Also in the box: a mint-condition copy of the book that Andreas Wackwitz wrote in 1931 about the history of the congregation of Anhalt, the original copy of his memoirs, the photo albums and travel diaries, the bright red notebook labeled *Exercise book*, in which my grandfather—at the time a prisoner of war in England—wrote down his hunting adventures in Africa (while Winston Churchill was fighting in the House of Commons for a mandate to destroy Adolf Hitler and his victorious Wehrmacht), and finally Andreas Wackwitz's diary from the First World War, a thick, lined school notebook with a sky-blue binding, the spine brownish and coming loose. From its pages fall drawings, photos, locks of hair, letters, feathers, official papers, and dried flowers. Private (later Lieutenant) Wackwitz wrote in this notebook every day of the Great War, from the first to the last, from the deceptive, easy weeks of success on the eastern front to the trenches of Flanders, where months suddenly turned into years—years that for his brother and so many others were their last.

Although I kept a regular diary during the war from the first day to the last, now, when I leaf through it, I wonder whether it will actually help me when I eventually write about my experience in the war as a whole . . . Now and then I noted a book that I bought in one place or another, or an organ that I played in this or that church, that I sat at a piano in a billet here or there in order to proclaim the fact that the expression "inter arma silent musae" does not apply in every case. Occasionally the diary alludes to various battle noises, and sometimes to blood and sweat. Now and then it devotes a few words to the foreign population, their character and behavior, their habits and customs, their houses, churches, museums, and cathedrals. It notes whether and how many letters and packages were received, and imparts with satisfaction where I shot rabbit, partridge, wild ducks, and sometimes even a wild boar. It distinguishes carefully whether I played Skat or Doppelkopp, drank a Bordeaux or a Burgundy, and happily goes on about the details of our shared lives as soldiers. All of that and much else is noted in telegram style, in strict chronology in two fat notebooks. Between the pages there are concert programs, battle sketches, military orders, official dispatches from the front, tickets, dried leaves, wild duck feathers, a medic's note, three charming letters from a young Frenchwoman, a lock of blond hair with a red ribbon, and the like—things one looks at after forty years with astonishment and melancholy. Only in the first weeks of the war does the diary go into great detail, describing the first battles, which were so exciting and so heavy in losses. An extended passage is also devoted to the devastation wrought by my brother's death. When I consider all this information and all these tiny facts, it seems to me that I wanted no humane and friendly hour to go unmentioned, that I felt it was important not to forget the small intellectual and artistic pleasures, or the occasional high-spirited expression of our youthful natures, and to contrast the hours in which we were happy with the trials of "service." The diary speaks only rarely of war's seriousness, of its problems and horrors, and then only by registering it. I don't think this was the result of indifference; more likely, it was the defensive reaction of a young man, a

kind of armor that one dons unconsciously to protect the inner per-
son. Those who wear this armor became weak or cowardly, depressed
or revolutionary. It was my fate to emerge from the war with the in-
ner person still intact . . .

Nothing in Paris or London resembles the old, nineteenth-century apartments of western Berlin. The ceilings are so high that you hardly notice them, as if one were sitting under the open sky outside. (Indeed, in Berlin, ceiling and sky usually have the same color.) A light like that which pierces the crowns of big trees enters through windows so tall that I couldn't reach the top even were I to stand on a kitchen ladder. Outside, the cars rush by. In such an apartment, on a windy April afternoon in the year 2001, I spread out the contents of the Uncle Tuca box. My aunt and cousins were walking the dog in the park; my son was playing on the basketball court across the street. Sitting at the window, I could see him between the trees, running, then pulling up and shooting. For fifteen minutes at a time, my feelings about my grandfather's war diary would seem like a confrontation with something still half alive, or perhaps alive at least some of the time (when no one is looking). These are objects that haunt or touch or warn or please us (or the mayor of Riva, or anyone else who looks at them), before they are washed away once again by the ocean of time. No one could call this dead storage.

My grandfather, who had participated from beginning to end in the decisive event of the twentieth century, described and reflected upon it with a sense of himself, with metaphors, quotations, a gruffness, and a sentimentality that stem directly and totally from the nineteenth century. After 1918, nothing was as it had been. Everything about our social world that interests us today has been passed on to the present as if backlit by the First World War. But it was with the hardness and coldness of the young man who understands himself to have come through death and destruction *intact* (neither *cowardly* nor as a *revolutionary,* neither *weak* nor *depressed*) that this light came closest to my family and to me. Sometimes, I think, so close that we were scorched by it.

In readers' heads, plots of books unfold in rooms, houses, and gardens all over the world, without the actual inhabitants of these spaces ever knowing it. All the horror stories and ghost stories I've ever read—for example Henry James's *The Turn of the Screw* or Shirley Jackson's *The Haunting of Hill House* and also Dickens's *Oliver Twist*—are set in the dark basement of a 1930s house on Hamburg's Orchideenstieg, where my grandparents lived from 1950 (after they were driven from the German Democratic Republic) until retirement. The house opens from the kitchen to a garden that I remember as perpetually foggy and rainy, in which there's a big cherry tree sheltering, under the damp shadow of a wall, lilies of the valley that grow—strangely enough—throughout the year. During my early school years, I was a compulsive reader of whatever ghost stories I could get my hands on at the public library or elsewhere—my mother's strict prohibition notwithstanding. I suppose that I wished to come closer by day to the terrifying dreams that haunted me at night and to track them down. And then, at night, I would often lie in bed for hours, immobile and sweaty, before I could fall asleep.

The first of these nightmares, however, occurred in my grandparents' house in Hamburg, long before I could read. In my memory, the house smells of cake and cigars, or the morning toast that we never had at home but that we could eat there with butter and jam. The upper floors had more light. There, my youngest aunt let me listen to jazz on a very white and modern Braun record player in her mysteriously girlish room, until her friend drove up in his Mini Cooper— and she would disappear for days. There, aged nine or ten, I spent an entire rainy summer afternoon reading *Die Abenteuer des Dr. Doolittle* and, once, *Lederstrumpf,* Cooper's *Leatherstocking.* This upper floor is my setting for more elegant and modern books (chapter seventy-three of *Man without Qualities,* about Leo Fischel's daughter Gerda, for example).

The heart of the ground floor's darkness was my grandfather's study—the black-lacquered bookcase, the desk big as a bluff, the aforementioned leopard's pelt on the floor in front of it, the dark Herero weapons, photographs of Windhoek and Luckenwalde, a Rembrandt etching (*The Mocking of Christ*) on the wall. I remember his brooding silence—he wasn't even sixty—over newspaper clippings, handwritten notes, drafts of sermons, and I have peculiarly precise memories of radio reports about uprisings in the Congo and the murder of the African leader Lumumba, which my grandfather noted with grim satisfaction and somehow fearful relief; of the death of UN Secretary General Hammarskjöld, whom for some reason my grandfather hated. There was a mocking ditty that I still remember: "Khrushchev and Lumumba/Dance the rumba./The UN hasn't a clue/What to do." Did my grandfather sing that himself? Probably it was we kids. And surely I had no idea who Lumumba was.

But I did understand then (and today more clearly than ever) the deep strangeness of that ground floor, which, I sometimes think, was thick with the spirits of the dead—unseen by my grandfather, because he did not want to be weak or cowardly, depressed or revolutionary. Then I experience the urge to summon these spirits against the silence that weighed on these rooms when my grandfather lived there, as if I had to mobilize the underworld. It was in these rooms that my weakness and cowardice, depression and rebelliousness had their beginnings, and whenever I am weak, depressed, or feeling cowardly and put upon, I return for a moment, a small, spectral boy, to this deserted place, where lives have long gone on without me, without any of us.

TWO SURVIVORS

On the morning of July 3, 1915, we move toward our offensive line, stretch out in the forest and have a bite to eat. At 4 P.M., we line up for battle. The Russian artillery attacks us from the left, and there is heavy loss of life. After we advance some 700 meters, a shell explodes 20 meters to my left at just the right height. I'm hit hard in the left knee and collapse. Two other men in my group also fall. As I unbuckle my backpack, a grenade falls before me into the dirt, but it doesn't explode. My knee begins to burn like fire. I notice that my boot is filling with warm blood. In that split second, I remember that about 20 meters back we'd crossed a fairly deep, dry trench. I leave my backpack, rifle, and belt behind me and crawl backwards on all fours toward the trench, screaming for a medic. When I reach the trench, I lose consciousness and am found by the medics with my head on the trench floor, my feet on the embankment. When I come to, they've cut open my trousers and boot and bound a tourniquet around my leg. They told me that Captain P. had jumped over the trench with the field officer calling behind him to the two medics, "The man can still be saved."

I had lost a lot of blood and was only vaguely conscious that other medics were there taking care of one of the two wounded men in my group. One poor fellow had taken three shrapnel fragments—in the chest, arm, and leg. The other had a hand wound and could make it on his own to the nursing station. Since the fighting was now further away, the two of us were brought back into the forest on makeshift stretchers that had been put together with two poles and some canvas. There, Dr. N. had organized a nursing station. We were placed on straw, and since we were among the first in the battle to be wounded, the doctor quickly turned his attention to us. I was in very great pain. According to what was written on the piece of paper that was attached to a button of my uniform, the doctor bandaged me as best as he could after he had sewn up the two main arteries that had been ripped through—the tourniquet had been around my thigh for 30 minutes. To strengthen my heart he injected me with 4 ccm ocleum camphori, and to ease my pain—I was screaming out loud as he was fumbling about in my wound—he gave me .02 ccm of morphine. On the piece of paper he wrote: "Attend to wound asap. Ditto injection of salt. Watch for blood loss."

My grandfather's survival, the passing down of his genes and his memories from my father to me and from me to my son is a story of solidarity. Class-consciousness, surely, played a role in rescues like that of Lieutenant Wackwitz by Captain P. A promising young lieutenant and fraternity man, even one lying unconscious in the mud, would be recognized by Captain P. I have always been flummoxed by this kind of solidarity and looked elsewhere for my origins.

On that Berlin afternoon in my aunt's apartment, I took the piece of cardboard that had been attached to the button of my grandfather's uniform in 1914 and held it in my hand. The size of a prescription form, it had pre-printed blanks for diagnosis, medication, and further treatment. At each edge was a red stripe, about as wide as a fingernail, separable by means of a large-gauge perforation. If both were torn off, the soldier could still march on his own. If the doctor had torn off neither, he couldn't even be moved. My grandfather had only one red stripe, which meant that he was to receive emergency care at the front, be brought behind the lines on a stretcher, and then restored to full health before returning to fight until the bitter end.

On that windy spring day in Berlin in 2001, the cardboard with the medic's pencil-gray, old-fashioned handwriting was in my hands and before my eyes, but I could not see the death that my grandfather had escaped. All those attacks that were "executed," the "advance fire," the "losses" are described in the same alien language with which he urged me to join a dueling fraternity in the 1970s. I would see death in war only through the eyes of my mother, who did not encounter it in the First World War, but in the Second. She, too, was able to transmit her genes and memories through me to my son by means of a chain of improbabilities. But I will never forget her story, because death revealed something to her in a dream about a future that she and I were to share.

My mother's younger sister, the only of the daughters from Esslingen who is still alive, is a wealthy widow now residing on elegant Euclid Avenue in Berkeley. She is the head of a large, complex tribe of daughters and grandchildren with whom I occasionally exchange enthusiastic e-mails, without the face and personality of my correspondent always being entirely clear to me. Sometimes I have the feeling that she is the only one of us who has met with real success— that she is where we have wanted to go for centuries; where, since the nineteenth century, many more bearers of my surname have lived than in Europe.

She was the family beauty, not the nice and good one (that was the oldest of the three, who was killed in a car accident in the 1960s), nor the gifted and rebellious one—that was my mother. It was the youngest sister who was the prettiest, and it didn't take long before one of the young occupiers with an irresistible smile and a well-ironed khaki uniform lost himself in the depths of her black eyes and abducted her to that country where nothing is as bad as elsewhere—not the winter, and perhaps not even death. (Such, in any case, is my American fantasy.) At that time, at least, there was no hunger in America, and after the war that was saying something. I have visited her there in her various houses, in Indiana and Connecticut, with and without my mother, as a child and as an adult, and each time I have had the feeling that the way she lived was how people ought to live. Her California house on Euclid Avenue is the only one of her homes I have never been to.

Instead she recently visited me, as she occasionally had in the years before. In all this time, she has never lost her homesickness for Germany. Since her husband's death, she flies to Europe almost every year and makes a side trip to see her nephew, who is now almost an older gentleman himself and her only living connection to the past. In my kitchen high above the Vistula, with the view towards Kraków's Royal Castle (for a long time now, I have had apartments that I like at least as well as I once liked her houses), we cook spaghetti and talk about Esslingen, my mother, life in California, my cousins, and the members of her California tour group who have been driven the sixty kilometers through the Beskid foothills to Auschwitz without her that day.

"You know, most of them are Jewish anyway," she says, a little defensively, vaguely confused. She knows she couldn't face the abyss that would open between herself and her travel companions, her fellow American citizens, the abyss that she has learned not to think of all the time, overgrown as it is by the deadwood and brambles of five decades of everyday life in America. But it is still there, it is still deep, she has known all along. And she is scared. "I'd just as soon not go there," she says. For decades now she has been the only one of us who has lived alongside Jewish neighbors, colleagues, and relatives. She says that in all these years she has never told any of them that her father was the leader of the local Nazi Party in Esslingen. But she probably hasn't gone into details about her father with anyone in Indiana, Connecticut, or on Euclid Avenue in Berkeley. For a few fractions of a second in these conversations with my mother's youngest sister, I have had the feeling that she was my mother; as if she hadn't died nearly ten years ago; as if she were sitting at my kitchen table. As if she had survived her cancer and were now living in California.

My mother was twenty-four when she saw death for the first time. When a person of my age gets to know a twenty-four-year-old woman, he is amazed, perhaps even shocked, at how fragile, unfinished, and vulnerable she still is at this age, how much can still go wrong. In truth, this is the best age to bear children, because the mother is herself still a kind of child. When my mother was twenty-four, she was childless, but she took a direct hit in an air strike. Flying over southern Germany in his Spitfire, one of the young conquerors with the irresistible smile and the well-ironed khaki uniform targeted a train that happened to be taking Margot Hartmetz to the front. As an aide in the *Luftwaffe*, she had volunteered to be a courier in exchange for the promise of a few extra vacation days. It is presumably the appearance of being both physically intact and invulnerable that makes men and women at that age charming and sometimes utterly irresistible. Unquestioned and unquestionable health. On a summer day in 1944 somewhere between Esslingen and Mainfranken, American weaponry strafed a moving train and tore apart my mother's shoulder and a large section of her right upper arm—in the years before the miniskirt, the most wondrously suggestive part of the female body.

That she would never again wear a swimming suit or an evening dress was, in the months that followed the attack, the least of my mother's worries. That she escaped with her life she owed only to an indestructible reserve of health. After some rudimentary roadside first aid, she was taken in the next ambulance to the hospital in Esslingen, where for almost half a year she endured operations, weeklong deliriums, cycles of seeming improvement and then relapse, swinging between hope and despair. Into the 1950s, wandering metal fragments would turn up in the most unexpected parts of my mother's body and would have to be removed by surgery. When she came home from the hospital, I, still a child, was allowed to touch these last souvenirs of the war. They were pieces of metal, melted smooth or maliciously jagged. In my hand they looked small, off-color, and absurd.

In later years, my mother would sometimes speak of the time in the Esslingen hospital as a no man's land between life and death. She would speak of the air attacks that had been endured by those who were too sick to move—the darkened ward, the bursting and screaming of the bombs, buildings crashing and burning all around them. She told of a nurse who stayed with her and held her hand. When my mother encouraged her to join the others in the shelter, she is supposed to have replied, "If I pop off, dear, it's all right with me."

She told of General O., a family friend, who visited her in the hospital and with whom she discussed the military situation. "It's not exactly a picnic," he said, "but we're doing what we can." She knew then that the war was lost. And she told of a dream that she had at the climax of her struggle against death, shortly before she somehow put the worst behind her, before the spring of the defeat and the new beginning in which she got to know my father and gave birth to me. In her dream, she heard the doorbell of the house in Esslingen that my grandfather had built in 1926 with the profits of his most successful patent. She opened the door and there, on the travertine flagstones, Death stood in silence, a skeleton in a black cycler's coat and with a scythe over his shoulder. My mother slammed the door shut and hid in the dining room. Instead, her youngest sister—at the time a *Luftwaffe* aide in northern Germany, from whom the family had had no news for weeks—went to the door, opened it, and said, "Go away. You have no business here."

And really, Death did not take my mother then. Two weeks later, the sister of whom she had dreamt (my future American aunt) showed up at her sickbed with chocolate and an egg. Her joy at her sister's reappearance, my mother always said later, was the turning point in her recovery. Shortly afterwards, her fever went down, she could eat again, and a few weeks later, her twenty-four-year-old constitution had defeated the bullets of the low-flying fighter plane. A few months more and Hitler was dead. Peace returned.

The summers of the first years after the war must have been of a phantasmagoric duration and beauty. The hot days over the rubble of the industrial zone of the Neckar Valley, on the vineyards between Esslingen and Stuttgart, were so gorgeous that it was as if they were mocking the hungry, homeless survivors. It would be another seven years before I was born. It had been just a year since Death had been turned away from my grandparents' house. My mother had not yet met my father. And still it seems to me as if those postwar summers became a kind of utopian backdrop to the atmosphere of my childhood memories: a sigh of relief, a feeling of a new beginning, a sudden premonition of luxury and distance, a dream of America.

A DREAM OF THE EAST

Patrolling the train from 3 to 4 one morning, I was suddenly overwhelmed by the sight of the snow-covered, flat distances—a starlit landscape strewn with miserable, cowed villages. It was the East, and for the first time I was really seeing it. As alien as it was, I nonetheless felt an inexplicable, mysterious pull of attraction. Was it the unconscious lure of the open range that I so often felt later in Southwest Africa, was it the pull of eastern space, waiting for action and submission, to which our medieval ancestors had yielded, or was my Polish grandmother calling from within me?

THE LITTLE HUNCHBACK

Without knowing it, on June 24, 1917, my grandfather Andreas Wackwitz came very close to meeting Adolf Hitler, army private and future chancellor. As an officer, my grandfather would not have exchanged even a word with an ordinary dispatcher, but it is possible that they marched past one another. Or perhaps the theology student trying to make his way into the shelter squeezed by the saluting, unemployed young painter. In any case, Adolf Hitler spent several days in the same network of trenches in Flanders as my grandfather, coping with fear, preparing for the coming attacks, and risking his life, as had my grandfather for several days before him. For a moment, history's ghost was that close to Andreas Wackwitz. He could know as little as anyone else that this was the scruffy, sunken-cheeked dispatcher of the 16th Bavarian Infantry Regiment with the dog and the strange moustache whose devoted, submissive, strangely veiled glance has been passed down to us in a photograph dated 1915. At the time, Hitler was a nothing, a private, and my grandfather, after all, a staff officer. Even in 1956, when he was writing down his experiences of the First World War and mentions in passing his company's having been relieved by the 16th Bavarian Infantry Regiment in a dugout near Teubrieleu in Belgium, he certainly would not have made the connection. Again, it seems to be left to his grandson to see the ghosts who crossed his path. But the longer I've thought about the meeting of Adolf Hitler and Andreas Wackwitz, and the more often I've read the relevant passage in my grandfather's journal, the more certain I am that something must have brushed against him, or touched him, not only then, but also when he described it in his memoirs in 1956. True, the pertinent passage mentions only very briefly what the duties of a company's deputy commander were and how he had had to meet his "damned responsibilities." And perhaps it is only a coincidence that his report becomes very dark at this point. The pale, awkward man who lived on the fringes of bohemian Munich, the future *Führer* and chancellor, the most famous political criminal of the modern age stood for a moment in my grandfather's life like the little hunchback in the children's song ("I go into the kitchen/ To cook myself a stew/And there's the little hunchback/ Who says, 'I'll have some, too!'"). Nowhere else in his entire account does he admit that there are images of the war that he never could quite shake.

The night was unusually black. As we were going off-duty—a job made difficult in any case by the crudeness of the Bavarians—there was considerable confusion, and we endured several painful losses. I attended as best I could to a sergeant next to me who was to survive the amputation of an arm that had literally been crushed by a grenade. His composure was admirable, and I saw to it that he was awarded an Iron Cross, First Class. Other images of the Battle of Wytschaete keep coming back to me: the bloated corpses of horses, the dead soldiers with black or blue faces, human bodies that had been blown to pieces, their parts scattered about, and a bleak, churned up expanse over which the English long-range grenades burst in a most horrible way.

THE END / WINTER MORNING
(FLOCKS OF BIRDS OVER THE HOUSE)

It seems to be one of life's rules that in peacetime men go through a manic-successful phase in their mid-thirties and then a depressive stage in their forties: a period in which their lives, if they do not fall apart (not an unknown occurrence), are irreparably cracked (death announces itself). Just as life at twenty-five consists of learning and new impressions, and at thirty-five of success, earning money, begetting children, and having a career (all of this suddenly seeming possible), so, at no later than fifty, men understand that they will die and—measured against what they really wanted— that they have failed. It is the age of heart attacks, divorces, problems at work, hopeless love for twenty-four-year-old women, the time of sleeplessness at dawn. (Through the winter haze, birds fly over the house. They come in increasing numbers, at first as points, hardly visible over the horizon. They fly toward the balcony and then over the roof, their weak wings stirring the air with a barely audible reverberation. They are flying toward destinations we long for but will never reach.)

In the meantime, I've read my grandfather's account of his retreat from France at war's end so many times that the thoughts and formulations of the twenty-two-year-old lieutenant have almost become my own. I no longer know whether I experienced it or read about it or heard about it as a child—or whether it hasn't come to me with other inherited characteristics—a big nose, a weakness for Havana cigars, a tendency to premature graying, and a world war. In the 1960s, my father, my uncle, and I, in a critical mood appropriate to the times, were combing through the most recently presented installment of my grandfather's memoirs, on the lookout for *reactionary passages*. We found, God knows, enough of them to upset us—the description, for example, of General Lieutenant von La Chevallerie—a *very tall, thin, white-haired man*, an allegory of an empire driven to insanity by disappointment (and becoming a kind of emblem to the rest of us):

With long strides he marched through the advancing soldiers toward the enemy, his red general's stripes shining. Brandishing an oak stick high over his head, he pointed with it as if with an unsheathed sword toward the burning village, screaming again and again—I had the feeling that he was frothing at the mouth—"Forward! Forward! If you love your Kaiser, follow me! Forward! For-

ward!"—The light eyes of his weather-beaten, aristocratic face shone fanatically in anticipation of death. It was truly eerie. But the soldiers followed him in a broad front through the exploding English grenades and toward the rattling machine guns as if pulled forwards by a magnet. If someone ducked and hesitated, the old man threatened him with the oak stick, and the fellow stood up and ran on in the direction of the enemy and the burning fire.

But this is the one heroic recollection of a retreat that seems otherwise to have consisted only of mud, French villages and fields, friendly fire from their own worn-out and broken-down artillery, incompetent orders from the German high command, and a general lack of morale. One of Lieutenant Wackwitz's more appealing qualities is the way in which he was able to understand how completely someone like General Lieutenant von La Chevallerie's had lost his marbles. Or—trained theologian that he was—that he noticed in the Prussian chaplain's expressions ("Helmets off for prayer") *the insipidly demythologized cliché of the alliance between throne and altar. Before the year was out, the throne would topple—and the only thing left for men who had grown accustomed to such talk was a total vacuum.* What was left for an educated man of the middle class like Wackwitz was music. *In a billet in La Ferte, young Lieutenant Gerhardt plays Chopin's E-flat Major Etude, with its sweet and melancholy beginning. A few days later, he is killed. Soon afterwards, the house comes under fire and the piano is overturned.*

Lieutenant Wackwitz was not yet twenty-three years old. But he had seen death, almost died himself, experienced success surging manically through his nervous system, and yet knew how hopeless it all was. By 1918, a war veteran had actually lived through pretty much everything. But there had been no time to give up the dreams, to watch the birds fly over the house, to be easier on himself and others, to raise children, and to see things as they were. My grandfather and his dreams did not have enough time to become older and weaker. In 1918, he did not yet know that the world would not go down with a bang but a whimper (and, what's more, that the world never really does go down).

I have the feeling that a revolution is due and write in the diary: "What's going to happen? It's stupid to even ask. Let everything collapse. Help, even, to bring it all down, and then build it anew. It will take centuries, but it will be worth it. Whatever else, not a patchwork job! At home: cholera, the plague, influenza, pneumonia. Lord, let this cup pass from us! As for the other cup: Civil war! Let the Reich break apart, we'll build a new one, the German spirit must once again be victorious, and may God save us from the rest. That is my only concern, otherwise I've come to terms with the situation and I hold my head high." My concern was for the salvation of our German essence and the inner strength of the German people.—The revolution came soon, but it was soulless, with red flags, dirty hands, and stupid demagoguery. Looking back, I ask: is it so strange that we veterans expected a revolution and then, almost to a man, experienced such a bitter disappointment that fifteen years later we thought our time had finally come?

The diary passage quoted by my grandfather dates from 1918; his commentary was written in 1956. The two texts are positioned behind one another like two lenses—one at a distance of forty-four years from us, the other thirty-eight years earlier, a telescopic alignment that gives me a close-up not only of the twenty-five-year-old of 1918, but at the same time of someone who was forty in 1933 and in 1956 sat as an old man at the breakfast table, mute and weepy—and still further in the distance, a small, vaguely contoured ghost: my own political confusion at twenty-four.

In 1918, my grandfather clearly wanted nothing less than a revolution. He writes as much quite straightforwardly: *we veterans of the front.* A revolution, of course, *of the German soul* and the *German essence.* It was, wrote my grandfather in 1956, concern *"for the salvation of our German essence and the inner strength of the German people."* These were the nationalist "ideas" of 1914—and of 1918 and 1956 and the rest of his life. It was when I read the passage in his memoirs about the end of the world in 1918, the German soul, the German essence, and the Revolution, that I understood for the first time what Hitler actually meant to his generation.

"That we lost it," was the answer Ernst Jünger gave before his hundredth birthday to a reporter who had naively asked him what had been the worst part of the First World War. The worst thing about the war that my country waged during the weeks when I was reading my grandfather's memoirs for the first time was the confusion that resulted in the evening's television programming from the endless special broadcasts about our involvement in Yugoslavia. The worst thing about the Vietnam War for young Americans was that so many of them returned crippled from South Asia; or they didn't return at all. Maybe the First World War is the last one about which the worst thing for the participants was that they were defeated. It is said that in the 1960s Ernst Jünger got up every morning, dressed formally, and sat staring straight ahead until bedtime. And it was probably just such a secret and bottomless depression I sensed in my grandfather even when I was a child, although at the time I would not have been able to say why he was so sad, so cold, insensitive, and strange. I recognize his sadness again on the onion-skin paper of his memoirs. It is a dangerous, veiled melancholy that men as different as Ernst Jünger, Max Beckmann, and Adolf Hitler brought back from the trenches, a mixture of monumental petulance, defiant and demonstrative insensitivity, self-righteousness, and occasional, uncontrollable rage. If one pays attention, one can see them in that generation's every deed, image, and word. Even before the war, my grandfather's fellow soldiers had not been able to make their peace with the men they had become or were in the process of becoming. A discontent fueled a four-year war with the British and the French, just as before and afterwards it fed their loathing of the Jews. Then it was too late. The revolution came, but it wasn't theirs. It was a revolution of democracy, of blue-collar workers, of avant-garde artists, of Jews.

Before my grandfather dismissed his "boy" Emil, handed in his weapons, was decommissioned and sent back into the world (although the world he had known no longer existed), he found himself stranded after a chaotic train trip in revolutionary Berlin, a city stirred up by soviet councils, street fights, and republican proclamations, a kind of in-between state in which anything was possible:

I took a short walk into the city. It was like a teeming ant colony. On my way back, a fellow with a red armband and a red cockade stopped me at the Friedrichstrasse train station and ordered me to cut off my epaulettes: all ranks had been abolished. I refused, and immediately I was surrounded by more fellows of the same type.

They weren't rude, and they weren't loud. They said they took their orders from another authority in the military. I realized that the rest of my journey was in jeopardy, and since there were in any case no officers with epaulettes to be seen, I had mine cut off. The fellow who did it was obviously experienced. I carried a pistol, and the Iron Cross was visible on my coat. They paid attention to neither, nor to the Prussian cockades on my cap. Not far from us there was a pile of guns and bayonets a meter high. Emil, too, had to throw his gun onto it. The Spartacus people probably helped themselves to them. The cutting off of the epaulettes filled me with mute anger. For many years, I really hated the Reds . . . I telegraphed home from Berlin that I was coming. In Breslau, I said goodbye to Emil, who traveled on to his home in Glatz, and I was reunited with my bride, who had come from Laskowitz. It struck me as strange that the telegraph and the trains were still working.—Our reunion took place on Repentance Day. We went to a pension on Teichstrasse, and on the way we drank a bottle of plundered champagne. By evening, we were in Laskowitz. I had survived the war.

But for the rest of my grandfather's life, both the mania of General Lieutenant von La Chevallerie and the depression of the formally dressed writer in the armchair lurked within him. At the war's end, he was still young and strong, but he was as disappointed as an old man. Only fifteen years later, in another kind of in-between state in which once again anything seemed possible, did the vague dreams, ideas, and phantasms of 1914 again come within reach. At the age of twenty-five, one can't yet see the flocks of birds flying away over the house together with one's life's dreams on early winter mornings. And at the age of fifty, Andreas still didn't understand that behind life's dreams, life itself goes on, without us. But perhaps it was all completely different. What do

I know? After all, he said nothing about this to me or anyone else. None of us knew what our grandfather was really
thinking and feeling when he wrote his *family romance* in the
fifties and sixties. What is left to me is to continue reading
the notebooks with their innumerable onion-skin pages.

The emperor, it is said, sent a message from his deathbed to you, and to you alone, his pitiful subject, the tiny shadow that fled from the imperial sun to the furthest distance.   —Kafka, "An Imperial Message"

8   In the Emperor's Palace

I drove to Laskowitz on an apocalyptically dark and rainy April morning in 2001. It was as cold as late autumn, and the low-hanging clouds blocked out all proper light until well into morning. I traveled the labyrinthine roads of the Upper Silesian industrial zone, past deserted landscapes of gigantic, rusting combines, iron smelters, and derricks, past the huge flying saucer-like disc of the Kattowitz conference center and the modernistic winged memorial to the Silesian rebellions, past endless rows of fifteen-story apartment buildings that from a distance looked American and elegant. I would find myself on smooth stretches of highway that had been completed only last year, and then on access roads sprouting weeds and mined with potholes deep as pig troughs. Morose laborers heading to the early shift were trudging along the muddy roadside, and pretty girls were freezing under bus shelters of galvanized zinc and iron poles. Next to the traffic light in a canyon-like thoroughfare somewhere between Bedzin and Dambrowka Goralksa, amongst high housing blocks wastefully adorned with caryatids, blackened bay windows, balconies, railings, Renaissance portals and busts, a fat old man was carefully and hopelessly cleaning the windows of his second-story apartment.

I stopped in Gleiwitz for a cup of coffee. Beyond Oppeln, the flat land stretched out into the distance. Tree-lined roads straight as a rod passed villages that would have looked no different a hundred years ago, with their sturdy, castle-like churches, half-timbered houses, ponds, baroque manor houses, and chimneys topped by stork nests. Behind classical gates, driveways allowed a clear view past hedges and high walls to small castles, which lay between distant hillocks and low outbuildings surrounded by trees. From a house-high bridge in Ohlau, the last town before Breslau, I saw the Wilhelminian train station below, its battlements and brick walls off at an angle between trees and train lines.

In 1909, when we children left Bunzlau for the long Easter vacation, we still had to travel to Ohlau by horse-drawn coach. When it came to fetch us, we felt very honored to see the coachman greeting us from his seat with a raised whip, as befitted people of high standing. Full of expectation and curiosity, we drove the fourteen kilometers toward our new home. First we went through the town of Ohlau, then over the Ohlau Bridge, past tobacco fields, through Ottag and the Oder Forest, through the forest and village of Jeltsch, and then finally down a long road lined by cherry trees, and over the Breslau-Oppeln train line then being constructed, crossing the village street at Schlosskretcham, through the gate to the estate, across the yard, past the forester's office, the tenant's house, the distillery, and the cheese factory, to the back of our house. Normally, one got out of the coach at the forester's office and went through the park gate flanked by two bronze lions.

I had assumed that it would all be gone. Next to me on the passenger seat lay the yellow cardboard notebook with my grandfather's memories of Laskowitz, written at the end of the 1950s in Hamburg—the first, the most detailed, the saddest, and, as I've always thought, the most beautiful and personal part of his memoirs. Small photos with brown spots and jagged edges are glued onto the thin paper (otherwise blank) between the narrowly typed pages of text. The forester's house. My great-grandfather, a man with a bulbous nose and a Vandyke beard, steeped in dignity and importance, wearing rubber boots and a soft, narrow-brimmed Tyrolean felt hat adorned with a chamois brush. He stands on the moor in a long coat next to his smiling young assistant, with his dogs, his rifle on his back, and his binoculars around his neck. My great-grandmother, looking much older than he does, wears a wool polka-dot dress; my grandfather, standing in front of the house, balances the antlers of an eight-horned stag on a campstool; a flower tub in the middle distance; the black and white, rustling foliage from the beginning of the century in the lordly park behind him.

As my grandfather was describing his childhood in this notebook, it appeared to him—as it does to everyone—as a lost paradise rising from the depths of his memory. Indeed, the Ohlau station, the tree-lined drive, the river plain, the old oak trees along the Oder River, the estate, the castle, the lions at the gate, and the forester's house had disappeared into the distances of history and were as invisible as if but dreamed. He had been exiled from the Garden, but by the time my aunt, his youngest daughter, was typing the Laskowitz memoirs in the 1950s, it was barred not by an angel with a flaming sword, but by an impenetrable barricade of watchtowers, minefields, and barbed wire. And on the last pages of his Laskowitz memoirs, he indulges in dark fantasies about the *extent of destruction and devastation* behind the world's last frontier, images apocalyptically inspired *by vague news that the head forester's lodge was burned down and all the furniture smashed and destroyed.*

But on that rainy April day, I found the village of Laskowice on exactly the same tree-lined road whose history and landmarks my almost seventy-year-old grandfather had described in 1959 in his dark, haunted Hamburg study as an invisible country that existed then only in his head. I left the car in a friendly little parking lot next to the lovingly restored village church, built in 1650, near the bronze lions of the park gate, in front of the completely unscathed, freshly cleaned neo-baroque castle. Walking casually through the lions' gate, I greeted the two watchmen dressed in black, who were guarding the entrance to the park and the Jelcz-Laskowice town administration now housed in the castle. I lost myself in the castle park of Laskowitz, comparing the trees, walls, paths, and buildings with the memory-landscape described in the yellow notebook that I repeatedly took out of my satchel.

From here a white beech-lined road goes past the castle toward a small neo-classical temple-like structure, in which a bust of Blücher stands on a pedestal. The beam bears the inscription: "1813—Unity Makes Us Strong—1871." Shortly before coming to this little temple, one turned to the right into our four-acre garden and toward the very friendly-looking house, with its glass-enclosed veranda beneath the room under the gable, two windows on either side of the veranda and antlers above it.

The Blücher temple was no longer there. But in the silence of the park, a woman with her bags from the day's shopping was biking on the softly crunching gravel of the beech-lined road past a gap in the trees at exactly the spot where the temple must have stood. I quickly found the *park's most beautiful feature,* as my grandfather had described it forty years ago, a red beech-lined road from the nineteenth century.

It began at the castle and went in a straight line toward a sandstone memorial four to five meters high, a crucifix whose pedestal bore an inscription to a Count Saurma who had been killed in 1866. It stood directly in front of the park wall, which was broken through at that spot and replaced with wire mesh, so that from afar you could see the cross rising against the open field and the horizon. The red beeches were planted so thick on either side of the road that one walked toward the cross as if through a forest of Gothic pillars. They were tall and thin and their crowns locked high above like the ribs of a Gothic nave. To walk down this road toward the cross always had a strong effect on the inner person.

The only thing that the Poles had changed since 1945 in this Caspar David Friedrich arrangement was that they had removed the wire mesh. And when I turned from the road shortly before the small clearing where the Blücher-temple had been on the right, it was a shock suddenly to see the forester's house, complete and with every detail intact, just as in the photos in the yellow notebook.

Our parents' house reflects the architecture of our soul. When we describe our lives, we do so in terms of rooms and houses. The art of memory has been allied with architecture for a long time. Old people, especially, sometimes feel transported back to the houses and interiors of their childhood with a precision that is unsettling even to them, so that for days they can't find their way out of its furniture, its views, its smells and atmosphere. This happened to my seventy-year old grandfather and his father's house in Laskowitz. While he was remembering and writing, it had apparently become the very picture of an order that it was his life's mission to maintain and which, in the course of the century, was lost to him. The description of his father's house is among the stylistic highpoints of his memoir. His emphasis of the fact that in the course of more than thirty years neither the position of the furniture nor anything else in his father's house had changed is no coincidence: everything was as immutable as it was in his memories, or on the closely-typed onion-skin pages on which he recorded them. According to Andreas Wackwitz, the house in Laskowitz that I stood in front of in the April rain in 2001 was a symbol for a world that should have remained as it was.

From the porch, one came into a vestibule, which led to a living room, my father's study, then two narrow guestrooms. My father soon extended the living room by half as much again, adding a nice, wide window. The domestic help lived in the guestroom that looked onto the garden. My parent's large bedroom was on the floor above, in front of it the aforementioned room beneath the gable, in which we children lived, initially all of us together, then I alone. There was also a maid's room and later an enlarged guestroom, more storage spaces and sub-attics, nine rooms in all, three of them very small. We needed a house with a lot of space, since we had help in addition to the maid, apprentice foresters in training with my father, and the guests who stayed with us during the hunting season. Next to the house, there was a roomy gazebo, and fifty meters away a very pretty bower surrounded by white beech where, when the mosqui-

toes weren't too pesky, we sometimes had coffee. The main floor of the house was raised—five or six steps led up to the porch—so that in the basement there was room for the big kitchen, the clothes wringer, and several storage rooms. A fly-wheel pump next to the kitchen was connected to the fountain outside and to the yard. A speaking tube, which to us children seemed a wonderful invention, went from the kitchen up to the dining room. Soon after we moved in, electricity was brought into the village, and electric lights were installed throughout the house. In the yard, there was a huge stall for small animals, a shelter for wood and coal, two wooden out-houses, and a walled dung pit. In the summer, Kurzer, the watch-man, split the logs for the winter and piled them into big stacks in the yard. Wood fueled both the tile stoves that heated the house and the stove in the kitchen. The yard was separated from the garden by a high wooden fence and enclosed on its other three sides by the park wall (two meters high) and the gable of the house.

Our parents had owned ample furniture in Petersdorf, so they didn't need much more to outfit the new house. My father bought a new, large desk and a round table with three simple chairs for his study. Otherwise they acquired nothing new, except for a cupboard, a large extendable table, a new piano, a few carpets, and curtains. When my grandmother Liebig died in 1911, my parents took some things from her house, like the pretty walnut cabinet in the living room. Until the death of my father—32 years after we had moved in—the arrangement of the rooms, the positioning of the furniture, etc., stayed the same. Whenever one came, one found everything in the same spot and felt immediately at home. Against the large back wall of the dining room under a jumble of deer antlers, there was a sofa and the large dining table with room for 14 to 16 people when the extensions were added. My father always sat on the sofa and presided over the dinner party, and as soon as everyone rose from the lunch table, he would lie down for a little nap. The dachshund crawled into the curve formed by his knees, and in the summer he covered his bald head with a newspaper to ward off the flies. On the other side of the room, the window side, was Grandmother Wackwitz's armchair, where my mother took her naps, her feet propped up on the footstool. She "didn't sleep a wink" because we made too much noise slamming the doors, stomping up the stairs, etc. But she was always very surprised when we told her that "she did a fine job cooking the peas," i.e., while sleeping peacefully, she made a little "blup" with each exhalation. Between the windows hung the pendulum clock and the wall clock, under which stood my schoolboy desk, built by a Petersdorf carpenter and placed there by my mother after I was living on my own in Anhalt. On the desk was a pretty, valuable inkwell perched on a green onyx plate with an eagle's claw, a shooting prize won by my father. My mother's sewing table stood at the other window, with a picture of Father and the children. A large walnut sideboard, a well-stocked linen closet, a flower table, and a serving table completed the dining room, where hunting dinners, so-called dinner parties, and also our wedding meal took place. In the living room were the piano, Grandmother Liebig's cabinet, a round table with two beautiful chairs, and a sofa, as well as a large baroque mirror, many knick-knacks, photos, etc. A painting of the Kaiser in a general's uniform was propped up on a wooden easel, a small round table with two wicker chairs stood in front of the sofa, and as a special ornament, a stuffed fox on a foot-high green plinth was placed next to the door to Father's study. My father had shot it from a great distance, and in memory of this triumph, it stood for years on its back legs and with its smart Reynard-the-fox face, holding a box with cigars on a silver tray. (To these I had free access whenever I was visiting home.) Later, the fox became the object of a certain interest—fearful at first—to our children. On the piano and on a shelf over the sofa, there were many photographs, some of them with inscriptions by various dukes and royals, vases, mementoes, and souvenirs—everything in the style of the time around 1880–1900, as indeed the whole room was decorated in a somewhat modernized bourgeois velvet-furniture style (with curtains at two doors!). Dusting all these things on the piano and the shelf was a time-consuming and tedious task. The picture of the dog "Treu" (who was poisoned in 1895 and memorialized by a stone tablet in my grandmother's garden) hung above the sofa. He lay in the grass, his head raised attentively, and my cousin Toni, who at the time was four, slept with her little head on his body—a picture in the sentimental manner of the Gartenlaube. My father had loved this dog a great deal, and thus this picture, too, held precious memories. Knowing this, I never felt the painting was all that sentimental. My parents felt a different and much stronger connection to the picture over the piano, a large oil portrait of my brother painted by the Breslau artist Carl Deller. Soon after my brother was killed in 1918, my father asked the painter—we knew him through his daughter, who had worked for a time as household help for my mother—to paint Matzen in the Laskowitz forest, wearing a hunting outfit and with a shotgun over his shoulder. Deller used photos of Matzen for the face and figure, but my father, too, served as a model, posing in a forest clearing in the Waldvorwerk hunting grounds. Deller made a present of the picture to my parents, and he also gave us a small study in oil, depicting a bit of pine forest, for our wedding. It went down with the other things from Windhoek, and the painting of Matzen was destroyed or burnt in 1945.

In my father's study there was a round oak table with three simple easy-chairs. Here Skat was played. Underneath the picture of the Kaiser in royal hunting garb stood the large writing desk, 1 meter by 2 meters. To the uninitiated it looked like an awful mess, but my father would get very annoyed whenever my mother tried to straighten it up, claiming that he could no longer find anything. The entire wall above the desk and around the picture of the Kaiser was covered from ceiling to desktop with antlers. There may have been 60 to 80 of them, with the date and location of the hunt indicated on each. On the wall's lower half, the antlers' spikes served to hang scales for weighing letters, tobacco pouches, tax receipts, appointment slips, unpaid bills, and the like. It looked lively and colorful, but my mother was less than enthusiastic about it. In spite of all the papers, files, writing tools, ashtrays, and letter trays, the desk still had room for a large number of pictures, e.g., of Head Forester Klopfer, Matzen, the Kaiser, of dogs, and God knows what else.

Above the door hung a picture of old Duke Friedrich with his little Bolognese dog. The Duke had made a present of it to my grandfather, who left it for my father in his will. Later I found a copy of this old steel engraving at an antiquarian dealer's in Hamburg and acquired it for 20 marks in order to bring the picture back into the family. The window immediately next to the door had a small opening through which the pipe spit was emptied—a procedure that was always accompanied by my mother's energetic "Pfui!" The rest of the furniture in this room consisted of a bookshelf, a cuckoo clock, a wing chair (from Grandmother Liebig), and a little bookcase. Over the bookcase hung a large painting of Bismarck (after the portrait by Lenbach), and on it stood a silver trophy, awarded in the war to each fighter pilot for his first hit.

One of the main pieces of furniture in the study was the gun cabinet. We had had it in Petersdorf, and I've already described it. In Petersdorf, we had a Steiglede triple-barreled hammer gun, a target rifle, and an old shotgun (used by me). To these, a Sauer & Son hammerless double-barreled shotgun and a rifle with a telescopic sight were added in Laskowitz. Matzen's guns, as well as a triple-barreled hammerless shotgun and a Browning shotgun, were also kept in the gun cabinet until Father's death. The entire room was permeated by a faint smell, more or less noticeable throughout the entire house, that emanated from three sources: tobacco, dogs, leather.

*Even entering the front hall, one could smell it amongst the dog
leashes, the old, sweaty hunting caps, the loden clothing, and other
hunting gear that were hanging on the antlers. Behind the curtain
were the oil-saturated hunting boots and, in the corner, was the basket for the big hunting dogs. I always liked this odor of tobacco,
leather, and dogs. It made me feel right at home, and without it a
forester's house is like soup without salt.*

I stood for a long time in my grandfather's fragrant, dripping
garden, the old yellow notebook in my hand. Its carbon-
paper lettering (dating from 1959) was beginning to dissolve,
blur, and soften. The spring leaves were still small, and their
light green color suffused the air between the branches of
the pear and apple trees. The ground was covered with
anemones. The interpretation of dreams teaches—as Freud
notes in his essay on *the family romance of the neurotic*—"that
even in later years, if the emperor or empress appears in
dreams, those exalted personages stand for the dreamer's father and mother." By contrast, the lonely man who was
dreaming in 1959 of Wilhelminian Laskowitz imagined all
his life that the empire and the *Kaiser* (*the German people's inner and positive strength* that made the empire worth belonging to) resembled his father's world and his father—a man
who was almost a Prussian district officer and whose dachshund would crawl into the curve behind his knees when,
after presiding at the dinner table, he curled up on the sofa
for his nap. The revolution, the world war, the enraged and
narcissistic destruction of a nation that had been tested in
war and proved wanting, and its vague and grandiose
restoration in future centuries fantasized by my grandfather
in his diary of 1918, and finally the new Reich of 1933—all
this, apparently, should somehow resemble the dachshund,

the sofa, the Chief Forester, and the nap. For his entire life, Andreas Wackwitz, in the vague, poorly thought-out, and peculiarly irresponsible way in which he formed his political opinions, seems never to have imagined a properly governed country any differently than the forester's house that smelled of dogs, leather, and cigars.

We, of course, cannot imagine what kind of new beginning the events of 1918, 1933, or any other time might have inspired. "No one gets through here and certainly not with a message from a dead man," I thought in the Laskowitz Park, while the raindrops fell on the onion-skin paper and the glued-in photos of the yellow notebook. However lovingly and precisely he had furnished it, the memory-palace of my grandfather appears to me as impenetrable and depressing as a junk heap. (One feels that my grandfather's documentary and biographical-apologetic interests coincide in these passages and give his account a golden background.) The emperor's message will never reach me. "But you sit at your window and will dream of it when evening comes."

9 An Island in the South Pacific

After having read parts of my grandfather's text a dozen times and copying them down, I find that I occasionally experience odd bits of detail as independent phenomena in my imagination—the furniture in the Memory Palace. It's a response that feels ridiculous, sometimes oppressive, and now and then very definitely weird. For example, the stuffed fox with the smart Reynard-the-fox face propped on a foot-high green pedestal and standing on its hind legs, presenting a cigar case on a silver tray, the *free access* to it that my grandfather enjoyed whenever he was visiting—this is an image that presents itself before my eyes for hours at a time in my own life, in which there are indeed cigars, if not trophy cabinets, rifles, and dogs.

I can no longer determine whether this fox really existed or whether it, too, isn't a kind of ghost that haunts the deserted rooms of the Wackwitz *family romance*. But what is unquestionably present in the Silesian landscape of my grandfather's memory is the allusion to death and an understanding of why life as it had been in the nineteenth century, whose last foothills and moraines are depicted in these memoirs, could not continue. Ernst Gustav Wackwitz, known in the family as "Matzen"—in his brother's memoir, his oil portrait hangs on the wall of their parents' home as a *memento mori*—is one of the young men whose life the First World War snuffed out. After everyone who knew them has died, the only traces left of them are a few photos, and usually even those have disappeared. One of Matzen's pictures that has been left to us, a brownish, smudged, and ghostly copy, shows him, perhaps twenty years old, in hobnailed boots and knee breeches, a hunter's hat on his head, sitting outside in front of bushes and trees that dissolve into a blur at the edges of the square little photo. He is smoking a long pipe with a porcelain bowl that extends almost to the ground. A large dog puts its head in his lap, another lies like a lion in the grass, and the young man smiles apologetically and embarrassed, as if he were not quite at ease—a guest in the reality of a viewer who is eighty years younger. Two other pictures in our family album (they must have been taken with a better and more modern camera) show him more clearly: in the company of a young woman wearing an elegant coat, fine leather gloves, and a fur hat, the features of her face so delicate, free of makeup, and pale that in a cool light they almost become invisible. It is a bright winter day; behind the young couple is a park; they stand between two columns of limestone or sandstone. It must be somewhere in Belgium.

The squadron sent his belongings home in his field trunk—his cameras, his diaries, his clothes, and parts of his uniform (belt and sheath), as well as some negatives from his cameras. I was also told that he had had "a little girlfriend" in Brussels, whom he visited several times when on leave. Prints from two of these negatives show them together. She was a pretty little person in a coat and fur cap, he, next to her, youthful and vital, free and open, at peace with himself and in the sense of privilege that youth confers. I found her address among his papers. Her name was Miss van Es, and we corresponded briefly. She wrote about the two of them and of her grief—tactfully and in a very agreeable handwriting. I don't know how deep and close their tie was, as he himself never spoke of it. But if it was consummated—as one would expect under the circumstances—it would make me glad that he should be granted this before his death.

Ernst Gustav, my grandfather's brother, was killed on July 16, 1918, at the age of 23, on a practice flight in his Fokker airplane. The crash was caused by a fault in the design—the plane that took Matzen to his death had been in use only since the winter of 1917–18. It must have been the Fokker Monoplane FIV, whose picture I am looking at in Meyers *Lexikon* of 1926. I read that under "the influence of Junker's ingenious designs, Fokker switched to a cantilevered wing with a strengthened cross-section. Its strong lift and wing span made the biplane construction superfluous, also in relation to the plane's ability to climb and maneuver. Thus, the Fokker airplane (Plate VI, 1) initiated a return to the mono-wing construction for fighter planes. By the end of the war, Germany, with its Albatross, Pfalz, and Fokker one-seater fighter planes, was in first place." The deployment of mono-wing fighter planes at that point was not, of course, of much use, extending the war probably by a few weeks and costing another hundred thousand young men their lives. And Junker's design was not quite as ingenious as described by Meyers *Lexikon*, for it functioned only on cool days.

*On the afternoon of July 16, the same fatal accident occurred some-
thing like a dozen times in several squadrons on the western front.
The panel separating those parts of the airplane that were very hot
from the incendiary ammunition was not sufficiently robust, and
in the course of this blazing-hot afternoon the ammunition ignited
and began to burn. At this moment Matzen's plane was already at
a height of 1000 meters. He immediately positioned it for a crash
landing, but at an altitude of 700–800 meters he must have realized that he wouldn't have enough time. The fire had spread to the
engine. So he baled out. But the parachute (perhaps already singed)
tore. The plane burned on the ground. When Matzen's comrades
reached him, he looked as if he were sleeping. On July 16, the afternoon of the accident, my fiancée was picking berries in the forest.
She was suddenly seized by a deep and inexplicable feeling of fear:
has something happened? Is it Andreas? Is it Matzen?*

It wasn't Andreas. It was Matzen. It was the beginning of
our *family romance.* Without ever having told anyone, my
grandfather discovered in the course of his research that his
brother was sacrificed to an airplane that had been poorly
constructed and insufficiently tested, but was nonetheless
widely deployed at the end of the war—a war that had been
lost long before and whose incompetent leadership was on
a panicked retreat forwards. But the rather obvious possibility that his brother was killed not as a would-be conqueror
but as a victim of a product safety test does not seem to have
occurred to my grandfather. The idea that it is permissible to
send people *en masse* to their doom in the interest of heroic
and hopelessly mistaken decisions was as taken for granted
by the strategists and soldiers in World War I as it was later
by the commander-in-chief at Stalingrad and his cannon fod-

der, or by the commanders and *Volkssturm* battalions of the battle for Berlin.

In 1940, in Westminster Abbey in London, again in the middle of a war, I read these words on a beautiful and stirring monument to the unknown soldier, and I thought of him: "They gave the most that man can give, life itself." These English words are more than the Horatian "dulce et decorum," and as long as men live, we will hold to them. My father held to them, and I, too, hold to them. Only the cowards, the base, the wicked, the "clever" ones want no part of it. At the time, I tried to console and fortify myself in my diary: "Being cheerful and vigorous, moving forward, seeking victory, and, if it has to be, dying—that was your heroic life. You are a brave and true fellow, a complete man."

In the meantime, my grandmother is picking berries in the Laskowitz forest, sensing, somehow, that at this moment her fiancé's brother is falling from the sky. In Berlin, I had her carefully transcribed copy of Matzen's diary on my knees, a series of matter-of-fact, stark, emotionless accounts of flight missions, sketches of barrack life, and conventionally heroic officer's mess wisdom. But a copy of the diary of one of Matzen's friends had been inserted among the back pages of the notebook. (Apparently it was not only the volunteers of the First World War who wrote nonstop until the last possible moment. After war's end, their wives, girlfriends, and admirers must have spent months and years copying everything all over again for one another and for posterity.)

Matzen's friend—his name was Rudolf Ilka—was killed just after completing his diary, on February 18, 1915. He wrote his last entry shortly before the assault was to begin. He was intoxicated by rage, terror, and adrenalin, and he knew that he would not survive the attack. "After a very turbulent night, at 6:30 this morning we received the order to storm the enemy. The infantry will attack at 10, and we will advance behind them to form a straight line. Now this diary is finished, and I won't be needing another. Maybe not. Godspeed, my golden, distant homeland; farewell, parents, brothers and sisters, friends, and my dear, fair-haired girlfriend, farewell to all of you. Death extends its thousand claws, a thousand arms want to tear me down from the sunny heights to a gruesome darkness—Mother! Mother, pray for your son, oh pray, for soon your son will be yours no longer. Lord our God, if it is your desire—I pray for an easy death, if death it must be—and for the success of our storm."

Indeed, Rudolf Ilka did not need a new diary. In the trenches of Flanders the sound of the word "storm" must have had its own demonic existence, nightmarishly detached from its actual meaning. Ernst Jünger describes the intertwining of idyll and death on the war's western front in a story that bears the title "Storm." (Like his famous *Storm of Steel* or *Copse 125*, it is in fact just a diary like those kept by Rudolf Ilka, my grandfather, his brother, and countless others of his readers and his generation, but Jünger's is elaborated as literature.) He describes the front as the natural habitat of arcadian demons: "At noon, when they squatted on the burned-brown clay benches of the lookouts and colorful butterflies swayed over to the trenches from the blossoming thistles of the rotting land, when the sounds of battle were silent for a few short hours and little jokes were accompanied by muted laughter, then a ghost crept out of the tunnel in a glowing light, looked one soldier or the other wanly in the face and asked, 'Why are you laughing? What are you cleaning your rifle for? Why are you digging about in the earth, like a worm in a corpse? Perhaps tomorrow all will be forgotten, like a night's dream.' Those to whom this ghost appeared were very easy to recognize. They became pale and dreamy, and when they went to stand guard, their view held unwaveringly in the direction toward which their rifle was pointing, toward no man's land. When they were killed, someone, a friend, probably, would utter the warrior's age-old words over their grave: 'Almost as if he had foreseen it. He was so changed recently.'"

It is completely quiet, and the butterflies sway in the air. An exploding grenade kills a hundred people, and then it's quiet again. For a long time I haven't been able to look at the two pictures of my dead great-uncle and his Belgian girl-friend without having them change like ghosts before my eyes. In contrast to the two smiling twenty-somethings in the photos, I know that the young man who is enjoying his good fortune and a seemingly timeless arcadia with the young citizen of a conquered country is a *dead man walking.* We are told that Japanese occupation forces were discovered on an island in the South Pacific twenty years after the end of World War II: they had not heard that the war was over. We imagine tattered uniforms, battle flags in the tropical wind, the heroic and senseless morning roll calls, the martial Robinson Crusoe–like existence beyond all battlefronts and hopes, the picture of the emperor in the commanding officer's hut, and the expression on his face when the discoverers of the scattered unit finally tell him that in truth there has been peace for all those years.

But there really had been a war, from which even the decommissioned survivors could no longer find their way home. The First World War was not over in 1918. It continued until 1989, and in a certain sense, not only my father but even I continued to fight in it, finding my way out only in the last fifteen years of the century. By war's end in 1918, an entire generation of German war veterans was beginning to try to transform their memories of gas attacks, fear, rage, torn-off hands and legs into something that these irritated and vaguely disturbed men could still call victory. ("They became pale and dreamy, and when they went to stand guard, their view held unwaveringly in the direction toward which their rifle was pointing, toward no man's land.") My grandfather was one of them, and his heroic idyll (his South Pacific island) lay in the Polish part of Upper Silesia, barely a hundred kilometers south of the new borders dictated by the Treaty of Versailles.

left: The author's grandfather, Andreas Wackwitz, in uniform, World War I.

below: The author's great-uncle, Ernst Gustav Wackwitz ("Matzen"), with his Belgian girlfriend, World War I.

The author's grandparents, Andreas and Luise Wackwitz.

The author's grandmother in the house in Anhalt.

The author's grandfather in Southwest Africa.

*The author's grandmother and aunts with a photograph of his father,
Gustav, then a prisoner of war in Canada, Christmas 1943.*

*above: The author's father and aunt
in Hamburg at the end of World
War II.*

*right: The author and his
grandfather, ca 1965*

10 An Invisible Country

A visit to Anhalt: the view from the highway is of deeply-lying marsh and swamp country, low birches, oaks, and pines in damp, reedy dells; meadows, fences, ponds, and bushes. A train line on the horizon, a derrick's flywheel in the distance, in the foreground the Dyckerhoff Company's white storage tanks. In the concrete forms of the 1960s, the Catholic church rises triumphantly on a slope—the cross aligned so that it can be seen as one drives into the town—as the sleek rental car rumbles across the narrow tracks next to the small train station.

It was a cloudy and windy summer day in 2000. My father and I passed the sign for HOLDUNÓW and drove into the small Polish town. From old photos, I began to recognize the street corners, rows of houses, and views out into the country, standing next to, in front of, or somehow even within the buildings, trees, and streets of the present. My father, then a boy of ten, had left all this in 1933 for German Southwest Africa, and in more than sixty years he had not been back. We drove at a snail's pace along the road to Pless, past the low baroque semi-detached houses built by the Seibersdorf refugees in the decades after 1770 and still standing after the fires and attacks of the Silesian insurrection of 1921. Now, of course, they have been resurfaced in plaster and the roofs are newly tiled. The procession of houses was interrupted by square, three-story, coal-blackened apartment blocks built during the years of the People's Republic. We parked two hundred meters farther on, next to a large school and prayer house (now covered in plastic siding) built by Friedrich Schleiermacher's father and inhabited by him until his death. We rested our arms between the sharp points of the barbed-wire fence at the edge of the garden. It had been enclosed since my last visit, and the frames of two new single-family houses occupied its space. As he explained to me whose rooms were where, my father began to tremble, his eyes filling with tears and his hands, as if in a gesture of horror or shock, rising to his chin and mouth. He remembered that when he was a small child, a large linden had grown on the very spot where we now stood. One night, from the deep darkness of their window, he and his sisters watched lightning literally split the linden in two. And then it fell. In the morning, shaken, they stood at the split and blackened ruin of the huge tree. "There were bees there," said my father. (The remark seemed a strange non sequitur.) "I've always remembered that." And for a moment he was unable to hold back his tears.

Wherever we went during the two hours we spent in Anhalt that afternoon, memory kept inserting itself in front of the remnants of the old weaver's colony, rendering it ghostly and somehow diminished. More than once, father and son had occasion to think about whether so-called reality, which we usually perceive as unequivocally concrete, impenetrable, and corporeal, isn't rather a loose and changeable web of memories, spirits, and moods, consisting only secondarily of facts and objects. The feeling of having landed in a zone of diminished reality became almost overwhelmingly strong when we asked the janitor, who was busying himself with rake, broom, and wheelbarrow, whether we could look inside. Accompanied by him, we stood in my grandfather's generously proportioned study (at one time probably the study of Friedrich Schleiermacher's father), now the consulting and meeting room of an ambulatory geriatric clinic. My father took inventory: here is where the bookcase stood, here was the desk, and there at the window, there had been a large leather armchair in which he read Karl May as a boy. The room was now furnished with a very clean glass-covered table and chairs of square steel piping, upholstered in a dark red fabric. A calendar with mountain views hung on the wall. For a moment, the brick and limestone church that had been torn down in 1986 (mine-tunnels had destroyed its foundations) seemed to appear in the window behind some large trees. (Its massive, confidence-inspiring but also somewhat unimaginative neo-Gothic forms had spread across the Reich from Berlin's Kaiser-Wilhelm-Platz all the way to Anhalt, the empire's most remote corner.)

What had been the children's room was now the accounting office. Next to it was the parents' bedroom. A low table with a bouquet of dried flowers stood between two chairs: in here, my father and his sisters had been conceived and born. Ghosts filled the air. It would not have surprised us if we had seen the "pastor in his cassock—he had died long before—sitting in front of the house, reading a big book. At midnight there would often be a sound of something creeping through the house, and unseen hands would turn the handle of the clothes wringer in the vestibule. Who did it and who the pastor was . . . no one knew." Laundry hung between the white-painted beams of the airy loft. We thanked our host and stepped back into the street.

Sometimes historic events, shaped by fleeting, mutable memories, come into being long after they have happened. Even so-called historical reality is only secondarily a matter of time and place. Today, for everyone on the planet, the word "Auschwitz" signifies an historical anti-matter that first came into being in the twentieth century. The Austrian name of this little country town evokes a black hole in the history of the modern world that sucks in all that comes near it, and whose borders, like a threatening horizon, surround everything that can be said about the last century and about history in general. But this was not always so. It is, in fact, something that has taken place only relatively recently.

Hardly anyone who was brought here by train in order to be murdered immediately (or, less commonly, worked to death) had heard of this place. (The trains came from Kattowitz to the north, passing so close to Schleiermacher's parsonage that they could be seen from it, or from Lvov and Kraków to the east.) Almost all survivors mention that the sign at the train station, visible through the slats of the cattle cars after the train had come to a sudden stop, meant absolutely nothing to them. And the policy of secrecy enforced by the murderous bureaucracy saw to it that few of the SS men who were stationed there, and few of the Germans who came to do business in the factories and offices of the industrial complex of Monowitz and Auschwitz, knew the location of this murderous place before they traveled there for the first time themselves. Postcards from the first third of the century show a picture-book small town at the northern edge of the Habsburg Empire, notable, if at all, only for the size and vitality of a Jewish community that constituted more than half the population. Even in the decades immediately after the war, most Germans would not have been able to say where Auschwitz was, or what had happened there.

But in 1964 and 1965, the years when my grandfather was writing his memoirs about Anhalt and Auschwitz, the historic event that had taken place in this obscure corner of Galicia burst forth in Germany as well. Its memories and ghosts converged in Frankfurt. There, in 1963, the State Prosecutor of Hesse, Fritz Bauer, set the so-called Auschwitz Trials in motion, so that those murderers and guards who were still alive, in Germany and at large, might be brought to justice. It was then that the name of the place took on the meaning in Germany to which it is now linked forever. Every time my retired grandfather opened his newspaper at breakfast (at the same dining table he had used in the Anhalt parsonage), he must have read something about the region in which his children had come into the world. Before sitting down at his desk to write his memoirs, he would have been reading about what had happened only five kilometers from the site of his first pastoral employment. (Theologians often refer to the beginning of their career as their "first love," an expression that Andreas Wackwitz, too, uses several times in a tone of gruff tenderness in reference to Anhalt.) It took the Frankfurt trials to confront German newspaper readers, and presumably my grandfather as well, with the fact that, from 1943 on, between one and two million people were industrially murdered an hour's walk from the garden in which my father played as a boy—their bodies disposed of by cremation, their ashes raining over the area. (As Paul Celan's "Death Fugue" has it: "a grave in the air where you won't lie too cramped.")

That the hard-working, war-decorated, nationalistically inclined 23-year-old assistant pastor Andreas Wackwitz got his first job in Upper Silesia, of all places, would not have been a coincidence, politically speaking. Awarded by the League of Nations to the recently founded Polish republic, it was, for German nationalists, something of a living symbol of the *Diktat* of Versailles. The guerrilla struggle in this area between the young Republic of Poland and various German Free Corps—climaxing in May 1921 in the battle of Annaberg, southwest of Oppeln—has long been forgotten, but in the Weimar Republic it became a myth of defiance, a kind of German Little Bighorn. The hated German Republic sold the victory—at least this is how the bitter young fighters saw it—to the League of Nations.

In 1921, Andreas Wackwitz took a position as assistant pastor in the plebiscite area, now belonging irrevocably to Poland. First in Antonienhütte, he then went to Anhalt/ Holdunów, where, still alone, he took up temporary residence in two small rooms in the southern wing of the house in which Friedrich Schleiermacher had grown up. A year earlier, retreating Polish rebels had devastated the German-speaking village and burned it to the ground. A few descendants of the Seibersdorf colonists had been killed, many had lost their livestock, and almost all had lost their homes. In this tense atmosphere, my grandfather's predecessor, who had negotiated with the Polish freedom fighter Wojciech Korfanty during the time of the rebellion, was no longer tenable as pastor of a German congregation. Carrying a single suitcase, Andreas Wackwitz took the mining train to the nearest station, where the pastor's servant picked him up. When he arrived at the house, the pastor was shaving: *He was expecting me and left for Kattowitz the same afternoon, which is presumably why he waited to shave until so late in the day. While* shaving, he told me the essentials, then packed his suitcase, wished me all the best, and was driven to the station.

Andreas Wackwitz wrote his description of Anhalt at the time of the Frankfurt Auschwitz trials, but in it one hears a final, dying chord from the nineteenth century. Though not noticeable at the time, the same wind of death that drove the bark in Kafka's story is stirring in the works of Stifter, Storm, and Keller. Everything that was beautiful to them would soon disappear, like the final stage direction of Chekhov's *Cherry Orchard* with its snapping string, "as if from the sky." And it seems that my grandfather had intended his Anhalt memoirs to be a literary counterpart to those awful eye-witness accounts in Frankfurt. It is as if—in defiance of the Chief Prosecutor of Hesse, Fritz Bauer—he wanted to call forth his own memory of this landscape, both for himself and for us. But the more carefully he employs his skills as a writer, the darker that melancholy undertone becomes, and the more clearly the pictures of death emerge from the Elysium of his memories.

At first I didn't have much time to look at the landscape, but I had a good view from the rise behind the church and the churchyard. There, the colonist Karl Chwastek had built a small windmill— later it fell into disrepair—from which one could see Imielin, a large Polish-Catholic village four kilometers to the east where we had our post office. This side of Imielin was the Protestant village of Neugatsch, founded in 1821 as a sister-settlement to Anhalt. Further to the north, the pine forest stretched into the distance, covering the entire horizon to the west. New-Anhalt, with 25 farms, was directly behind the rise, just a few kilometers to the north. Looking further to the west, right next to New-Anhalt, one could see the small settlement of Swinow, which had approximately equal numbers of

Protestant and Catholic landowners; this side of it, on the road from Anhalt to Kostow, was the Martineum orphanage. The churchyard and the church with its beautiful pointed towers lay low to the west, and on both sides of the church, Old-Anhalt extended from north to south with 44 farms. Beyond its southern end, two kilometers away, rose the derrick of the Heinrichfreude mine. The panorama was completed by the Polish village Smarzowitz to the southeast. The wooded hills of Emanuelssegen ascended in the distance to the northwest, while in the west one saw the smokestacks of Böerschächte, and, in the southwest, crowned by a pretty baroque church, Mt. Clemens rose commandingly, on its southern flank a spring that was well known in the world of Silesian sagas. Beyond the coalfields with their haze, smoke, noise, and traffic, about 15 kilometers to the north at Myslowitz-Schoppinitz-Kattowitz, etc., there was in every season a beautiful 360-degree view into the distant Upper Silesian landscape. The landscape around Anhalt was peaceful, the coals mines of the area emitted little pollution and were, with the exception of the mine at Heinrichfreude two kilometers away, in or behind the forest, and on the two roads to Kostow and Imielin there was hardly any traffic. Straw-covered houses and barns nestled under trees and, depending on the season, children tended flocks of geese, sowers worked in the fields, reapers harvested corn. Herds were led to the communal field in the morning and back to their stalls in the evening, wagons returned to the barns with the harvest, potatoes were dug up, the smoke of fires rose into the clear autumn sky, and in the winter the sleigh bells rang through the village. For sowing there was also a jointly owned seed drill. The field work was done with a horse or cow, or by hand. There were no tractors yet. The grain was threshed with a stick, the grain cleaners were worked by hand, several farmers also had a horse gin for threshing. There were centrifuges in the house, but butter was still churned by hand. Probably nowhere in Germany today does one wake up

at six in the morning to the measured clanking of the neighborhood
flail. But the flail gave off a nicer sound than the electric motor or
the threshing machine does now, if indeed a harvester isn't brought
out onto the fields.

But I digress. I wanted to say that this entire landscape around
Anhalt breathed the peace of the quiet world of ordinary farmers.
The dead rested in the shadow of the church, and the living pursued
their modest livelihood working their farms, still unspoiled by mod-
ern technology. The basis of the peasant's existence was small: in
Anhalt, since the beginnings of the Colony, every farmer owned only
3.5 hectares (in Grasch it was a little more), which is why so many
men went to work for the railroads and in the mines. Their homes
were small and the families were usually large, but I was always
surprised how peacefully and patiently these people lived together,
always two families under one roof in houses identical in form and
size, and how, in spite of their poverty, they looked impeccable when
they went to church on Sunday.

Occasional echoes of Johann Peter Hebel's story "Unexpected Reunion" are unmistakable in this passage of our
family romance. (". . . and the farmers sowed and reaped. The
millers milled, the smiths hammered, and the miners dug
for veins of metal in their subterranean workshop.") And,
as my grandfather writes, it is first of all the dead who rest
in the shade of the church that come to his mind—an association that moves me as do the uncanny features added by
Stifter to his cozy descriptions, or by Hebel to his idyllic story
about the resurrected miner of Falun. The sinister quality of
the area around Anhalt has become almost unbearably intense in the decades since my grandfather wrote these paragraphs, and whenever I'm there, I find that I'm relieved to
be returning to Kraków as soon as possible. The spectral at-

mosphere of this seemingly typical Polish village cannot be explained away by the obvious devastation and poverty of the Silesian industrial landscape. The sadness of the derricks, smokestacks, potholes, video parlors, beer halls, kiosks, and outdoor carpet markets along the road where many of the old thatched double-houses of the weavers colony have been replaced by the huge apartment blocks of the People's Republic of Poland (which in the meantime has itself been replaced)—I have seen similar landscapes in the Midlands of England and in Belgium. The feeling in Anhalt is different.

I liked it at bedtime when my grandmother would tell me what my father had done as a small boy, how he had played, and the mischief he'd got into. Children love stories of this kind: imagining that their parents, too, were once young seems almost as reassuring, amusing, and strange as a fairy tale or the story of the small boy who flies through the air on a goose. Only now do I really understand how odd and truly terrible it is that my grandmother did not mention one single time what had happened in this same place only ten years later—giving it not even as much attention as my grandfather did in his account of 1964 and 1965 with its subliminal note of death. The black hole of the century's history sucked up the geography of Upper Silesia and dragged a small, pregnant silence along with it into our family's discussions. The more explicit the society around us became about the event this silence pointed to, the more extensively it spread out beneath us, and the more were conversations and objects, people and places seized by it—until apparently we could speak only by observing strict rules, rituals, and safe distances. Around "Anhalt," where my father was born, where he had played these pranks and said these funny things, the geographic uncertainty that had come to charac-

AN INVISIBLE COUNTRY   123

terize our country's eastern borders became as dense as an impenetrable fog. When I grew older, I liked to think that my father came from Thuringia, where there was also an "Anhalt." Eventually, I forgot about it and made my peace with the fact that he came from a small village in an invisible country.

In July 2000, my father and I went up the slope from the parsonage to the cemetery, over the tree-covered terrain where the absent Wilhelminian church has been replaced by its ghost. Behind wooden fences surrounding low brick houses, the leaves of the poplars moved ceaselessly in a light wind, making the village noise of central Europe. Gravestones, among them Schleiermacher's father's (the sandstone cross that had been smashed after the war was replaced a few years ago by one of concrete), even a war memorial under a linden—Andreas Wackwitz would have still seen it—bear German inscriptions: "Resting place of Carl Heinrich Lorenz, respected teacher and organist at the school and church of Anhalt. He first saw this world's light in Dyhrnfurt on March 28, 1798 and was called to eternity by the Lord on October 15, 1848. John 11: 25"; "To the memory of our fallen sons and brothers, 1914–1918." We left the cemetery. A very light rain had begun to fall. Football slogans—"GKS Katowice forever" and "GKS Katowice rules OK"—had been sprayed on the wall. It grew dark as we drove home, past Pless and Auschwitz, into the valley between the Vistula and the Sola Rivers and through the hill and cliff country around Kraków.

In memory of six liberals: my parents and grandparents

—Richard Rorty, Dedication to
Contingency, Irony, and Solidarity

11 *Five Professors, Dreams of Jürgen Habermas*

On an elegant summer day in Tokyo—the weather as hot as a tropical jungle—my wife and I rode our bikes to Kanda for a Saturday afternoon in bookstores. "Yes. It was a happy time. For such a long time afterwards, I felt clearly that it was happy." (Lars Gustafsson, *The Tennis Players*.) But evoking the intensely brilliant quality of the Tokyo summer on a dank, cold March morning in Poland is not so easy. The Malayan, damp heat. The unrestrained, tireless shrieking and grating (part animal, part machine) of finger-long cicadas in every tree and bush. The unearthly white, mile-high mountains of clouds stretching into the hot, pale blue sky and far over the Pacific. The warm ocean wind that smells of exhaust, seaweed, and flowers.

In Tokyo, bikes are permitted on the sidewalks. On our hour-long ride over the hills and across the flat parts of the city—for a Western sensibility, the layout of Tokyo is not only disturbing, but also somehow disturbed: dense, sprawling, and confusing—we rode along canals that were absolutely straight for miles on end, past video cameras guarding the steel fences and moats of the Emperor's palace, underneath dark and intertwined multi-tiered highways reminiscent of Piranesi, across bustling plazas, through residential areas quiet as country villages. Sometimes the sidewalk was so empty that we could pedal along in high gear, while in other areas, we had to push our way at a snail's pace through masses of chic young businessmen and women at the height of their deceptive, transitory wealth, going in and out of expensive boutiques and bistros.

The Kitazawa Bookstore in Kanda, at the foot of the Ochanomizu Hills (five universities founded in the nineteenth century lie scattered on their heights), is quite different from the ones of downtown Tokyo. It is a real bookstore, well managed in the "old" European style, specializing in literary texts and books on the humanities from Britain and the United States. On countless Tokyo Saturday afternoons, we flee behind the ceiling-high store windows of this venerable firm into its air-conditioned coolness and peace, as if into a dream of Bloomsbury. Japanese gentlemen—serious, dignified, dressed like the faculty members of an exclusive American east coast university—direct their customers to obscure publications that one can leaf through for hours in well-worn leather and wicker chairs. The smells are of dust, paper, and coffee. Between the rows of bookshelves, pretty Japanese doctoral students wearing sweater sets appear and disappear. In the gallery, two American professors discuss John Dewey in soft voices. Outside it may be boiling July or stormy November—Kitazawa Bookstore is a European book paradise at the other end of the world.

On the afternoon I want to describe, dusk arrived early and quickly. We biked back home. In the wire basket behind me was Richard Rorty's *Essays on Heidegger and Others* (2d edition, Cambridge University Press, 1991). From the book's back cover, the white-haired, suntanned University of Virginia professor (dressed in a light summer suit and sitting in front of a bed of bright pink azaleas) smiled into the camera. He looked relaxed, like a grandfather on summer holiday: a man who had found in teaching, publishing, reading, and writing, not only professional happiness but personal happiness as well. I read this book in the cool dawn hours on our terrace and looked at azaleas that were of the same color as those behind the grandfatherly face smiling from the back of the book. The happiness that this book gave me in the following days and weeks (and that lasts to this day) consists of a contagious atmosphere of ongoing theoretical democratization that makes one smile, laugh, and think. In the certainty that everyone—student, professor, school teacher, street cleaner, politician, housewife—understands all philosophical problems, takes them seriously, and makes their own decisions for their own lives, it is a stimulus to goodness and courage. Since then, whenever I open a book by Rorty, I find myself enveloped in an ethics and politics of philosophical inclusion.

Rorty's American pragmatist philosophy is a potent antidote against the German tradition. He is not interested in finding the ultimate, unshakeable foundation for our thoughts and actions (not even for democracy, philosophically rooted by his German friend and counterpart Habermas in intersubjectivity). There is no better reason for being a liberal, said the white-haired, suntanned American professor, than solidarity with all other liberals. Let's be who we are, said he, and convince or fight our enemies. Let's not waste our precious time by trying to find the foundations, the granite, unshakeable ground of conviction, the philosopher's stone. How liberating that was for me that autumn. Maybe one has to be German to understand. Maybe one has to have been surrounded for a lifetime by the teeth-grindingly tiresome, never-ending, ever-frustrating, ultimately futile search for certainty that is the German philosophical tradition.

Tokyo's seemingly endless summer holiday weather was followed by the sunny autumn that often lasts until Christmas in this part of the world. I bought and read everything that I could find by Richard Rorty. The early 1990s in Germany were the years of the great normalization, the time in which the country found its way back out of the *Sonderweg*, the "special path" of remorse, repentance, and arrogant guilt, into the strangely fluid, inconclusive, ambivalent, and personal notions of truth and morality that prevail in real democracies. In hindsight, it seems it could only have happened by some instinctive process, as if moralists and lovers of truth like Heinrich Böll, Rudi Dutschke, Peter Brückner, and Walter Jens had lived in an entirely different era—say, before the war.

Our country was reinvented once again. Precisely because I was living far away, I felt that I was participating with particular intensity in what was happening there. I read *Der Spiegel* and the dailies that arrived by airmail half a week late. I was outraged by the writer Botho Strauss's right-wing, intellectual manifestos and horrified by the crimes of the skinheads. I took books by the hero of German liberal philosophy Jürgen Habermas with me on walks along the Pacific, reading them in Denny's Restaurant on the beach of Shin-Zushi. So far removed from my own country, I understood for the first time—with the help of books by Rorty and Habermas, and my fantasy-relationship with these two professors—that we have to create not only history but truth itself. It is not enough to simply possess it.

Rereading my old diaries, I'm reminded that I even dreamt of Habermas and Rorty, often and in detail, proving that my obsession with this pair of white-haired intellectuals, who were separated from me and one another by two oceans, seems—psychodynamically speaking—to have gotten slightly out of control.

October 17–18, 1993. Dream of Habermas. Am at a convention in which I say—to general amusement—that Marcel Reich-Ranicki is wrecking all German thought and writing that deviates from his pedantic and old-fashioned, German-teacher standards. Habermas has left the auditorium. I see him in the corridor and engage him in conversation. He says that he was tired and that his young assistants had told him to leave, that he needed to regain his strength. But now he'd return. I think: "Will he help me against Reich-Ranicki?" Then he talks about his discussions with Rorty and about his daughter (suddenly we're talking about "habitation" as understood in its Heideggerian sense). This daughter has a child who says, "We love each other so much that I live on Mommy's shoulders." His advice to me: Let my son live on my shoulders. The experience of "lifeworld" is irreplaceable, especially in raising a child. Then: An esoteric appendix was added to a few copies of his latest book, *Between Facts and Norms*, in which H. tells fairy-tale-like parables. Perhaps he can send me one of these copies. I think: "Then I shall belong to the Order of the Knights of the Cross of Reason." In front of the window there suddenly appears an expansive city landscape like the Ernst-Reuter-Platz in Berlin. Stones lie on the street, and in the sun a bicyclist rides between them. I say: "'Summer's here and the time is right for fighting in the street.'" Putting his hand through his white hair, Habermas replies with a melancholy smile, and I think: "Now he's misunderstood me." What I had meant was that things might break open again and start anew. It was only a few days ago, when I remembered and then looked up the dedication in Rorty's *Contingency, Irony, and Solidarity,* that I understood what I was really looking for in that summer of 1993.

After 1970, my grandfather and I had finally reached the point where we shared no conventions (beyond the most general social rules), opinions, or illusions. There was no room for negotiation, even if in the course of such negotiations we had allowed ourselves to shout or to bang doors. Family rules seemed to prevent us from breaking off all contact, or even from putting our relationship on hold, resulting in the indescribably futile and alienating encounters and conversations between us that accompanied my adolescence and almost all my university years as regularly and unavoidably as summer vacations and Christmas.

On a foggy October day in 1973, for example, as the last volumes of my grandfather's memoirs were being written, I was visiting my grandparents in Lörrach on the Swiss border, sitting in front of that black-stained desk on which my grandfather kept his marksmanship trophies. His rifle hung on the wall. The old man on the other side of the pitch black, cliff-size desk had apparently resolved yet again to engage his evasive and vaguely stubborn grandson in conversation, if not to come to actual agreement. When I reread my diary entries of that afternoon and evening a quarter century later, I realize with some astonishment that, following adult conversational strategy, I did my best to avoid controversial themes and arguments and concentrated instead on the cigar and the wine, on weather and health. Not that it helped me in the slightest. Because my grandfather, doing everything he could to start a fight with all the allusions, subjects, and turns of phrase at his disposal, must have been truly enraged that all the while I was contemplatively sniffing my wine and blowing smoke rings to the ceiling.

He could no more lure me from my reserve with provocatively elaborate descriptions of the delights of fraternity life in Breslau than he could with a detailed story of having accidentally shot—he was about my age and hunting—a "peasant," whom his father then managed to mollify with sweet talk and the gift of a hare. And on and on, but I wouldn't rise to the bait. While this was probably just what the old man secretly wanted, his twenty-one-year-old grandson, however calmly he acted, felt that by giving in to conventional pressure, his manliness had been challenged: he had stilled his thirst for battle and his instinct for self-defense, exercised consideration, let his grandfather's harangue wash over him uncomplainingly, and responded with friendly and hypocritical interest. That much is clearly expressed by what I wrote at the time. I wasn't allowed to defend myself; my grandfather, it seemed to me, had transformed me into a woman, or at least into a coward. Previously he hadn't noticed me. Now he rendered me defenseless.

I read in my 1973 diary: "When he's there, I feel (as I always do in the presence of authority) clumsy, listless, shrill, ridiculous, inarticulate, insecure, stupid, ignored." As long as my grandfather kept talking, his country was stronger than mine, and the past was more real than the present or the future. But he would not be talking for much longer. We both knew it. In the last years of his life, my grandfather, after saying almost nothing for so many years, displayed (and not just toward me) the kind of provocative, calculated, and absolute tactlessness that one might expect and perhaps tolerate from very young men. He was a ghostly, Wilhelminian, pubescent eighty-year-old, a geriatric teenager rebelling against my country as he never had against his own father, a young rebel from the nineteenth century, an old man in revolt.

In the last of these memories, my grandfather tries to draw out my girlfriend of the time (we had stopped off at my grandmother's funeral on our way to France so that she could meet my extended family): "Come into the light, my girl, so that I can look at you." I knew that he would think she was wearing too much makeup, that upon examination he would ascertain the absence of a "Christian core." Both she and I laughed when, after looking at her for a moment, he turned away saying, "Well, so much for that." We were still laughing about it at the Loire and in Paris. In the following years "Well, so much for that" became a running joke between us, one of those formulaic gags that friends and lovers have only to summon in shorthand—giggling, and savoring their shared history and conspiracy against the world, yet again.

But in retrospect, it strikes me as sad that I could not take my grandfather more seriously, that he was not even able to annoy me any more. "Well, so much for that" was his legacy to me. They were his last words, at least to me, for he died that same year, without my having seen him again. Rebelling against a thoroughly well established German Second Republic preoccupied with itself and completely uninterested in his enmity, my grandfather became an object of fun, and this did not make the farewell from him any easier. For it is not true, as Karl Marx claimed, that people part cheerfully from their past when the plot and the cast, after their first serious or even tragic appearance, return for a comic reprise. When my grandfather was alive, I always knew that in the face of the unintentional comedy of his monologues and behavior I would rather have cried than laughed. And twenty-five years later, reading his 1973 and 1974 description of his trip to the United States in 1966, I know it again. Especially regarding his depictions of the American "Negro," to which I initially responded with a smile, snorting and giggling, but that actually made me feel quite hopeless. In his last notebook, he wrote page after page about those "Negroes," discussing them in meticulous detail and with angry earnestness (and unintentional humor, as if the words had been written by the comic German writer Eckhard Henscheid). My grandfather probably dished out his racist diatribes so unashamedly in the hope of provoking his reading public, that is, his sons—as if my father or uncle would ever have read these pages with anything other than a shrug of the shoulders, in a helpless mixture of sadness and comic despair.

Pennsylvania Avenue leads from the White House directly to the Capitol. The closer I got to the Capitol, the more often I was surprised by the neglected state of many of the facades, entryways, side streets— a sure sign that Negroes live there. Lots of windows are boarded up, paper and garbage lie about, black street urchins are running around or hanging about on the corners. When you leave the Capitol for the area around the main train station, the disorder and neglect get worse and worse. Washington has a black population of more that 50%, and for some time it has had a black mayor. And yet the Negro proportion of the USA as a whole is only 10%! Since the abo-

lition of slavery in the middle of the nineteenth century, the Negroes have poured from the southern states and its extensive agricultural areas to the great industrial cities, increasing the size of the industrial proletariat and adding to the general criminality. The areas in which they live become disorderly, unhealthy, crime-ridden slums. The government builds them their own neighborhoods with massive, multi-story buildings with plumbing, green spaces, playgrounds, etc., and in just a few years it's in ruins. I drove past such housing complexes with Bill, and between the buildings we saw a lot of garbage. I said that within ten years it will all have gone to seed. Bill growled bitterly: it won't even take five years! Of course there are Negroes who have succeeded socially—officers, staff officers, even generals, I think—there are black doctors, lawyers, government officials, professors, etc. I already mentioned that the mayor of Washington, the capital of the USA (!), is a Negro. We saw Negroes and Negresses who were dressed in a thoroughly elegant, European style and were obviously employed in responsible jobs, driving around in expensive cars and sport cars, we saw cute little Negro girls playing with white children on playgrounds and having a good time, we were served by black waiters and maitre d's who are maybe even better at their jobs and have more savvy than their European counterparts, and some of the old ones carried themselves like privy councilors. We also saw white saleswomen serving arrogant Negresses politely and with patience. But when a Negro manages to buy a house on a street in which whites live, all the whites rush to sell their houses before they lose their value. This has nothing to do with "racism"; it's simply a sure thing that within a few years the house inhabited by Negroes will have gone to seed and no white person will want to live wall to wall and fence to fence with Negroes in such an uncivilized neighborhood. In no time the street that until now was "white" has become "black." After what we've observed in the USA, it's nonsense to speak of racism and oppression, of white priv-

ileges and withholding of civil rights. A situation in which 20 million Negroes out of a total population of 200 million are almost all concentrated in the large cities and exhibit such a huge gap in civilization and education can't end well. I don't believe that the existing problems can be solved other than by closing the gap within a few decades—faster than this is hardly possible—and the Negroes will have to do their part. Saying this, I am by no means approving of a biological mixing of black and white. But if black and white are going to live together in harmony, I can't imagine any other way than that the Negro rises to the standards of the average white person. There are enough examples of their achieving this, but the question—it seems to me—is still open whether it is in their nature to hold to this standard once they have attained it, and whether those who achieve it are not exceptions. Maybe it won't take decades but centuries to find valid answers to all these questions, and maybe there aren't even any answers. They will have to continue to live with these and other problems—the human condition is such that its problems can't be addressed like a simple two plus two. By way of further commentary on the Negro problem in the USA: when we drove out in the country, we saw lots of small towns—in Pennsylvania, for example—that looked like European country towns. On a Saturday afternoon, the inhabitants were sweeping the streets! Negroes were not to be seen there. Lancaster, a city with a population of 60,000 and with lots of industry and beautiful residential streets is a model of order and cleanliness, and only 2,000 Negroes live there. Also Orlando in Florida—it, too, a large town—seemed to us in good shape, undisturbed by Negroes. Alexandria, on the other hand, close to Washington, was fairly ruined by Negroes in some places.

So much for my grandfather's insights into the life and character of "the Negro." Had I come across these paragraphs in

1974—and in truth I had given up reading his memoirs a long time before—I probably would have just rolled my eyes. But the closer my grandfather came to dying, the more provocatively and urgently he tried to make himself understood with testimonies of this kind—both orally and in writing, and his unrestrained reflections on the "Negro problem"—though he was by then a very old man and in fact quite indifferent to issues of this kind—were just such an attempt. He must have met with the same reaction to his writing that some people experience in nightmares: the louder he snarled in his fear of the present, the more muted were our responses, the more solicitous and indifferent our behavior. The more my grandfather wanted to call attention to himself, the less he seemed to be present. It was too late; he wouldn't survive the decade. And during the mid-1970s at the latest, he became (for us) a lunatic whom we felt an obligation to protect, whom we couldn't contradict, so instead avoided. Even my aunts, for decades his most loyal audience, began to shake their heads and to look, instead, to their children. My country had won. Our lives were important, difficult, and beautiful. Even before my grandfather died, we began to forget him.

Then it was summer in Kraków, twenty-five years later, the last year of the twentieth century, and I was almost fifty. I sat in my office, unable to forget my short trips to Anhalt and Auschwitz, spending my evenings reading the memoirs of a dead old man and thinking about the time when my grandfather had begun to glide slowly and irrevocably from his country's future. "Yes, it was summer. The ancient chestnuts opposite the District Commissioner's house only moved their dense green broad-leaved crowns in the morning and evening. In the daytime, they remained motionless, gave off a bitter scent, and spilled their spacious, cool shade over the road. The skies were never anything other than blue. Invisible larks trilled unremittingly over the silent town." In the morning I walked to work along a street lined with chestnut trees like the one in this passage from Joseph Roth's novel *The Radetzky March*. [Trans. Michael Hofmann.] Morning dew lay on the grass and on the rose bushes around the famous Renaissance castle, and the city's countless young women transformed its squares, streets, courtyards, parks, and gardens into an erotic open-air performance unburdened by either Protestantism or feminism. In Kraków on mild summer evenings, I sometimes really don't know where I should (or am allowed to) look.

In 1921, my grandfather had just turned twenty-eight and taken up his pastoral duties in Antonienhütte, a small congregation of workers and miners in Upper Silesia that had just become Polish. Did he also have experiences like those of his grandson in the erotically charged Kraków summer of 1999? Such erotic fireworks—low-cut blouses, short skirts, high-heeled shoes, blazing eye makeup, and intentionally visible brassieres—such orgies of flirting, all-night dancing, and high fashion (depleting entire savings accounts) are probably possible only after wars, dictatorships, and revolutions like those of the twentieth century: people can express their relief and their reclaimed vitality with the rewards of a highly developed consumer society. (This is probably why, in the victorious and liberated parts of the world, the early 1950s—one thinks of Marilyn Monroe and Jane Russell—and the last decade of the twentieth century were such celebratory and crazed periods of open eroticism, years that saw an increasingly mass-oriented and globalized redemption of the promise that the Roaring Twenties in New York and Berlin had made to the women of the world.)

Antonienhütte in 1921 was surely nothing like end-of-century Kraków. But the peasant girls and the young Polish working women of Upper Silesia who had suddenly acquired their own state and a new self-confidence were surely ready to enjoy life, and my grandfather was a handsome man. (Though he was engaged to my grandmother, a young woman of the right class and the right morals, she—waiting for the wedding and the chance to start a well-run household—was separated from him by a day's journey and two complicated border crossings.) Maybe the looks, the encounters, the dusks, and the spring days of a postwar German-Polish village in which everyone knew everyone else were at least as suggestive as the market square in post-socialist Kraków. In any case, my grandfather tells a story of his time in Antonienhütte, where he began his professional life and his career as a German abroad, that is one of the most peculiar parts of his entire memoir. And though he probably did not know it at the time or when he wrote it down, it is a story whose undertone and implications are unambiguously erotic.

At the service in Antonienhütte—it must have been Christmas or New Year's—I suffered an enormous shock: as the congregation was singing the Lord's Prayer, after "for thine is the kingdom," etc., a young woman with a child in her arms was suddenly standing by the church door. Slowly, to the rhythm of the hymn, she began walking toward me. According to old German law a newborn child was laid at the feet of its father, who, lifting it, would legitimize it, and thinking that she might place the child at my feet, I was seized by a

kind of panic. I didn't know the young woman, and I knew of course
that I was completely innocent. But might it have been a malicious
mystification by a group of fanatic Poles? After the congregation had
sung the Amen, she stood in front of me, at the altar, with the child.
Fortunately old Kutta was in the church, in the first pew in front. I
looked at him anxiously, and silently he lifted his crippled hands in
a gesture of blessing. It was as if a stone had been lifted from my
chest. I, too, raised my hands and said the age-old biblical blessing
from the fourth book of Moses over mother and child and into the
congregation. The child didn't stir, and mother and child returned
into the congregation during the closing verse.—Later it was ex-
plained to me that just that week the child had turned one, and that
in such cases the mother comes with it to the service so that it might
be blessed in this manner.

The origins of the panic attack that my grandfather suffered
at the altar of Antonienhütte are more complicated than
he would ever have allowed himself to admit. When he
returned to Flanders after becoming engaged to my grandmother while on leave, he stopped seeing his Belgian girlfriend. But I read the young woman's letters from that Uncle Tuca banana crate with the broad-brimmed, grinning
Bananes-Originales logo. They may have been devoid of
content, but they were full of feeling, as such letters are—
hopeful, confused, overwhelmed by herself and, so to speak,
morally breathless. They lie next to what is still today a very
blond lock of hair bound with a little red ribbon, tucked between the pages of the pale blue war diary, written in a thin,
intricate, and swirly woman's hand that conveys impotent
devotion. The greatest worry these letters express is that
"cher André" would see her as superficial and morally unserious after she had gotten "involved" with him. (Who

knows to what extent?) And my young grandfather did not seem to feel that he was any less a conqueror in enemy territory when he was in Polish Upper Silesia than he had been in occupied Belgium.

I was on my way to the train station in Kostow early, at six or seven, when I could hear gunfire flaring up at intervals from the direction of Imielin. Soon I could hear shooting coming from other directions as well. I needed to be in Kattowitz for a meeting and decided to proceed and see how far I would get. For days there had been talk in Anhalt that trouble was brewing. Even before Meyer [my grandfather's immediate predecessor] had come to Anhalt in early April, the people there had been afraid of impending attacks on the German enclave—the position of pastor was vacant and they had no other leaders—and they fled to Kattowitz. Only the old people stayed behind. The refugees had been given shelter in a school, where they spent Good Friday. The next day they returned to Anhalt, and on Easter, March 27, Vicar Ruschke came from Kattowitz. Of him it must unfortunately be said that he was a notorious coward and loudmouth. He drove to Anhalt for Easter service in an Italian military vehicle and in the company of Italian soldiers—the district of Pless was in Italian-occupied territory—and returned immediately afterwards to Kattowitz, again with Italian soldiers (who themselves were scared out of their wits) for protection. With the arrival of Meyer, the congregation became less nervous. As soon as a pastor was in the parsonage, the people of Anhalt took the verse from the first Epistle of Peter to heart: "Casting all your care upon him, for he careth for you." Years later one of our neighbors, old Frau Pokluden, once said to me: "Oh, Pastor Wackwitz, it's good to have you back. When there's no pastor in Anhalt, it's as if the sun is no longer shining." So I continued on my way to Kostow in spite of the gunfire . . . I wasn't afraid for Anhalt. Instead a kind of curiosity and the wish to be where the action was drove me in the direction of the coal mines. I didn't know, for example, that on this morning in Antonienhütte more than a dozen German country police had been killed in a most gruesome manner. They had barricaded themselves in the guesthouse with some of the leading Germans, including the two school directors. A huge mass of fanatical Poles shot in the direction of the guesthouse. The only result of telephone calls for help from the French occupying troops was that they stopped before actually reaching Antonienhütte. When the last cartridge was spent, the besieged men negotiated with the Poles and were given free passage. As they left the guesthouse, they were beaten to death one by one and their bodies defiled by Polack women in a most horrible way. The Catholic school director was able to escape with a broken arm and a few other injuries; the Protestant saved himself by hiding. If I had been in Antonienhütte at the time, I, too, would probably have been among the besieged.

The train left Kostow more or less on time. My fellow-travelers— laborers and office workers on their way to their jobs—were worried, and in their conversations there was no lack of gallows humor. After we had passed Myslowitz, the journey ended in Schopinitz, about six kilometers short of Kattowitz. Whoever wanted to continue had to get a przeputsku (a permit) in the gymnasium. In the gym, there were Powstancy of martial but not very confidence-inspiring appearance, carrying pistols and hand grenades on their belts and acting important. I showed my passport and explained that I was a clergyman and had to get to the church offices in Kattowitz. After looking at me critically and mistrustfully out of their spiteful and basically insecure eyes, they gave me the przeputska I'd demanded. Later I heard that in this gym a sizeable number of Germans were terribly mistreated, not to say tortured. This experience taught me once again the old truth that he who is afraid, has lost the game from the outset.

From this and other passages in his memoirs, it was clear to me that my grandfather was a courageous young man, even though I know that some details of his story probably call for closer scrutiny. The rebels of Upper Silesia were not to be fooled with, but my grandfather was not afraid of them. The stories of his neighbor, old Frau Pokluden, also evoke the bravery of the Seibersdorf refugees and their pastor, whose Protestantism was the religion of their resistance (a Lutheran chorale from a remote, eighteenth-century forest fades away . . .). Why, then, was he so afraid of the young woman in the church in Antonienhütte who was walking toward him with her child as the final chorale sounded? (I imagine the scene as a Renaissance ballet, with the young Polish woman, about to have her child blessed by my grandfather, dancing a kind of German-Polish blessing-minuet to the tune of this Protestant resistance chorale. In its steps, perhaps, the better possibilities of our countries had become visible. It might have been a dance that resolved the history of the Germans and the Poles, instead of what really happened.) What was it that my grandfather was so afraid of on that Sunday morning between the wars? And what was the contest that was, as a consequence, lost from the outset?

Books can come into people's lives by means of various and complicated detours. Their readers or victims are not always able to say where they bought, borrowed, read, or dreamt of them. Maybe they've never even held it in their hands—and yet without this one particular book their lives cannot be understood. Sometimes it is precisely those books that are of greatest consequence for their lives that people will have read without having ever opened them. In my second summer in Kraków, I spent some evenings on my balcony and over wine in the street cafes on the main market with a learned, older friend who called my attention to a book that I desperately needed. (Inexplicably, those books that were useful to me turned up at what was seemingly the exact right, and sometimes truly portentous, moment in my life: suddenly, there they were.)

The learned friend had come to visit me in Kraków for a week in May. The sun rose over the large garden of the Bernardine monastery, the morning wind stirred the curtains of my bedroom, and in the high trees in front of my kitchen windows, titmice were pecking at the budding blossoms. In the evenings, we sat on the balcony or took walks on the hills that encircle the old part of the city. My fatherly, or at least teacher-like, friend talked about having read Johann Gottlieb Fichte's *Addresses to the German Nation,* which he and his reading group had studied during the months of German reunification in the early 1990s. (It is strange how the literary social forms of the early nineteenth century have been resurrected in our reunited capital—now, of all times).

Two mornings later, I was sitting at breakfast with the little poison-green volume of Fichte's *Addresses.* (I was able to find it right away in the library of the Kraków Goethe Institute. It was the only one of Fichte's works in the collection, and I was the first person to check it out.) The further I got into Fichte's bossy, peremptory, peculiarly Adolf Hitler-like fantasies, digressions, resolves, appeals, and demands, the more clearly I felt I understood not only my grandfather's "Negro" nonsense, but also his response to mother and child in Antonienhütte; his journey amidst the rebels; his pride, stupidity, courage, and fear. I felt that I understood the lindens behind the parsonage in Anhalt, the dead who were resting in the shadow of the church tower, the winter evenings that rose over the pines and birches behind the house, and perhaps even the ghostly pastor who is said to have been seen reading a book there. I do not know whether my grandfather read Fichte's *Addresses to the German Nation*, but it is as if Fichte knew my grandfather and described him in the little green book—his desire to be German, deep, serious, Protestant, brave, childish, indomitable. A mighty fortress. And completely different from the French, the English, and the Negroes.

Johann Gottlieb Fichte, the *Wunderkind* and founding father of early German idealism, was hounded from his Jena professorship at the beginning of the nineteenth century. One consequence was that he became irritable as only toppled and aging prodigies can be. Rejected by Kant, abandoned by his most significant student, Schelling, he embarked on a project of single-handedly uniting the splintered German nation—a nation that he would forge in the fire of his rhetoric with three famous lectures held in Berlin, giving it a consciousness of its mission and its greatness, and leading it in its struggle against the French occupiers. (This project at least resulted in the restoration of his professorship and even a promotion to the directorship of the university in Berlin.) The most important theoretical pirouette of the *Addresses* and also of the lecture series that preceded them—entitled *Characteristics of the Present Age*—is the notion of the Germans as a chosen people or, as Fichte puts it in one of his characteristically pallid and loveless expressions, a *normal Volk*. And, according to Fichte, because the Germans were never completely conquered by the Romans and never absorbed Latin as a medium of communication, they belong to a nation that is especially close to its own language and essence—while the Romance language-speaking French, Italians, English, and Spanish use a dead idiom and are cut off from their roots. It comes down to this: Europe's only true *Volk* are the Germans, and therefore it is their mission to conquer other nations and to liberate them for the sake of their own individuality. After all, inspired by the purity of their language, their "normality," their naturalness, and their fury, under the influence of Martin Luther's world historic speech-act (the model for Fichte's nation-building *Addresses*), they found the true—German—form of religion once again.

After Napoleon had been vanquished, the construct of Fichte's theoretical nationalism was forgotten for a time in the nineteenth century. But before and after World War I, it was put to work again as a set of elusive but "normal" convictions, "that lived on malignantly inside people, scuttling like the claws of crabs" (as Peter Handke once wrote about similar sets of convictions—at that time coming from the Left—in the late 1960s). A vague feeling that everyone and everything German was superior—a superiority that may have been abused, unrecognized, and dormant but was indisputably genuine—and an empty pride in an unreachable German depth and courage are what galvanized my grandfather's generation. Andreas Wackwitz's remote life in Anhalt, his feeling of responsibility for the descendants of Seibersdorf's first refugees, his memory of the war, all seem to have amplified the scuttling sound of the German crab claws within the politically disappointed young lieutenant into a booming certainty that would lead him ever further astray and would not be stilled until his death many decades later.

Making everything still more complicated, impenetrable, and illogical is the fact that had Fichte's forgotten *Addresses* been taken at their word, the term "normal *Volk*" would have described the Poles rather than the Germans in the 1920s. Inspired for centuries by just those romantic ideas of purity of language, culture, and *Volk* that had inspired Johann Gott-lieb Fichte, the Poles fought for their own country in 1918, reclaimed it, and found themselves on the path to European normalcy. But to the losers of World War I, the Polish Republic was a bastard fathered by Versailles. To overthrow it became their calling, as they followed the illusory glory before their eyes and the nationalist-*volkish* crab scuttling in their inner ear.

Similarly, Vladimir Ilytch Ulianov/Lenin, whose army Jósef Piłsudski beat back just short of Warsaw in 1921, developed a strange, chiliastic, world-dominating obsession with the advance of the Red Army toward Warsaw "proving irrefutably that the pivot on which the entire post-Versailles world system rests lies somewhere in the vicinity of this city." Tukhachevsky's order of June 2, 1920, postulated that "the road to a general world conflagration proceeds over the body of White Poland." Nineteen years later, the German army took this road. The destruction of the Polish state was to be the signal for both the proletarian and the *volkish* revolutions. If the Germans despised the Jews most of all, Polish statehood came next. The reasons were similar: the Republic of Poland symbolized the victory of western, Latin-Catholic, transatlantic, or British-imperial modernity—it was a protégé of countries with dead languages and desiccated roots. The Jews had devised a clandestine plot to control the world—so whispered the scuttling crabs' claws—and its political incarnation was the Polish state, where so many Jews lived. For both Communists and Nazis, Poland of the 1920s and 1930s had a valence similar to that of Israel for Arab revolutionaries. The destruction of Poland was the Holy Grail of both forms of European totalitarianism, the object of their ceaseless hatred. Between the Soviet

Union and Germany, the Polish Republic of 1918 never had a chance.

My grandfather, who in 1921 had braved the gunfire of the Silesian rebellions to catch his train to Kattowitz, acquired a disability that conditioned him for the rest of his life to those peculiar, obsessive, fatally racist remarks and seizure-like attacks of which I was the victim during my student years and until his death. He wrote in his memoirs in 1964, for example, that *after the Hitler-German invasion in 1939, the Poles were brutally robbed of their rights. This horrified me when I visited Upper Silesia in 1940.* But a few pages later, writing about a favorite family dog that disappeared inexplicably in 1933, the German-nationalist malady strikes again (he writes, alas: *probably some Pole caught and ate it*), like a Tourette sufferer who is impelled to yell "Fuck, fuck" in the most delicate social situations.

It was a compulsion and a disability, and when people (like his grandson) wouldn't take these kinds of things seriously (had I done so, for consistency's sake I would have had to break off contact with my grandfather), there was nothing left but to see Andreas Wackwitz from his unintentionally comical side. Perhaps the forced, defiant self-assurance that vented itself in his lifelong, *volkish* Tourette syndrome (and the older he was, the more unintentionally funny it became) was his equivalent of the idealistic *Tathandlung* ("fact/act") on which Fichte had built his life (in deed and thought) before he decided to become a speech-act politician in French-occupied Berlin and invent the "normal *Volk.*" Life is hard, people want something secure to hold onto, and my grandfather grabbed on to what he took to be the root source of his country, his culture, and his religion. But during the 1930s and 1940s, and for the rest of his life, while he held with a cramp-like reflex to his bravery, his Protestantism, and his unintentionally comical, *volkish* nonsense, events took place against which almost no grasp-reflex is effective, and certainly none that is *volkish*. And as the Auschwitz Trials in Frankfurt proceeded, my grandfather, too, wrote down his memories of Jewish Oświęcim:

Whenever we had visitors, we arranged a group tour, usually of Emanuelssegen at Niemanns or of Oświęcim, the town later known as Auschwitz, which had a Jewish population that was probably over 50%. Our visitors could not have been more surprised when on market day they saw how primitive it all was—the dirt, the Jews in their kaftans, caps, payess, velvet hats, and red beards. They observed the Jewish women bargaining over chickens and ducks, they read the most incredible Jewish names on the store signs, and listened to the men with the phylacteries on their arms and the little wooden cubes on their foreheads as they bobbed up and down in the "shul," babbling and murmuring their prayers. Then, finally, from the bridge over the Vistula, our visitors watched, shuddering, as the rabbi slaughtered the poultry bought at the market, the chickens leaping back and forth, jumping a meter high and beating their wings, until they finally lay still, as if exhausted. If the kaftans and the spouting forth of the psalms must have seemed strange and repulsive to someone witnessing this for this first time, no one seeing this slaughtering could resist feeling that here he was encountering a strange and very different world. But he who had the occasion to inform himself more deeply would also see that the family life of this Jewish population, though strict, was clean and honorable. It is a good thing that man cannot see into the future.

Ever since I first read this passage, the extraordinary moral incompetence and coldness of its last sentence, its emotional sloth, have marked the divide that separates not-wanting-to-look and not-wanting-to-speak from moral brutalization. But there is solace in knowing that in our family's and our country's past there is someone whose memory I can hold onto and about whom my grandfather and I might agree, were he still alive—in whose memory it would have been worth not fighting over the brutality of that sentence.

It was a beautiful, warm, and peaceful summer. The rebels were far away at Annaberg, and I often spent the evenings in the garden with the teachers Miemietz and Schäfer under the lindens planted there in 1794 by old Schleyermacher, Anhalt's first pastor, and we discussed political events and prospects.

I am writing this in the library of my apartment in Kraków. In the mornings, the light in front of my windows brightens between the Habsburg-yellow baroque towers of the Kraków Bernardine monastery, while swarms of dark crows fly over my apartment toward the Vistula, and a strong, unnaturally warm *föhn* wind blows the leaves from the orchard of the Bernardines into spirals so high in the October sky that without looking closely one cannot tell birds from leaves. Another time, the morning light of an unnaturally spring-like Sunday in February shines on the orchard of the Bernardine monastery. The bells of the Wawel Cathedral are ringing, and in the distance a white plume rises from a high smokestack into the still air. I light another cigar, pour myself another cup of tea, read what I've written, and think about Friedrich Schleiermacher, who, as a small boy, stood in the garden of the Anhalt parsonage and thought about the possibility that the entire history of antiquity, like all myths of origin, might just be fiction, that every country was invented, that every *Volk* is a coincidence and every tradition merely a story that might develop otherwise. That as we continue to write history, we can change it.

Later, in the early nineteenth century, Schleiermacher and Fichte became enemies. It is no exaggeration to say that the two famous Prussian professors hated each other. I was not able to find out much about this enmity and its causes in the libraries that I visited almost every week, often for entire afternoons, while I was writing my *family romance.* But I'm convinced that something important was at the bottom of their differences, namely two fundamentally different conceptions of the German tradition. Fichte claimed to have found the origin of the German "essence" in the national character, in the language, in the *Volk* that the Romans could not vanquish and over whom Napoleon could not sustain an enduring victory. Schleiermacher, on the other hand, it seems to me (this is how I want to invent our tradition), tried to remain true to the uncertainty that he had experienced under the lindens of the Anhalt parsonage garden where, before the second great war, my grandfather sat with his colleagues over wine and cigars in the evening, and where my father lay in his cradle as a baby.

Schleiermacher was altogether more interested in the ways our tradition had been invented than in locating its origins. He was, perhaps, our early nineteenth century Rorty, a Prussian *liberal pragmatist,* a German intellectual who was not obsessed with origins and their exclusions. After all, he had spent his childhood with the Seibersdorf refugees in an area where the most varied people got along and had to hold together, and where one could recognize truth and tradition as coincidental or invented—as had been the case in the wide spaces that had been settled by the ancestors of the American pragmatists. Friedrich Schleiermacher knew in any case that we understand ourselves by understanding the past and the old texts and that nothing—not who we are, nor where we have to go—is forever fixed and determined.

In the Bavarian State Library in Munich in the spring of 2000, on a cold and brilliant April morning on a visit back home, I finally found, photocopied, and read Friedrich Schleiermacher's review of Fichte's *Lectures on the Characteristics of the Present Age*. (It had been published as the first article in the philosophy section of the January 21–23, 1807, issue of the *Jenaer Allgemeine Litteratur-Zeitung*, the *New York Review of Books* of its day.) At home in Kraków, I had been doing research for several weeks before in the reading room of the Jagiellonen Library, where nothing has changed since the early 1930s, not the big clock at the front, not the little brass labels on the shelves, not the cast-iron lighting fixture at the top of the ceiling or the railings on the encircling galleries where the books are kept and from which one can look down onto the reading tables in the football field-size rectangular room. Burgundy red leather writing surfaces, black-lacquered desk lamps with flexible necks and silver screws seem to have traveled through time from the 1920s, unchanged and unscathed. Outside in the streets and over the park named after the philanthropist and social reformer Henryk Jordan, the March sun shone through the coal dust, the early spring rain was falling, and buds were sprouting on the trees. Archived somewhere in the stacks are the papers of Rahel Varnhagen, who frequently saw Fichte and Schleiermacher in Berlin and probably knew better than I ever can why they loathed each other so.

Now in Munich, I sat under a high ceiling supported by cleanly designed columns, in front of glass walls, on a comfortable new chrome and black leather chair. The laptops around me were humming and clicking quietly, the air was good and the street outside machine-swept; in the park in front of the clean windows the first leaves were already green and the attractive doctoral students were wearing open shoes with high heels. Schleiermacher's 1807 review of Fichte is written with an elegance and wit that would make it suitable for reprinting in a current *New Yorker*, were not all the concepts, problems, and language-games that were central to the beginning of the nineteenth century as forgotten today as the Epic of Gilgamesh or Hammurabi's Law. All that has remained of Fichte's elaborate constructions and "fact/ acts" is the idea that, as a German, one is a more genuine and better being than a Turk, a Jew, or a Vietnamese. And of Schleiermacher's ripostes, parrying, traps, and ironies, we come away with the idea that one constantly has to reinvent oneself and others in a friendly, ongoing, reciprocal story. The great hermeneutist used a polemic technique that seems to have been employed for the first time in his Fichte review and (as far as I know) not perfected until Karl Kraus: the ironic quotation, the art of criticizing something by leaving it unaltered, making fun of something by taking it seriously. (Somewhere Kraus wrote that the article written by his enemy was "the strongest measure that I've ever undertaken against him.")

Many of Schleiermacher's friends (maybe including Rahel Varnhagen) apparently found his polemic method too unserious, clown-like, or, as we might say, Rortyesque. Defending himself in one of his countless, perfectly written letters, he asserts that he "always resisted making the thousands of jokes that suggested themselves, and if some are still there, I'll bet anything that they aren't mine but Fichte's."

Schopenhauer, who disliked the first German speech-act politician at least as much as Schleiermacher had, drew a little chair in the margins of his copy of the *Foundations of Transcendental Philosophy* wherever Fichte wrote that he "posits" himself. And no doubt it says something about German idealism that, after hearing of Schopenhauer's small pencil drawings, one can never again read Fichte's chef-d'oeuvre without grinning.

The controversy that raged in the *Jenaer Allgemeine Litteratur-Zeitung* is now so remote and incomprehensible that most of us will come away from Schleiermacher's demolition of Fichte with only a vague sense of his wonderful elegance and humor. (In targeting his actual enemy, the great man exposes not only my grandfather and his ideological heroes but also more than one contemporary politician and thinker.) But as I sat on the chic chair of the Munich library, my mind went back to the summer of 1993, when I read the contemporary German conservative-romantic Karlheinz Bohrer's essay in the journal *Merkur* while sitting on a park bench along a Beijing canal. It was about the expulsion of the early romantics' ironic, fragmentary, self-referential, and playful language by the languages of earnestness with which Fichte and later Hegel committed the Protestant Prussian educated middle class to the humorless search for the unrecoverable origin of all thinking and all lives. I still remember that at the time I felt defended by Bohrer against the very same Michael Rutschky, our most outstanding essayist—who almost a decade later on my balcony in Kraków, referred me to Fichte's *Addresses* as the key to my grandfather's (and Adolf Hitler's) inner life, and who had earlier given me quite a going-over on account of my 1993 budding Rortyism. "I see myself as supported by Bohrer against Rutschky. Beijing, August 6, 1993, 5:30 p.m." is what I wrote in the margin of my *Merkur.* And I admit that ten years later, on that spring morning in the Munich State Library, I was proud of Schleiermacher, almost as proud as I sometimes had been on Japan's Pacific shore when I looked out over my copy of Habermas's *Theory of Communicative Action* toward the tropical ocean, proud of Jürgen Habermas and his American sparring partner, Richard Rorty. I had discovered one of us. Here was someone who would help me against my grandfather.

So I didn't really dream of Friedrich Schleiermacher in the spring nights of 2000. But for a moment in the Munich State Library, the pastor's garden in Anhalt surrounded me, and I saw not only my father smiling and playing there but also the small boy from the late eighteenth century who had worried in that same garden about whether "all the old writers and with them the old history had been invented" and about "this remarkable thought that tormented me, that I kept to myself, deciding that it would be confirmed or refuted by the discoveries that I would make, for myself, in time."

12 Abandoned Rooms

I was still a young child, walking with my father from Stutt-gart's Killesberg toward Pragsattel on a March afternoon in the 1950s. A spring wind blew in the dry, gray streets. Pine trees stood in front of the bright facades and roofs of the Weissenhof settlement, a modernist model housing develop-ment from the 1920s, while acacias and elders stretched their branches over wooden fences toward the street that curved and headed into the valley. We were looking toward a city that was bigger than anything I could have imagined. Above it, the colors of pale sky moved on. The Weissenhofbäck bak-ery, the yellow streetcar, Frau Fischer's grocery store, the art academy with its pale murals painted on yellow stucco—all under this sky as father and son nestled into the wind. But the sky stretched on into the distance beyond us. In my imag-ination, it spread under fast-moving clouds over American prairies teeming with buffalo, or over African savannah, where old-fashioned biplanes flew and eagles took wing. The entire world encircled me, and beneath my feet, grass was just beginning to grow between the cracks in the sidewalk.

As we stepped into the rusty revolving gate, we could see ahead to a second gate, with a recumbent lion and the gilded inscription "Rosenstein Park" on its pediment and beyond that, disappearing between the trees, seemingly boundless meadows that continued on at each point where one would have expected them to end. There are two kinds of night-time excursions that have recurred regularly since my childhood. Each time I experience them, I'm preoccupied and pleased all the next day and even afterwards. One of these recurring dreams leads me into rooms, houses, or apartments that I've forgotten when awake and then, in my dream, suddenly rediscover. I enter on stairs, or through concealed doors or passages that happen to open or that I chance to catch sight of, and with a slight sense of trepidation, I proceed to walk through these attic-like, sparsely furnished, and peculiarly neglected rooms. I ask myself how I could have forgotten this place so completely for so long and how I will be able to reconcile my life here with those dwellings in which my wakeful and conscious life unfolds.

The other dream that has recurred with several variations in the decades since my childhood transports me to a park or into a landscape that begins as a park but that ends nowhere and is limitless: there is no wall, fence, or street, not a person is to be seen; it just extends deeper and deeper, infinitely far into a world from which I will never emerge or never have to return. I find it strange that the two pictures of happiness preserved in the deepest, most instinctive and inaccessible part of me—entering so rarely into consciousness that they are long remembered, indeed unforgettable— are concerned with the condition of being both different and elsewhere. Once, on a late winter night during my years in Japan, I was in one of those dreamed landscapes and came upon an ocean beach utterly devoid of people. I walked along the shore for days until I saw a huge wave of completely translucent emerald-tinted water crashing onto the beach in all its loneliness, while a loud voice in heaven or in the head of the dreamer said: "I am not who I am," expressing, perhaps once and for all, the essence of my deepest happiness.

That it is possible, even in this life, to be freed of the imprisoning self—in abandoned rooms, while walking through infinite parks: this I've learned, or perhaps more accurately, inherited, from my father and grandfather, though by what roundabout psychological detours I don't know. And I have the feeling that this image is linked not only to the memory from the 1950s of that walk in Rosenstein Park but also to memories that are, properly speaking, not my own, but that were told to me by my father or that came to me from my father's and grandfather's memories by some other means, perhaps at a very deep layer where all memory and consciousness are one, and no longer distinguishable.

My father and I went through the squeaky iron turnstile under the lion's gate and walked to the Rosenstein Nature Museum. We had entered a park that would never come to an end. Passing through gates on which animals sat, we would keep on walking through ever-new infinities, And at the same time (in reality almost fifty years later) I was in Poland—now an adult and headed toward old age—standing in front of those black, cast-iron lions on the pillars of the Laskowitz castle gate. Beyond them, the infinite depths of the park had begun for my father when he was a child. My grandfather wrote that he couldn't forget, even in the 1960s, *how protected and safe I always felt lying in bed in the evening, the castle watchman, Kurzer, telling the hours on a soft and dark-sounding flute that sounded like the call of a stock pigeon.*

If he went on watch at 10, he would start calling the hours then, and he continued every hour until 4 in the morning. He circled the castle and also went some way into the park, sounding the hour several times at short intervals. His brother, the watchman at the farm, answered him from the farmyard or from the stalls. From time to time one heard a dog barking in the village or a train rolling in the distance. If there was no wind and it was summer and the windows were open, I could also hear the clanging of the clock in the village church tower. The guard Kurzer still walks with his flute in every park that I've known since. On Hampstead Heath, in the Bois de Boulogne, in Munich's English Garden, in Central Park, in all these artificial landscapes (that in reality comprise an infinite space within our souls), I sometimes imagine myself after I'm dead, walking with my father and my grandfather. Sociologists tell us that the memories and dreams of fathers and sons and grandfathers fold into one another like the tubes of an extendable telescope, and that probably no one really lives his innermost life on his own.

I think it was Frenssen's book Peter Moor's Journey to Southwest Africa that gave me the impulse, my grandfather wrote at the beginning of the chapter "Why Africa," introducing the memories of his years in Southwest Africa that he put to paper between the summers of 1965 and 1968. As so often is the case when dealing with "life" and its supposed spontaneity, it was probably literature that inspired my grandfather to decide to go to Africa. His African memoir imitated *Frenssen's book* but so, probably, did his real life in Southwest. Another model may have been the brown volumes written by the proto-Nazi German novelist Hans Grimm. (My grandfather had looked up Grimm in a hotel in Kattowitz before leaving for Africa. They had dinner together, and my grandfather was apparently negatively impressed by a degree of vanity that really must have been ghastly. *Volk without Space, The Oil-Prospector from Duala, Lützerland:* they are Gustav Freytag-like, shockingly bad and actually almost unbearably programmatic novels, throbbing with late colonial rage and a longing that by 1933 was completely delusional.)

Perhaps it isn't even true, as I believe Woody Allen and Arno Schmidt have written, that our lives imitate cheap novels. Perhaps cheap novels are an experimental spiritualist medium, wherein the voices of the dead communicate to us. "What befell the merchant is what befell so many Germans whose bodies had united painfully with the hard, hot earth of Southwest. Like most of his fellow countrymen, he did not exploit the Negroes. Nor was he violent, nor a conqueror, nor a brave adventurer. He was a diligent citizen of the lower-middle class, who sought to rise more quickly than was possible in his homeland. Like the others, once he was in possession of his greater freedom and on his new, sunlit path, he moved closer to Fate. And one day he suddenly stood facing it. Alone. Standing before the inevitable he, too, of course, was heroic." Thus Hans Grimm, ad infinitum and, in those years, at every possible opportunity. But (once again): *Patrolling the train from 3 to 4 one morning, I was suddenly overwhelmed by the sight of the snow-covered, flat distances – a starlit landscape strewn with miserable, cowed villages. It was the East, and for the first time I was really seeing it. As alien as it was, I nonetheless felt an inexplicable, mysterious pull of attraction. Was it the unconscious lure of the open range that I so often felt later in Southwest Africa, was it the pull of eastern space, waiting for action and submission, to which our medieval ancestors had yielded, or was my Polish grandmother calling from within me?*

I have to admit that I have sometimes asked myself similar questions thinking about my grandfather and his memoirs. For example, when I read the last sentences of his memories of Polish Anhalt (*slowly the shore retreated into the distance, the waving people became smaller, and as it grew dark, we had already passed Cuxhafen. Africa lay before us*), I think about how late one afternoon in the early fall of 1990 I was in the Frankfurt airport drinking a *Weizenbier*, looking through the picture window at the jumbo transports of the American air force that were taking off and landing in the midst of the buildup to the first Gulf War. The first leaves were falling from the trees. Our furniture, books, and clothes were already on the high seas, somewhere between Cuxhafen and the Suez Canal. We would never return here. We were off to a new start. Japan lay before us.

Or I think of the summer night in the sleeping car from Stuttgart to London in the early 1980s when I, with nothing more in the luggage rack than two large suitcases and a traveling bag, left my friends, a tenured job as a high-school teacher, and the city of my childhood forever, with no security other than the fairy-tale belief that I was only thirty and whatever I found would in any case be better than death. Or I think of the evening heat and the red, hazy sunset I saw on a late summer day over the suddenly endless stretches of grain fields and bluffs, after I had finally passed Bratislava and was driving toward southern Poland through a country that somehow seemed Roman. ("Pannonia," I thought with emotion.) Suddenly, I came upon a large, very yellow hotel with double windows, wide stairs, and high stucco ceilings in the center of a small town above the steep bank of an unknown river. Musicians were playing in the market square under arbors that dated from the Renaissance, young women and men were sitting about, and the shadows from the foliage of acacia branches fell on the pavement in front of street lamps. High up in the gray cliff walls of the same canyon in which the hotel nestled, I was later to come across the proud inscription of a Roman scouting patrol from the time of Marcus Aurelius, who once had followed the river far into the barbarian foothills. For the rest of my life such moments will mean more to me that any "homeland."

Southwest of Meissen, between Leipzig and Dresden, lies the village of Ziegenhain. The very fruitful sand and loess landscape is called "Lommatzscher Pflege" and is named after the holy Oracle Lake (since disappeared), whose waves were thought to be linked to the fate and future of the Sorbs who lived there until well into the late medieval period. Thietmar von Merseburg described its location and magic power as follows: "Lommatzsch is a spring no further than two miles from the Elbe river; it feeds a lake that frequently brings forth wonderful apparitions, as the natives and many eye-witnesses attest. When the lake is covered with wheat, oats, and acorns, it is a harbinger of peace and a bountiful harvest, and brings joy to the people of the area who often gather around it. If on the other hand, the wild storms of war are erupting, it foretells the certain outcome with blood and ash. The people of the area honor and fear it more than they do the churches."

A short walk outside the village of Ziegenhain lie the late-baroque houses, offices, and outbuildings of a large farm. The castle-like, three-story main house was built in the seventeenth century over much older cellars and walls. The road leads to it through a rounded archway topped by a stone urn or vase on a pedestal, with a globe-shaped, ornamented cover. Carved onto its front surface, within a laurel wreath above the year 1802, is the entwined monogram of the wealthy landowner Christian Gottlob Wackwitz. In 1791, he bought the estate of Lindight from his brother Johann Christian—after he had already expanded his family's property four years earlier by acquiring two large estates that had gone into debt when the peasants were freed. The size of the property was equal to any of several smaller counties west of the Saale River and was almost coterminous with the borders of the agricultural collective that took it over in the 1950s and proceeded to run it into the ground.

As far as we know, everyone who carries my name comes from this area, indeed from this estate. Today most of them live in America. I look at the reproduction of a Biedermeier oil painting on the frontispiece of a four-hundred-page volume entitled *A Pictorial History of the Wackwitz Family 1402– 1988* that a Frederik Hendrik Wackwitz from Van Alstyne, Texas, sent me sometime in the 1990s, sharing the latest results of his very extensive and detailed amateur genealogical research. There are stone globes on the masonry pillars of the wall around the estate's vegetable gardens, very white walls under the hipped roof of the main building, a small onion-dome—perhaps a kind of chapel—that towers over the inner courtyard. In the background is the massive roof of a barn. The horses are black, the trees, classically thin, and geese are scattered across the sunny grass in the foreground, like something out of a story. The sky takes up more than half the picture.

But distant as this image is from me and little as it seems to say to me across such an unthinkable remove of time, it is equally distant from the earliest owners of the Lindighthof. The first of my ancestors to be named in a document, strangely enough also a Stephan Wackwitz (in the spelling of the early fifteenth century, "Wagkwicz"), was, in turn, the descendant by several centuries of an enterprising young man who came to this place sometime between 1050 and 1250 from the Rhineland or Flanders or Thuringia. He crossed the Saale with all his earthly belongings, cleared a patch in the forest under the protection of Meissen Castle, built himself a hut, planted, went hungry, and brought in the first harvest. By 1402, Stephan Wagkwicz's immediate ancestors had had enough time to acquire four farms—any one of them would have been sufficient for a family—and the acreage was already twice the usual size. Were they obtained by marriage? Or were they purchased? Or awarded for bravery in killing Sorbs, burning their property, and selling them into slavery? Who will ever know?

When I was four or five, my favorite Grimms' fairy tale—in the blue, cloth-bound volume from which my mother read to me when I was as old as my son is now—was the one that was longest. (And when my son was four or five, he knew the same story so well that he could tell it completely and correctly, in all its complexity and crazy logic, to anyone willing to hear it, with wide eyes, finger-stretching gestures, and a narrative voice that a succession of generations has somehow validated.) It is called "The Two Brothers," and I loved it especially because it took almost an entire Saturday afternoon to get through. "The brothers kept on, and finally they came to a forest that was so big that getting out of it in a day would have been impossible. So they remained there the entire night and ate what they had put into their hunting bag. They kept going the second day, too, and they still didn't get out."

"We come on the ship they call the Mayflower/We come on the ship that sailed the moon/We come in the age's most

uncertain hour/And sing an American tune"—Ever since I
heard this song by Simon and Garfunkel (with only a slight
change in rhythm to the tune of the Reformation resistance
chorale "O Haupt voll Blut und Wunden," by the way), I
have been happy in the thought that from the very beginnings of humanity we have not simply come from someplace, but that we have also always arrived at someplace at
some time, "in the age's most uncertain hours"—by ship
along the coast, on foot through dream-infinite forests and
steppes (through parks) that finally come to an end after all,
when the struggle and the actual work begin and we bear
children, who bear children, leave us, and move on in turn.
And I know today (and in reality have always known) that
the infinite landscapes that I sometimes see in my dreams
include not only the Namib desert that my grandfather saw
in 1934 (We rode on, through endless herds of oryx and zebra,
mountain ranges to the left and the right); not only the Laskowitz
park that my father saw when he played in his grandparents' garden and from where my grandfather would hear
Kurzer the castle watchman's flute while he lay in bed; not
only the never-ending Rosenstein Park; but also the spot
near the oracular spring not far from Meissen, where a man
perhaps not so different from me, a German living abroad,
eight hundred or a thousand years ago in the High Middle
Ages, did not want to trek any further (or could not, or was
not allowed to) and settled down (for a few centuries).

He knew nothing of the endless wanderings of the generations before him that brought down the Roman Empire,
settled in Greece, left Mesopotamia (in Neolithic times, having acquired the skill of cultivating grain), proceeded through
the deep jungle that then covered the continent, came as far
as England and the Atlantic and pushed Cro-Magnon man

back into the Basque country. And he didn't know that around 1770 his descendants would make their way via Bremen to Amsterdam and then sail over the ocean to Brooklyn. But it seems to me that he, too, must have sometimes dreamt of deserted rooms and infinite forests. "And when they sat down to their evening meal, the two brothers said to their foster father, 'We won't touch our food or take a bite until you have granted us a wish.' He asked, 'What is your wish?' They answered, 'We have learned all we can. It is now time for us to go out into the world. So please allow us to leave and to journey.' Then, in joy, the old man said, 'You speak like noble-spirited hunters. What you desire has been my own wish. Go. You will do well.' Whereupon they ate and drank joyfully together."

I remember the picture vividly even now. It was taken from the summit of Hira, with a corner of Lake Biwa like a mirror far below. Down over the steep slope, broken here and there by a boulder, stretched a brilliant field of mountain rhododendrons. A sort of astonishment swept over me, I have no idea why. A volatile, ether-like excitement stirred a corner of my heart.   —Yasushi Inoue, "The Rhododendrons"

13 The Jacaranda of Madeira

When a person leaves the life he knows and sets out for the unknown—which has to be better than death, whatever happens—it may be the right decision, or one that is pleasurable, or even the only decision possible. This was the tradition of my ancestors, and it was completely consistent with, and perhaps even secretly waiting for, the ideology and actions of the Nazis. The dreams and fantasies so violently released during Hitler's climb to power became stronger than caution, reason, a sense of responsibility, or conscience; above all they were stronger than the ability to look closely and to assess risky endeavors realistically. Perhaps one has to imagine them as a state-sanctioned and state-protected dream afflicting 60 million people simultaneously: the castle park of Laskowitz joining with millions of other childhood memories of infinity, and suddenly stretching from the Atlantic to the Urals. Once exposed, such megalomanic fantasies are buried in the shame they have left in their wake. And today, we see only the dreamless ruins brought about by recklessness, blindness, and criminality, and we are no longer able to understand them.

Nor do memoirs like my grandfather's make sense of them. Instead, they present doubts and momentary flashes of realism as having been as manifest in retrospect as they surely ought to have been in actual fact, but unfortunately were not. At the critical moment—inevitably—people forgot or (for one reason or another) never got around to voicing their doubts and hesitations. Such are the exculpating strategies with which we struggle to maintain our self-regard. So it is not only because of my own sense of shame and family loyalty that it seems impertinent, if not somehow unsportsmanlike, to quote from volumes of the "African Homeland Calendar" dating from 1938 or from other dangerous years of this calendar—which, for all I know, is still being published.

Andreas Wackwitz—erstwhile Lutheran Propst for Southwest Africa, the Church Superindent for Luckenwalde, later Hamburg hospital chaplain, and finally Lörrach pensioner—published his best literary writing from 1933 until well into the 1960s in this "homeland calendar." Friendly, straightforwardly precise, and emotionally tumultuous, written in the manner of Johann Peter Hebel, these short stories are accomplished reflections and essays—in fact, calendar stories—on local and world-historic events of that year. In 1938, for example, my grandfather's contribution was entitled "Austria? Austria!" Reading it, I experience with a new immediacy the truly hair-raising imperceptibility with which the Hebel-like tone glides from the illusions of German nationalism into a completely brazen and unrestrained Nazism, an imperceptibility that in 1938 governed not only my grandfather's style but, indeed, his life.

What interested me more than these poisoned texts among my grandfather's papers was the description of his second encounter with Adolf Hitler. By this time, the great man was no longer a mere low-ranking dispatcher but, as of a few hours earlier, Chancellor of the Reich. And my grandfather was not a young officer, but a German-nationalist pastor who served outside the country, had just turned forty, and did not really know quite what to do with his life. Should he return to the Reich and be near his aged parents in the Silesian parish of Grosshartmannsdorf? Or should he follow his dreams and take a position in the former colony of German Southwest Africa, since 1918 a British mandate? Windhoek or Grosshartmannsdorf? I would not have found this a difficult decision. But my grandfather, too, probably knew exactly what he would do, and I believe that what he experienced on January 30, 1933 (again like Leonard Zelig, recognizable somewhere in the background of the historic tableau), strengthened his resolve to leave home, parents, and an "awakened" Germany, an awakening that was not only contemporaneous with his decision but secretly in league with it.

There was no word from Windhoek, and in Gross-Hartmannsdorf they were waiting for me to accept their offer. I was in the position of a man with a bird in the hand and unable to decide whether to let it fly in order to grab the two in the bush. Following V.'s advice, I decided to go to Berlin to see what I could find out from Senior Consistorial Councillor H. When I arrived, he was ill and in bed. He told me that among the numerous applicants I had the best chance, but that the executive board of the church in Windhoek had not yet declared its preference. But, he said, he would send a cable and urge them to make a decision. In the meantime, I should lay my cards on the table in Grosshartmannsdorf and ask for a few weeks' deferral.

I spent the night in Berlin. The following day was January 30, 1933. The Schleicher government had resigned, and Hitler was at the Hotel Kaiserhof on Wilhelmsplatz. I went to the Foreign Ministry to see von Grünau, the former General Counsel of Kattowitz. We spoke about my Africa plans, and I asked him about the new government. He said that everything was perfect—Hitler was chancellor, and the Government had been sworn in. I asked about Schleicher, and von Grünau responded with a shrug of the shoulders: "They gave him his top hat and showed him the door." He had had too many irons in the fire.

As I was standing on Wilhelmstrasse, the street vendors were already selling the special editions printed up by the newspapers. In the afternoon, I was at H.'s again, and I wanted to catch the 10 P.M. night express back via Breslau. By evening there were posters everywhere urging people to join the torch-light parade that was gathering at the Great Star in the Tiergarten and about to go through the Brandenburg Gate, along Unter den Linden and into Wilhelmstrasse, past President Hindenburg, Hitler, and the new ministers. I took a position on Unter den Linden, near Pariser Platz. The SA and other Nazis in uniform, the Stahlhelm, and all kinds of other groups marched in very long columns of four with flags, music, and torches. Berliners were standing in a dense crowd, four or five deep in front of me and with several more rows behind me. As the first SA unit passed, many called out "Heil!," hands were raised, hats were waived. I stood in my fur coat and fur hat and, since it was cold, with my hands in my pockets. Suddenly someone hit me over the head with an umbrella, and I heard something like "Take off your hat!"

I turned around and pushed my way out of the crowd. Taking a detour, I reached the Wilhelmsplatz (later called Reich Chancel-

lor Platz). A lot of police were there illuminating the Chancellor's Palace with searchlights. I worked my way through the crowd and saw Hitler at the open window above the ground floor with others standing next to him and at the adjacent windows. Holding the flag high, the SA trooped by with a calm, steady gait, blaring military marches. Hitler raised his arm again and again. The crowds cheered, and from a human pyramid people threw roses that were caught by a man standing next to him. I pushed further into Wilhelmstrasse where old Hindenburg was standing at a closed window in the wing where Bismarck had lived. He was wearing a black frock coat and was illuminated from the side by lanterns. He stood tall and straight, as if carved out of wood.

When SA troops marched by, he nodded his head in greeting, but if they were Stahlhelm formations, he waved. The sight of Hitler did not move me especially. All I could think was: Well, let's see how he does. I found it reassuring that old, conservative politicians like Hugenberg, Seldte, etc., were in his cabinet. But the sight of the old man in Bismarck's official apartment made a very deep impression on me: against his convictions, but not wanting to violate the Constitution, he had appointed the "Bohemian private" after all. I grew serious and had the feeling that I was witness to a historic moment. Gradually, the time of departure drew closer, and I worked my way back to Friedrichstrasse.

In spite of his skepticism, caution, and even disapproval, subtle signs in my grandfather's description betray a feeling that his country and the entire world were becoming young once again (perhaps in the way that happens to some men of his age when they get to know a young woman one more time). Once again—"Lo, how a rose e'er blooming/From tender stem hath sprung"—a rose bloomed from the stem of the wooden Field Marshall and Reich President, from the stem of the Laskowitz forester's house, the German Empire, the Old World. (Hindenburg's fat, grumpy face looks at me from a postcard that the young Andreas Wackwitz, or perhaps his bride, pasted, with other souvenir pictures of World War I, onto the first page of an album. Hindenburg is sitting at a desk and staring ahead sullenly, presumably looking as one should after recently having lost a world war.)

Andreas Wackwitz was skeptical—something that was very important to him, in retrospect. But he also hoped that the treacherous Republic would not remain the last word in German history, that Anhalt would be returned to Germany, that the country would regain its greatness (and its African colonies). This hope must have been seductive, indeed almost overwhelming. (On the other side of the shamefully shrunken borders the *inexplicable, mysterious pull of attraction* of *the East, waiting for action and submission to which our medieval ancestors had yielded* and *the unconscious lure of the open range that I so often felt later in Southwest Africa*.) The seductiveness and hope (and the beckoning of expanded career opportunities) must have been so powerful that my grandfather's doubts did not have much impact. I would guess that Andreas Wackwitz would have needed more than one cognac in the dining car of the night train through Silesia to still his excitement. Perhaps the sacrifice of his brother had not been in vain after all. Perhaps his country would get a second chance.

I have often read this scene in my grandfather's memoirs, and each time a cold, ghostly wind blows through it. The wooden general, who had been placed leaning into the window, like a corpse. The strangely silly, erotic, and circuslike feat of the "human pyramid" from which men threw roses, a rather unimaginable configuration, like something out of Kafka. The blow to the head, the waiting night train, the cold. The impressions that the diarist took with him onto the train to Breslau on January 30, 1933, are contradictory: the petrifaction of the general and the arousal of the rose-throwers; depression and mania. My grandfather claims that he reacted to the German dilemma with skepticism on the one hand ('Well, let's see how he does. Good thing that he's surrounded by reasonable German men'), with melancholy reflection on the other (*the feeling that I was witness to a historic moment*). The emotional distance—symbolized by the waiting night train—dates from 1954, when this passage was written. But in 1933, my grandfather may well have been as depressed and as manic as his fellow-countrymen on Unter den Linden, shouting to the heavens and sad unto death, and the strangely galvanic liveliness of his memories of that January 30 evening still gives the reader a sense of what his mood must have been at the time.

Initially and for a long time, Germany would expand without having to go to war, and when Andreas Wackwitz went to distant southern Africa, it seemed that he had been justified in having put himself, heart and soul, at the disposal of the irredentist cause during the last twelve years of the German Republic. Maybe this abandon was not as scandalous from the vantage point of 1921 as it seems to us, who know where it was all headed. No provision of the Treaty of Versailles was as compellingly criticized at the time and seems as unreasonable today as the division of Upper Silesia between Germany and Poland, against which my grandfather directed all the decisiveness he had acquired during the First World War. It is not necessary to quote Lloyd George, who is supposed to have said that giving Silesia to the Poles was like handing a pocket watch to an orangutan—my grandfather, of course, quoted this saying *con gusto*—for even a liberal like the future German foreign minister Walther Rathenau had spoken of the partition of Upper Silesia as a "wound in the middle of Europe that would never close." (Five years later, he would be gunned down in an assassination planned in part by the right-wing Annaberg veteran Ernst von Salomon.)

And in 1920, Max Weber wrote, "For compelling economic reasons the mixed-language areas of Upper Silesia . . . belong to Germany: the economy of the entire region depends on them, and if you separate them, the stunting of the economy of the entire region east of the Elbe will be the consequence." Later, after this separation had been decided on, he warned that after a few years German workers and intellectuals would inevitably think once again "about the revolutionary means of self-determination that had been employed by the *Irredenta* and how a people of seventy million could use them more extensively and effectively than Serbia or Italy had ever done." The great sociologist's prediction is especially moving and disturbing—it's as if, shortly before his death, the *eminent Wilhelminian* had seen not only my grandfather, behind him, but could already vaguely recognize Goebbels and Hitler.

Even in 1935, at the time of the plebiscite on the annexation of the Saar region to a stronger, re-arming Reich, it seemed that Hitler and Goebbels were nothing worse than realistic, deliberate, and not particularly revolutionary irredentists. After the successful vote on the unification of the Saarland, my grandmother in Windhoek described to her in-laws in Laskowitz how she and Andreas had arranged for the church bells of the Southwest African desert highlands to be rung as they were in Germany. "The boys who were to ring the bells were at our place by quarter to nine, but they had to curb their enthusiasm for another two hours, because Andreas and the consul had decided that the bells could be rung only after the consulate had received official world and hoisted the flags. But the English radio brought the news at about 9:30, flags were raised everywhere, and our phone was ringing incessantly. Everyone was asking why we, too, weren't sounding the bells since they were already ringing in Germany. At about 10:45 the consul called. We rang our bells, and the Catholics rang theirs, and every good German thought and said: When will the bells be sounding for Southwest as they are now ringing for the Saarland? And we thought about poor Upper Silesia and the suffering of the Germans in the Polish area. I didn't know if I should cry out of happiness for the Saarland, or out of sadness for Upper Silesia. Both feelings were mixed in me, and in the back of my mind I was wishing to be here long enough to see the handing over of Southwest.—On Andreas's orders the bells were rung until 11. While they were still sounding, Frau Gutknecht called from Regenstein, saying that she wanted to hear the pealing bells with her children. Very touched by the thought of this good German woman, I held the receiver out the open window. After a while, Frau von Michaelis, the woman who supplies our milk, called from Avis, and I let her hear the bells in the same manner, which gave her and her employees great pleasure. And something else touched me: a phone call, also at about noon, from an old, deaf lady, Frau Dr. Kaempffer, who lives all by herself on the edge of the city. She's the mother of Hans Kaempffer, the 'young German' whom Hans Grimm wrote about in his book on Southwest. She said she just wanted to exchange a *Heil Hitler* with someone, that she was so happy about the Saar that she just had to talk to someone."

But it's not the seemingly important events like the 1935 Saarland plebiscite that I remember from the African chapter of our *family romance,* nor is it the political developments or the career decisions. It seems in retrospect that what actually mattered throughout my grandfather's life were the small and unimportant events and impressions that are suddenly illuminated more than half a century later (as in Yasushi Inoue's great story, "The Rhododendrons," and in all lives). "The azaleas were beautiful today as we came past Keagé. Possibly, since they belong to the same family, the rhododendrons are in bloom at the summit of Hira. Somewhere high on that slope, the white flowers are blooming. The great white clusters spread over the face of the mountain. Ah, how much more at peace I would be if I could lie there at the summit under those scented clusters! To lie with my legs stretched out and to look up into the night sky—I am happier even at the thought of it. There and only there, I somehow feel, is what could rock me and lull me, give me peace. I should have gone up there, at least once. It is too late now. It is no longer possible for me to climb mountains." (Trans. Edward Seidenstricker.)

On April 26, we docked at Madeira for two hours, and Gutschu and I went briefly on shore, where magnificent blue jacaranda were blossoming and the islanders used sleds. On one of the following days, we reached Las Palmas, and in the evening I went on shore with Mother. We strolled under the tall palm trees and admired the glorious flowers in the parks. We returned to the ship on the launch.

Or:

Cape Town lies on the Atlantic side. First you drive south with the Atlantic Ocean on your right; at the Cape of Good Hope you turn toward the Indian Ocean and drive along the wonderfully expansive bay (on the right side) beneath the cliffs. For the most part, the coast is rocky. The view from the highway, wending along the sides of the cliff like a road in the Alps, is stunningly beautiful. On the one side, the cliffs climb steeply and mightily, on the other, twenty, or thirty or more meters below, the surf thunders onto the rocks. The road goes up and down, through forests and large park-like stretches, past vineyards, through wealthy residential towns and resorts. The view of the surf and the ocean is indescribably beautiful. The closer one gets to the Cape, the more desolate the landscape becomes, heather of all kinds and sizes covers the cliffs, shrubs and bushes with gorgeous, tulip-like blossoms (protea, or sugar-bush, as the Boers call them) grow in boggy soil, low shrubs like alpine roses adorn the mountain slopes, ocean fog and drizzle brush against the lonely expanse, and finally the Cape lighthouse comes into view.

Or, yet again:

Patrolling the train from 3 to 4 one morning, I was suddenly overwhelmed by the sight of the snow-covered, flat distances—a starlit landscape strewn with miserable, cowed villages. It was the East, and for the first time I was really seeing it. As alien as it was, I nonetheless felt an inexplicable, mysterious pull of attraction. Was it the unconscious lure of the open range that I so often felt later in Southwest Africa, was it the pull of eastern space, waiting for action and submission, to which our medieval ancestors had yielded, or was my Polish grandmother calling from within me?

I have only to erase this passage's strange, *volkish* arrogance from my mind (an arrogance that was to make my grandfather so useful for the Nazi movement twenty years after this moment along a snowy stretch of Galician train track) for it to become apparent that he and I have something else in common, as if we shared the same memory, as if I had been with him on that winter night in Galicia. Because the distances of the *East*, needless to say, were waiting as little for *action and submission* as were the Cape of Good Hope, the jacaranda of Madeira, or the blossoming flowers of Las Palmas. They were simply waiting for Andreas Wackwitz, just as in my time other flowers, countries, and distances were waiting for me, and as I would have given up and ruined my life had I—unlike my grandfather (or like him, but completely differently)—not followed its *pull* (or whatever else one wants to call this attraction). (Scenes from the *Education sentimentale* of a German family living abroad.) "I said to myself that someday I would stand on the little steamer, depicted in a circular inset on the same page, that several times each day made its way from hamlet to hamlet up the lake coast; and, looking up at the jagged lines of Hira, I would climb to exactly the spot on the peak from which the picture was taken. I do not know how to explain it, but I was quite sure that the day would come. It would come. Without fail. My heart had made its decision, shall we say—in any case, I felt not the slightest doubt."

THE JACARANDA OF MADEIRA

October 25. A few nights ago Carl saw a fiery apparition just beyond the foot of his bed. It seemed as if an invisible hand were describing a zig-zag in the air in long horizontal bands with a white-hot coal or a glowing fingertip. Whereupon one heard a strange creaking.

—Eduard Mörike, "The Ghost in the Parsonage of Cleversulzbach"

14 Tale of the Snake

Events transpire in the histories of peoples and empires, in almost all lives, and in some books, that seem random and disconnected. But at times their very existence as verifiable facts becomes meaningful in itself and evolves into something akin to the raw material of literature. We then understand that a particular turn of events in a life or in history takes on its significance (and sometimes it becomes all-significant) as a consequence of its being self-contained, consistent, and accidental, apparently following its own necessity—a closed if perhaps also completely inexplicable or shadowy event "system" (like Elser's failed assassination attempt on Hitler in 1939, or the death of the Victorian general Charles George Gordon in Khartoum in 1885). The life or epoch in which the event occurred seems to be so conclusively summed up in it that it is as if the individuals or nations concerned had never experienced anything other than this small, illogical occurrence. Unlike symbols, legends, and riddles, such events are not circumscribed by particular meanings and do not point inevitably to certain conclusions.

They are simply occurrences in the real world. And the peculiarly irrefutable significance and evidentiary value that link them to the lives in which they take place are as mysterious as the unkempt old man in Tolstoy's novel whom Anna Karenina sees several times in her dreams and then once more before she throws herself in front of the train (when he suddenly really exists).

My grandfather's famous tale of the snake narrates such an event. On the one hand it is just a memorable hunting experience of the kind that was told around a campfire in Southwest (or, later, with his sons over wine). Yet reading and thinking about it, I find it difficult to shake my first impression: my grandfather came to see what he had experienced with a cobra at Waterberg in 1938 as a kind of paradigm of his life and (even if he never would have expressed it this way) as the interaction of a demonic threat and divine providence (or something like that—these stories are always difficult to nail down with semantic precision). Certainly, anyone who knew my grandfather would believe his assurances that this story really had happened as he told it: whatever else may be said of him, he was the opposite of a liar and a hysteric. So I have little choice but to acknowledge that such things apparently do happen—especially, perhaps, in strict, Protestant homes and lives where, confronted with the inexplicable, one strives for the greatest and most rational distance from the occult—which, in turn, might feel obliged to engage in occasional pranks or acts of vengeance.

Driving on a work-related trip to the north, I brought along an engineer named Gerhard from Okahandja to Otjiwarongo, where he had some surveying to do. We passed Waterberg and went to the cemetery where German colonial soldiers who had been killed in the Herero Uprising were buried. We left the car and the Herero boy in the bush and walked in the sand to the walled cemetery. A cobra, about one and a half meters in length, was sunning itself on one of the graves. As we got closer, it began to move away from us. I immediately hit at it with my walking stick, but at too sharp an angle and with too much force; the stick broke through in the middle. Gerhard quickly grabbed a palm frond that was still lying there from the last memorial service, and he, too, began to strike at the snake. After I hit it several times on its spine, it could no longer move. Quickly, I put my foot behind the snake's head and, absolutely furious on account of my broken walking stick, I speared its iron tip through the cobra's head, pinning it to the ground. Once it was still, Gerhard took it by the end of its tail and held it high, head hanging downwards, and I photographed him in this pose. Then he squeezed its neck between the thumb and index finger of his left hand so that its mouth opened. With a little wooden stick he bent its needlelike fangs, which normally lie flat to the back on the upper jaw, and the pressure forced the clear, slightly sticky poison to flow out of the glands.—We brought the snake back to the car, having decided that we'd strip and then dry its skin. The Herero boy was sleeping under a tree. Gerhard said, "Let's put the snake in the car and then wake him up and have him get into the car; watch how he'll turn gray from fright." So he put it on the empty back seat—the other was full of suitcases and blankets. Since the car had been standing in the sun for a long time with its roof open, the leather of the seat was not just warm but very hot. Hardly was the snake placed there, when it began to move, and before we could blink, it was hiding under the blankets. We found ourselves cheated out of seeing a terrified boy and instead were rather scared ourselves. Fortunately a piece of the tail about the length of a hand was sticking out from the blanket. Gerhard grabbed it quickly and decisively, pulled with all his strength, and with a flourish threw the snake high over his shoulder and away from the car. The boy and I just had time to jump to the side. But the snake had hardly touched the hot sandy soil, when it slithered quickly under the car. At first we were so surprised that we could move neither hand nor foot, but we positioned ourselves as quickly as possible around the other three sides of the car to see where it would appear again. But it didn't come out, and there was no trace of it in the sparse grass under the car. So I sat inside and drove a bit further, whereupon the boy pointed to a hole in the ground: "Mister, onjoka in here!" A meter-long branch was stuck into the hole, but only half of it would go in—the hole was blocked, or it curved to the side. We got a spade, started to dig and reached the bottom of the hole. Where was the snake? We all three lay on our stomachs and looked under the car, we opened the hood, took out all the luggage, examined the side pockets, the tool box, looked under every seat—nowhere was there any trace of the snake. Shrugging our shoulders, we gave up and reassured ourselves with the thought that it must have escaped from the other side of the car before we could reach it. After all the bags had once again been loaded into the car, we drove the twenty miles to the Flotows', where we wanted to spend the night. The car was put in an open shed, we inspected the Flotows' plantations, and after enjoying a nourishing dinner and relaxed conversation —naturally, we recounted our adventure with the speared snake—we lay down to sleep, Gerhard and I each in a room of the guest house. The next morning we drove on, I dropped Gerhard off at Otjiwarongo and promised to pick him up a week later. When we saw one another again, he reported that in the meantime old Flotow had been in Otjiwarongo and had told him on his honor the following, incredible story: on the morning after we left Waterberg, Frau von Flotow walked into the garden, to the little house that is both well-known and essential. When she was about to return to the farm house, she suddenly saw the raised head of the cobra directly in front of her. She quickly retreated to the *little house, slammed the door shut and, in a loud and shrill voice, called for help. One of the Flotow sons beat the snake until it was dead. All the Flotows present saw clearly that the head of the snake had been pierced. It was our snake! We had brought it with us in the car for over twenty miles! Where had the scoundrel been hiding? But now the story gets very strange indeed. I went to the hotel's yard, looked for my Herero boy and told him what Mister von Flotow had reported. He said that this didn't surprise him at all, because early on the morning of our departure he had seen the snake's trail coming out of the shed in which our car was standing and then making several turns and circles in front of the gauze curtains behind which Gerhard and I were sleeping, finally disappearing from the garden! The entire story sounds as incredible as it is strange, but once again: every word of it is true, and it happened exactly as I've described here!*

I want to say at the outset that, often as I've read and thought about my grandfather's story of the snake, I do not understand it, but what should I have expected? I have the feeling that the meaning of this story is both precise and very important, but it eludes my grasp, and I have to be content with a few additional details, parallel instances, and reflections to help untangle the meanings of this *unheard-of event*.

What jumped out at me immediately was the astonishing fact that my grandfather seems to have missed his story's most obvious implication entirely. Its only tangible point (insofar as it has any point at all) goes back to the statement of the "Herero boy," who claims to have seen the trail that the cobra left from the open shed to the gauze-covered bedroom windows of the von Flotows' guesthouse. The two whites had intended to play a stupid, gruesome, and dangerous trick on this nameless Herero (as he surely realized), and he would have had every reason to frighten them in turn, as if to show them that he and the snake were, like his country's demons, in league against them. It is important to understand that this man was one of the last of a great, self-confident, and famous nation of warriors that the German colonial troops had crushed thirty years earlier at Waterberg in Wilhelminian Germany's only war prior to 1914. The Germans then drove the Hereros into the murderously arid Omaheke Desert where, after wandering about for weeks, some eighty thousand of them, including women and children, died a miserable death. This was one of the "late Victorian holocausts" that are as much a part of European colonialism as the genocide in the Belgian-ruled Congo described by Joseph Conrad in his novel *The Heart of Darkness.*

This descendant of the slaughtered Hereros, working as servant, guide, and errand-boy for whites like my grandfather and the surveying engineer Gerhard, probably felt that the sons of the Wilhelminian killers (paying their respects to the dead tormentors of the great black chieftains and warriors) had encountered the ghost of Samuel Maherero or one of the other great Bantu heroes in that soldier's cemetery. His silence in the face of the cobra, its pierced head hissing softly and rocking back and forth in front of the masters' bedrooms, evokes, when I read and reread my grandfather's snake story, the ominous silence of the Omaheke Desert, which in 1904 seemed to promise salvation to almost one hundred thousand defeated Hereros but in reality delivered them to death.

Nor, when reading this story (repeating it to myself, or elaborating on it in the shower, on my bike, or in the office) can I overlook Freud's assertion that the snake represents "the most significant symbol of the male genitals." Of course, as Freud ironically notes elsewhere, a cigar is sometimes just a cigar. But the story's small, telltale details suggest strongly that the Waterberg cobra was not just a snake: my grandfather's strange, inexplicable fury over the broken walking stick, stronger than any fear of this most dangerous of southern Africa's poisonous snakes; the cruelty of the phallic schoolboy prank devised by two grown men, who can think of nothing better than seating the unsuspecting and sleepy Herero in a car next to what might be (and then, in fact, was) a highly dangerous cobra, and this in front of the gravestones of the murderers of his people; photographing the surveying engineer with his booty, all one and a half meters of it. And one page further in his notes, my grandfather reveals that, as far as he was concerned, *this* African snake was not merely a snake—something he observes with a candor possible only in a man who had nothing but contempt for all forms of psychology and psychoanalysis.

Once when we were in Karibib sitting in front of the door at our friend M.'s, someone suddenly said, "There's a snake in the room!" The snake, about a cubit in length, had probably crawled through the open door toward the lighted lamp. I immediately ran to it and stepped on it so that the side of its head was visible next to the sole of my boot. Then I pulled out my pocket-knife and, with the greatest satisfaction, cut off its head, having learned this from my father's encounters with vipers. I wiped off my knife on my trousers, shut it, and put it back into my pocket. The women present admired my manly decisiveness, and when they heard that I was about to use the same knife to cut off the tip of a cigar, I saw in their faces a reaction of respect mixed with repugnance.

There's no way around it: the knife that he cleans off on his pants after successfully decapitating the snake, and that he intends to use soon afterwards to trim the cigar (here surely much more than just a cigar), noted by the women with a mixture of revulsion and admiration; the *greatest satisfaction* when he cuts off the snake's head; the memory of his father (of all people) instructing him in killing snakes. One can't read it in any way other than that Africa, through the medium of the ghostly, immortal cobra of Waterberg, showed the two white heroes of the snake story that the humiliated continent, *waiting for action and submission,* still had a hard-on (one that was not just large but possibly immortal and capable of a twenty-mile pursuit). *She quickly retreated to the little house, slammed the door shut, and in a loud and shrill voice, called for help.*

But the final or conclusive meaning of the cobra is to be found neither in its political role in our *family romance* nor in its psychoanalytic-comedic symbolism. Because the snake, of course, is not only the "most significant symbol of the male genitals" but also the most significant Christian symbol for the devil and for evil, for Lucifer, whose head the archangel Michael pierces with a lance and holds down with his boot, before pushing him down to hell. *But now the story gets very strange indeed.* It is clear to me that my grandfather, had he ever entertained such thoughts, would have seen evil (vanquished but still lurking) in the Hereros (in his view quite properly condemned to genocide) and in the dangerous, rebellious ghosts of their dry, hostile, and strange country. But in 2001, his grandson knew this with absolute certainty: the evil that was so stubbornly and invisibly close to his grandfather for such a long time (the soft hissing of the pierced head rocking back and forth, the poisonous snake in front of the gauze curtain), the evil, whose undistorted reality and repercussions he had escaped by a whisker again and again, had in reality been waiting for him at home. He didn't encounter it in Africa, but in his own country, where he returned in 1940, after the sinking of the *Adolph Woermann*, after that cigar on the high seas, after being interned in England, after being separated from his family and his seventeen-year old son, who was on his way across the Atlantic to Canada as a prisoner of war, where for five years he would fell trees.

"For murder, though it have no tongue, will speak
With most miraculous organ." —Hamlet

15 Murder

The German Democratic Republic had not yet gone out of
business, and the oddly worthless-looking aluminum coins
and small bills, like play money with portraits of Goethe and
Müntzer, were still in circulation. It was the spring of 1990,
and friends had lent me their red Lada, which I drove south
from Berlin on the car-length concrete slabs of a rural road.
I was on an inspection tour of a country that was suddenly
supposed to be ours. A few kilometers before reaching the
Zinna monastery, which is what I really had come to see, I
suddenly yielded to a vague, sentimental, familial impulse
and turned onto the road leading toward the town of Luckenwalde. I left the red Lada on the sand-strewn cobblestones
of the market square and wandered for half an hour through
the streets of the small town. Its mood seemed vaguely hostile. Trying the handle of the entrance to the late-Gothic
Johanniskirche, I found it locked. In no apparent physical relationship to anything else, a bell tower or watchtower with
a baroque hipped roof stood in the dusty and very bright
morning light. I realized that I knew this scene from a water-

color that hung in my grandparents' living room when I was a child. Almost no one was out on this morning of the GDR's last spring, and I still remember standing on that market square and wondering why it is that at every time of day and in every season of the year, towns like Luckenwalde seem to embody the eternal recurrence of despair and damnation. I gave no further thought to the fact that the infant Rudi Dutschke and his mother had arrived in town exactly fifty years earlier (at the same time that my grandfather, who was then as old as I am today, had come with his family).

In the late fall of 1940, Germany was at the vertex of its brief period of world domination. Poland and France had been defeated, occupied, and partitioned. At Dunkirk, Britain's armies had fled in panic. The Netherlands, Belgium, Denmark, and Norway were occupied. "During 1940 the twin obsessions of Hitler—'removing the Jews,' and *'Lebensraum'* had come gradually into sharp focus," writes Ian Kershaw. "In these months the twin obsessions would merge into each other. The decisive steps into genocidal war were about to be taken." *(Hitler 1936–45: Nemesis.)* And in the very same months during which the groundwork for Germany's final defeat was being irreversibly laid in the brand-new and splendiferous chancellery of the victorious Reich thirty kilometers to the northeast, two people came to Luckenwalde whose shared presence there was to shape my own life. With the help of the invisible bond between them, I hope to convey a better understanding of the history of my age and generation (far beyond my *family romance*) and to be able to cast it in a consoling light. Imagining that I know something about my grandfather's life in Luckenwalde (with what justification, God only knows), I can tell myself that I am also shedding new light on the charismatic, peculiarly boy-like, and sometimes really childish man who for a time was the uncontested political leader of my generation.

I examine the black-and-white photos that my father glued into his copy of my grandfather's Luckenwalde memoirs (noted on the flyleaf: "Begun in the summer of 1969, completed in the spring of 1970 in Lörrach"). My youngest aunt, then a small child, stands in front of ominous-looking, oversize corn or, more likely, tobacco leaves that point almost like a yucca plant into the air of the pastoral garden. The hipped roof of that bell tower or watchtower is in the background. My father's younger brother, my uncle, is wearing his Hitler Youth uniform: short pants, boots, short-sleeved shirt, and a tie that suggests both the military and the youth movement but is loosened casually, giving him a touch of the dandy. He sits with his arm around the shoulder of his sister, whose hands are folded demurely in her lap. My grandmother is next to him, wearing a floral dress. They sit on the three steps that lead from the house into the garden and smile as if nothing bad could happen to them for the rest of their lives. But a thick white arrow in the picture points to a buried cellar window, where the rescue teams were to search when digging for survivors under the ruins of the house.

The interior of a house with closed curtains. A brass ashtray and a small vase with hyacinths grace a grand piano. The leopard skin with the stuffed head and glass eyes. A sofa bed on which I slept when I was in Lörrach, into the 1970s. My uncle, by now a young man, on the organ bench of the *Johanniskirche* in Luckenwalde and wearing civilian clothes, is turning toward the camera, his hand resting on the music stand. Although he never really spent any time with me, indeed, hardly even seemed to notice me, he was always my favorite uncle: distracted, reserved, melancholy. The authoritative, confident movements of his hands and feet on the keys and pedals when, later, I sometimes turned the pages for him and the casual, sanctioning nod when, having read ahead and taken note of the last bar or two—although he had not yet played them—he came to the end of the page: the signal for me to turn it.

The scratchy-looking woolen-and-silk stockings of the many women and girls in this family. (The more ladylike and adult my aunts, the less woolen, the more transparent the stockings.) I can discern the complete works of Luther on the bookshelves and the gray-brown of *People without Space* (the same color as those silk stockings). I am struck by the eternally heroic smile and optimistic stare into the camera that is preserved in these pictures. (Only my uncle usually looks sad, and sometimes my grandmother is staring into the distance, as if thinking of her first-born in Canada.) Why does all this strike me as so inexpressibly melancholy? They have returned from the blossoming flowers, smells, deserts, animal herds, from Africa's spaces and its adventures to a country that the great liberal journalist and historian Sebastian Haffner once described as being like a family meal where, on the edge of the plate next to the good meat, the solid potatoes, and the healthy vegetables, as if it were a kind of mustard or cranberry sauce, sits a bit of shit. But it is strange how oppressively close these shades of brown and gray feel; the scratchiness of those stockings; the suddenly vivid memory of that sofa's dry, dusty odor.

Only after 1945 are my aunts and uncles smiling again, smiling into the camera as people in my country smile. (And then my father, too, is back in the photos—thin, incredibly young, optimistic, relieved, beaming—returned from captivity on the other side of the ocean.) My oldest aunt, standing in front of the partly bombed Hamburg Museum of Applied Arts, looks like one of my old girlfriends. Dressed in a scarf and a heavy coat (once a winter uniform), she is so graceful that she could be posing for a fashion magazine. My father stands next to her, positively draped in coats, jackets, and shawls, his thumbs hooked under the straps of a backpack as if ready for any adventure. He laughs in a manner so liberated and happy that one can't look at the picture without at least smiling with him. The lost war looks good on both of them. My aunt will soon follow my uncle to his American home. (In 2001, he was buried in Arlington Cemetery.) Soon my father will get to know my mother, whose background was as remote from a Protestant pastor's house in Prussia as it was possible for another German's to be.

Although I would not be born until well into the next decade, I have only to leaf back to those oddly oppressive photographs from 1943 and 1944 to know—despite what could reasonably be expected or even conceived—that I have it in me to feel like a contemporary-in-spirit to that vaguely depressing Luckenwalde pastor's house idyll. I, too, know something of the paralysis, the unease, the suppressed feelings of guilt, the unacknowledged fear of the future that characterized this period and that was present in the itchy stockings, in the gray and brown of the streets and interiors (suddenly penetrated by the white, red, and black of those ghastly Nazi badges, armbands, and flags). I knew that there was something disturbing in the melancholy of the Chopin march that my grandfather and uncle played on the grand piano in the living room, in the thundering of the Bach chorales in the *Johanniskirche* on Sunday ("O Eternity, Thou Word of Thunder"). Something moved in the shadows of the leaves on the parsonage's coal-blackened wall.

What must have been very disturbing indeed for both children and adults during the years of Nazi rule was the sudden presence in an idyllic small town like Luckenwalde of people who, though living, were as if dead. Wearing their yellow stars, the town's Jews may have walked about with everyone else, but their isolation was unbridgeable and irreversible: they were in another country. After 1938, they were the living dead, and in 1943, they disappeared altogether, namely into the vicinity of Anhalt. And even aside from the Jews, it must have seemed in Luckenwalde and everywhere else in the country as if the gates of hell had opened. After 1943, every household and every business could order for their own use one forced laborer (or more), be they Russian, Ukrainian, Polish, or French. Not unlike the paradoxical sleight-of-hand of corpses and ghosts, the slave-laborers were both present and absent. They embodied this paradox daily and in full public view. Mute, without rights, unpaid, they were given shelter somewhere and taken care of (or not) as their keepers saw fit. People weren't allowed to touch the "laborers" (as if they were defiled) or to let themselves be touched by them. "Apparently," wrote Rudi Dutschke, "Mother taught me as the youngest not to let myself be carried by the prisoners who came to work the soil every week in the gardens of our neighborhood, to have no close contact with them"—which is why he hit his father in the face, when the strange, unshaven man in uniform, on leave from the front, wanted to carry him on his arm. (This was one of the few childhood memories that Rudi Dutschke later spoke of. It is a "screen memory": the father, too, was a visitor, a ghost from the lowest regions of the dead.)

But of those who were half-dead or merely potentially alive, it was my father whom my family loved most and missed most painfully. Only rarely did a letter arrive from the prisoner of war camp, and for the duration of the war, his future was as uncertain as it had been in the months when it was assumed that his ship had been sunk on its way to Canada by his own country's submarines. In a 1943 Christmas picture, my grandmother and two aunts, the younger perhaps seven or eight, the older already a young lady, are gathered around the framed drawing of a young man (who, as Thomas Mann wrote of Joachim Ziemssen in *The Magic Mountain*, "would have been downright handsome, if his ears hadn't protruded so"). The purposeful and solemnly ruminating expression in the faces of the three women almost attains what the Nazi death announcements for fallen soldiers described as "proud mourning." And so they appeared and disappeared—Church Superintendent Wackwitz's POW son (who remained seventeen years old for the entire war), the fathers on leave from the front, the foreign workers, the maids from Minsk, Leningrad, and Lublin, the Jews, those marked for selection, leaving no trace, disappearing, as is said of ghosts, quick as a flash, and inexplicably:

Finally we arranged to have Russian girls sent to us. They worked hard. The first, named Marja, was a strong, strapping thing with a full head of black, curly hair and strange eyes. When a military doctor who happened to be at our house saw her passing through the room, he asked whether she was causing us problems—he thought she suffered from serious hysteria. And, in fact, there was something about her that wasn't quite right: she sometimes had attacks of defiance and anger, and when I once had some kind of to-do with her in the laundry room (I can't remember why), she became so enraged and out of control that I slapped her. Facing the wall, she cried loudly, sobbing ceaselessly for her mother. Then I was sorry and wished I hadn't hit her.

But of the inhabitants of death's kingdom who were brought into proximity with the Germans, the untouchable slaves of house and garden were the closest to life. Further removed into the land of the dead—though somehow still alive—were the men and women wearing striped overalls, wooden shoes, and the humiliating, clownish caps. Although the authorities hardly tried to hide them, after the war everyone claimed never to have seen them. And perhaps that is not simply an excuse. Just as these death-actors (or "figures," as their murderers called them) were there and, at the same time, no longer existed (for they were, according to the logic of the situation, as good as dead), they would have been both seen and not seen as they trudged along the country roads or, with movements slowed down by hunger, wandered like ghosts on public construction sites.

In the machine shops, there were lathes, a lot of electric motors, moving conveyor belts, laborers working at the machines, supervisors going back and forth. The workers wore the striped clothing of concentration camp prisoners. They didn't look badly nourished, their faces showed neither anger nor despair, and they seemed completely absorbed by their work. Their foremen were the so-called Kapos from the concentration camps. In answer to my question, the chief engineer assured me that the laborers had regular hours, weren't overworked, received cigarettes and occasional treats, that they worked willingly and were easy to get along with. Nonetheless, I wasn't really comfortable with the whole thing. Later, Dr. W. told me that in concentration camp M., along with the Jews, there were mostly political and homosexual prisoners, among the latter Dr. P., who until 1933 was a famous sprinter, a kind of German Nurmi. Once, I was on a train passing M. and saw a column of Jews working on the tracks. I have to say, they looked very wretched and starved, and I was deeply shocked and depressed.

I discovered firsthand how easily and willingly people allow themselves (and want) to be duped when making supposedly spontaneous inspections of sinister places that are as carefully prepared as Potemkin villages. Shaking my head in disbelief, I read the diary that I wrote when touring the GDR in 1974 as a member of a "delegation" of the MSB Spartakus. I remembered how, on my first evening in this socialist Germany (which, in a certain sense, consisted only of Potemkin villages), in the bed of some union holiday lodge not far from Luckenwalde, I lay in futile panic and brooded about how I could decently extricate myself from this student group that I had joined only shortly before, thoughtlessly but also as a provocation, and as an experiment. Accomplishing this was to take me several years.

I was, perhaps, never closer to my grandfather than in 1974 in that union lodge in Communist-ruled Brandenburg and, indeed, during the very years in which I wanted to put the greatest possible distance between myself and him and his views. It was the time of my flirtation with the other totalitarianism, which (to my own detriment) I embraced as an act of provocation. Of all of us I am, perhaps, the least justified in accusing my grandfather of blindness, for I know all too well how a person can accidentally peer behind the facades so skillfully constructed by National Socialism and then German socialism (a skill neither ever devoted to the real business of governing), see reality, and then try in vain to forget it for weeks afterwards, reacting with *shock and depression.*

On the other hand, Andreas Wackwitz was faced with (and closed his eyes to) more than the suffering and gloom of an oppressed people who may have been fettered and robbed of their autonomy but were otherwise more or less taken care of and left in peace, at least as long as they played along. (Similarly, in the early seventies, the innumerable "democratic forces" in the Federal Republic—who remember none of it now—closed their eyes in turn.) In Luckenwalde in the 1940s, he also chose to look away from neighbors who disappeared without a trace and without explanation, to look away from the open enslavement of foreigners in Luckenwalde's homes. And he chose to look away from mass murder, though people knew all too well what was happening, what with the rumors and reports passed on under a seal of silence.

No passage in my grandfather's memoirs is more alarming than the good-humored, memory-gilded descriptions of two trips with his children from Luckenwalde to the village of Anhalt, near Auschwitz (Anhalt was long since German again), and from there further south to hike in the Tatras, whose stations, mountain huts, and train connections I, sitting at my desk in the year 2001, can look up and trace in the pages of *Baedekers Generalgouvernement* (second edition, 1943). When I found this handy travel guide with its golden letters deeply embossed into the faded, blood-red, grainy cardboard cover for a few zloty several years ago in an antiquarian bookshop in Kraków, I could hardly believe my eyes.

What is creepiest about it is perhaps not even that a book like this was written and published, but that the details of *Baedekers Generalgouvernement* are so reliable that even now, in all seriousness and suppressing a mounting horror, I sometimes take the pocket-size volume into which all the strangeness and false innocence of the 1940s have, as it were, been concentrated, and look up a location—a mountain route or a church—before one of my trips or excursions, or after I'm back home. Especially hair-raising is the observation "now *judenfrei*" that appears on the same yellowing, beautifully printed pages as the high-quality information in the section on Kraków's medieval Jewish quarter of Kazimierz, or the preface on the climatic, geographic, and historic conditions of a country where the Germans were then in the process of killing one of every five citizens. ("This new volume in our collection was published at the suggestion of Herr Generalgouverneur Reichsminister Dr. Hans Frank. It was with pleasure that the editor welcomed the opportunity to publish a handbook that conveys the scale of the achievement, the progress and the order that the German Reich has brought to the Vistula region in 3½ years under difficult wartime conditions.")

In conversations with my successor, Pastor Gustav Uibel, I discovered for the first time that only twenty kilometers away, in Oświęcim (now called Auschwitz again) there was a large concentration camp, and that many Jews were interned, died, and were cremated there. When one asked about the fate of a Jew whom one had known from before, one was told, "He went up through the smokestacks at Auschwitz." If, badly shocked, one asked further and demanded an explanation, the reply was a shrug of the shoulders and vague allusions, and I assumed that he was trying to say that there were many deaths due to bad care and mistreatment and that the dead were cremated. Even that seemed bad enough, and I didn't want to believe it. The so-called final solution of the Jewish question, i.e., the killing of thousands in gas chambers and the cremation of the bodies in special ovens had, in 1940, not yet begun, not even in Auschwitz. On one of our trips to the Beskids, we once drove by a section of one of the camps. What one saw from the train looked no different than military barracks, except they were surrounded by a high wire fence.

Still today, a traveler can see the watchtower-like main gate with the railway entrance, the barracks, and the fences of Auschwitz-Birkenau from the Kraków-Vienna Eurocity train. The experiences that Andreas Wackwitz, and in all likelihood his children (however unconsciously), brought along with them on their excursions to the high Tatra—the remarks about the Jews going up through the smokestacks, the sight of the concentration camp (which, defying credulity, he remembers as strangely depopulated)—will befoul their loveliest childhood memories in the remote corner of their soul to this day, like that little piece of shit on the edge of the plate with which Sebastian Haffner so fittingly compared the subliminal but ever-present knowledge about the kind of country they really lived in.

The three children wrote sweet accounts of these trips for Mother, which I have now re-read with great pleasure and emotion. Elisabeth made drawings for hers, and Beate did what she could, gluing in photos and pictures. The awakened memories of these hikes move me greatly. Not only because the magnificent landscape of the Beskids and the Tatra opens up before me once again, but especially because these reports enable one to recognize how much the children enjoyed

nature and being together with me. Again and again, they write—
Dad said—Dad explained—, and everything we did is told as a se-
ries of paternal intentions, actions, decisions. And yet there is room
for criticism and resistance, e.g., when it's time to get up in the morn-
ing, refusing to take naps, having to eat large plates of porridge
boiled only in water, etc. But all in the best of spirits and trying to
see the silver lining on the dark paternal cloud.

It's as if my son and I had passed concentration camps on
our way to our summer biking and camping trips. And even
in the Arcadian high mountain landscape of the Tatra,
death—spread by the Germans over all Europe and with a
particularly intense degree of evil in the region of my father's
childhood and dreams—left its mark and said: I too am here.

It was a pretty, very simple room with two beds. The man and the
oldest daughter had been sent off to Silesia as forced laborers. The
woman, who had five young children, managed the small inn. There
was a notice affixed to the outside of the house saying that it had
been expropriated and belonged to some German agency. The woman
told us that she had to pay rent and could be deported to the east-
ern part of Poland at any moment. Here, for the first time, the bru-
tality with which the Nazi state acted toward conquered peoples con-
fronted me. Initially I thought that I hadn't understood the woman
correctly, but there was no doubt about the truth of what she said.
All of these little mountain farms were confiscated without compen-
sation. It was naked theft and a crime against humanity, just as the
Poles were to carry out to a much larger extent after 1945, when
they expelled many millions of Germans. The woman and the other
Poles with whom I spoke took it fatalistically. As I could speak Pol-
ish, I gained insights that I would not have had otherwise. In Bielitz,
I saw that the Poles all had to stand aside for Germans at service

counters, etc., and when we were cooking a meal in the village of
Sol in the following year, we met a German peasant who had been
resettled from eastern Poland and received seven small Polish farms
in exchange for his one. The wooden houses stood empty, the own-
ers had been dispossessed and relocated to eastern Poland. The new
German owner answered our question about what he intended to
do with the empty houses with a shrug of his shoulders—eventu-
ally he'd probably burn them down. He didn't seem all that pleased
with his new property. Such observations shocked me a great deal,
and the longer the war dragged on and the less certain the outcome
seemed, the greater grew my secret fear of the vengeance that would
one day be visited upon us by those who had been treated so un-
justly.—But to return to our Skrzyczne hike in 1940. The girls swam,
although the water in the Szczyrk swimming pool was still quite
cold. In the evening we ate scrambled eggs. Rosalie had gotten the
eggs. The girls slept in one of the beds, and the next morning Beate
claimed that she had found a dead flea. I assured her that dead fleas
don't bite, but she wanted to hold onto the thrill of the horror and
chose not to believe me.

My Aunt Beate, whose seventy-fifth birthday we celebrated
in November 2001, was fourteen when she found a real flea
or one that she dreamed of (in the bed, maybe, of *the oldest
daughter who had been sent off to Silesia to work for the Germans*).
But it wasn't the living or dead fleas in that night lodging
that *horrified* her. Maybe the source of her nocturnal horror
was something other than the squeamishness of a young
lady. Maybe we should think of the flea of Szczyrk as belonging to the same genus as the cobra of Waterberg—it is,
of course, much smaller and to be taken lightly—or the weird
animals that appeared in the Lobnitz "Jews Meadows" between Auschwitz and Anhalt during the nights of Advent.

In any case, the twilight so familiar from home also charac-terized the Tatra mountains—people were present and then suddenly gone, and one couldn't tell whether those who were manifestly present were alive or dead, like the flea in Beate's bed in Szczyrk. And the challenge—whether in Luck-enwalde or in the Tatra—of transporting the living dead to the beyond, where in the view of the state authorities they should have gone long ago and, indeed, were already, must have been understood in both places as a technical problem, or one of hygiene (so to speak) or pest control.

It must have been some time prior to this that members of the con-gregation twice showed me written notification from clinics to which mentally ill relatives had been moved shortly before, from their pre-vious asylums. The clinic administration wrote that the patient had died suddenly of a contagious illness and that for hygienic reasons (Ordinance number such and such) the body had been immediately cremated. The urn would be sent upon request. This concerned the notorious killing of "lives not worth living," which claimed many of the mentally ill as victims. Medical commissions came to the clin-ics and selected those who were "unfit." Some Christian clinics were successful in preventing their removal. For example, one heard af-ter the war that, at Bethel, Bodelschwingh was able to save all his patients. It was because they were afraid of the worldwide scandal that an action against Bodelschwingh and Bethel would have caused. When I read the above-mentioned notifications, I had already known from official sources in the Church—in strictest confidence!—that such killings had been undertaken. It was a state secret, men at the highest levels of the church were demanding incessantly that these measures be stopped, and there was reason to hope they would suc-ceed. For a time, it was also rumored that Hitler had ordered that the killings cease, but I don't know whether there was any truth to this. Some families, perhaps, were not so distressed by the death of an incurably mentally ill relative, but others, who suspected or knew what had happened, were horrified. But they didn't know what to do, and they were afraid. In both cases that were presented to me by congregants, I tried to calm and console them as best I could.

"The condition under which the feeling of uncanniness arises here," wrote Sigmund Freud in 1917 (when my grandfather and Adolf Hitler, though unknown to one other, had taken turns at their post in the muddy trenches of the grenade-churned Flemish front), "is unmistakable. We—or our primitive forefathers—once believed in the possibility of these things and were convinced that they really happened. Nowadays we no longer believe in them, we have *surmounted* such ways of thought; but we do not feel quite sure of our new set of beliefs, and the old ones still exist within us ready to seize upon any confirmation. As soon as something actually happens in our lives which seems to support the old, discarded beliefs we get a feeling of the uncanny; and it is as though we were making a judgment something like this: 'So, after all, it is true that one can kill a person by merely desiring his death!' or, 'The dead do continue to live and appear before our eyes on the scene of their former activities!', and so on." ("The Uncanny," in *On Creativity and the Unconscious*.) *Some families, perhaps, were not so distressed by the death of an incurably mentally ill relative, but others, who suspected or knew what had happened, were horrified.* My grandfather keeps his distance, maintains the trust in authority that he had relied upon his entire life, tries *to calm and console them as best I could.*

Having read my grandfather's memoirs and looked at photographs from that time, I know today how powerful, strange, and wonderful it must have been to experience the dreams of German glory and world empire, the dreams of an Anhalt restored to Germany (the bells ring over the Saar and Southwest)—the fulfilling of the dreams of a Laskowitz castle park extending over the whole of Europe. But what also came true were other wishes, secret and evil, that people sometimes entertained before falling asleep, in the shower, or when vacuuming the house: that the sick neighbor would finally croak, and the rich Jew next door, too, so that we can get his apartment. The town was inhabited by ghosts. And the authorities of this deeply strange and oppressive country told people what to do and to be silent about what they had hardly even dared to think or wish. But reading those thin pages, I also discovered that the murderers themselves knew what they were really doing, and they couldn't forget it.

In the summer of 1943—or was it in 1944?—a police officer from Luckenwalde came to my office and asked to see me privately. He was a man of over 50, short and very strong. He said that he was now on vacation from his tour of duty in the East with the so-called Security Service, a unit of Nazi police, and that he had experienced terrible things that would not leave his conscience in peace. He had to participate in mass shootings of Jews. Women were among the victims. He told me details. I had heard hints of this, but I had asked no questions: there was so much daily business to attend to, and what could I have done! And now it was before me in all its ugliness. The man asked me: "What should I do?" For a moment I was afraid that he might be an agent provocateur. But the man's distress seemed genuine, and I believed him. I advised him to refuse or to call in sick, but he thought he couldn't risk it, that it would endanger his life. I advised him to shoot between the people or above their heads. He thought that might be possible, he had even tried it, but his very participation in such executions would not leave him in peace. He had a wife and children, and during his vacation he wanted to be with his family and to rest, but even here there were nights when he couldn't sleep. Then I spoke to him of sin and mercy and of God's forgiveness, and it seemed to me as if that might give him some enduring consolation and maybe ease his conscience. He left in a burdened frame of mind, and I don't know what became of him.—Now I knew, too, but I felt that I shouldn't speak to anyone about it since the discussion had been a kind of confession. And whom would such information have helped? Very probably I would have put not only him but also myself in serious danger.

Thirty-four years went by. In 1977, I was twenty-five, as naive and malleable as only a boy from the educated German middle class can be at that age, having seen and experienced nothing more than classrooms and lecture halls his entire life. And in the lectures, conversations, thoughts, articles, films, and books of those whom we took as our models—a sizeable and influential minority of professors, journalists, and teachers, both our age and older—there lived the conviction that at this time in our history we were not citizens of a democracy, even a very imperfect one. Murders, about which no one had wasted a word when they were being committed, now cried out, belatedly and with wondrous voices. The elections—whether general, secret, or free; the newspapers—however critical their reporting; the police—who restrained themselves even at the height of the angriest and most oppositional demonstrations: it was, so went the whispering in our heads, all for show. The veil would be torn off soon enough, and the horror would come to light. What mattered now was to provoke the system to reveal itself for what it was, while we were together and could defend ourselves collectively. Woe to those whom they would later catch alone. Woe to those whom the darkness had already swallowed. In the real world that lay behind the appearance, somewhere in the inner heart of reality (the horror), the murder and torture, the transformation of human beings into bodies, continued—not only in South America but also behind the doors of German prisons, police stations, and university hospitals.

"Torture in the Federal Republic of German: On the Situation of Political Prisoners" was the title of the journal *Kursbuch*, no. 32. The bizarre title referred to supposedly unjust imprisonment conditions for members of the Baader-Meinhof gang, a left-wing guerrilla organization that for months had terrorized the country in the early 1970s. According to the propaganda of their numerous radical chic sympathizers, these people were victims of sinister (and, as it later turned out, complete fictitious) experiments of "sensory deprivation." The mask was torn from the secretive and terrible "Special Research Division" of the Psychiatric Clinic of the University of Hamburg-Eppendorf, behind which—this is what Margrit Schiller wrote and believed as late as 1999— "research in re: conditions in our prisons" was being conducted. "After about 6 to 8 minutes people became so terrified that the organism's entire hormonal system was upset. After 10 to 15 minutes the experiment had to be terminated, because the blood began to dissolve." They, the men behind the scenes, the real rulers of our country, dissolved the blood of their enemies. They tortured a woman who had fallen into their hands: in her secret message that was smuggled out of prison, Ulrike Meinhof writes of the "feeling that my head is exploding (the feeling that the top of my skull would tear or burst off)—the feeling that the marrow was being squeezed from my spine into my brain . . . , the feeling that I was standing constantly under an imperceptible current, I was being steered remotely, the feeling that I was pissing the soul out of my body, like when one can't hold it in—the feeling that my prison cell is moving . . . Raging aggressiveness for which there is no release. That's the worst. A clear awareness that I cannot survive, and the complete inability to communicate that."

Once I saw the Sibyl of Cumae with my own eyes. She was hanging in a cage, and when the boys asked her, "What do you want, Sibyl?" she answered, "I want to die."   —Petronius

16 Minor Prophets

At that point, Ulrike Meinhof probably had been mentally ill for quite some time. But for a while, we believed that in Pythia's stammerings we were hearing the voice of the dead: the writing on the wall, the ghost of Hamlet's father, the whimpering of living skeletons, Marja's sobbing, her face to the wall: "The political concept for Cologne's death-wing is—I'll say it straight out—gas. The Auschwitz fantasies I had in there were . . . realistic." And Gudrun Ensslin wrote, "Difference beween death-wing and isolation: Auschwitz to Buchenwald. The difference is simple: more survived Buchenwald than Auschwitz . . . We who are inside, to say it straight out, can only be surprised that we were not sent to the showers. Otherwise nothing can surprise us . . ."

Before Holger Meins starved himself to death in Stammheim Prison, he managed to get a note smuggled to Jan-Carl Raspe (as well as to the German public). Raspe, who had also embarked on a death-fast, had briefly become careless. Meins wrote, "*If* you *know* that with every PIG VICTORY they are more likely to actually murder—and then you decide to give up and save yourself, you *thereby* give the PIGS a *victory*, meaning you hand us over, then you are the pig . . . so . . . better just be honest (if you still know what that is: honor): 'I'm alive, down with the RAF, victory to the pig system . . .' —either human or pig/either survive at any cost or/fight unto death/either problem or solution/there's no middle ground . . . still, everyone dies. The only question is how you lived: FIGHTING THE PIGS as a MAN FOR THE LIBERATION OF MEN: as a revolutionary, fighting—as much as you love life: disdaining death, this for me: serving the people—raf."

I don't know how long I brooded over these terrible pronouncements. In the spring of 2001, I was with my son, taking the train to Berlin to get my grandfather's papers from my aunt's attic. Something dreadful and archaic, as if coming from a great distance, emerged from between the lines of these peculiar formulations, so unmistakably cobbled together from bits of German sociologese, street slang, and Luther's Bible. I read them again and again, murmuring certain phrases to myself (my son looked up, disconcerted, from his Mickey Mouse comic), putting the book down and staring out the window. Its considerable power—still palpable today—derives from an old and honorable rhetorical style, with its rolling cadences and insistent pulse, its pauses and eruptions that reach for and then finally find the tradition of *inspired speech*.

No longer does Holger Meins speak as a politician-turned-criminal. Starving and on the threshold of a coma, he speaks as a prophet, not because he claims to see the future (where prophets have never seen anything more substantial and interesting than the richly deserved downfall of the mighty), but because he claims to show the real world—the awful, guilty world behind the veil of deceit—to the *Volk* and its the evil rulers (in my erstwhile fantasy, the government of Germany). It was not only Jan-Carl Raspe whom Hoger Meins wanted to confront for desiring to live and for lacking the resolve to starve himself. He wanted to show all of us the sin of our participation in swinish, whorish Babylon, a system that would soon meets its awful, deserved end thanks to RAF-delivered death, whether by bombing or starvation.

Having long played a pernicious and slightly ridiculous role on the German Left, this particular tradition of inflammatory rhetoric derives from Fichte and fortifies a prophetic style with intensely arrogant demands on the audience's time, compliance, and sense of guilt. In all likelihood, Holger Meins, half-dead, was already hallucinating when he wrote this letter. Deep in his conversation with the ghosts of a Nazi resurrection that materialized before his crazy eyes, he is not speaking so much as intoning, like a medium in a trance, or Isaiah in the Old Testament. The shamanistic sing-song, the call to political murder evokes from our common past and literary memory not only Fichte's *Addresses to the German Nation*, Hamlet's soliloquies, and the Old Testament, but also the poetry of those torn pamphlets of the *Storm and Stress* with their dashes, ellipses, and exclamation marks that inspired Schleiermacher's father to move from Breslau into the wilderness north of the Duchy of Auschwitz. Speaking from the pulpit of his open coffin, Holger Meins breaks his sentences into poetic lines and, employing a style familiar at the time from the writings of Heiner Müller and Volker Braun, bursts into capital letters at the climaxes of prophetic excitement.

The man was half starved. He knew that he had done terrible things and therefore had to slander his opponents and victims as Nazis and pigs. And he was still politician enough to avail himself of that hellish machinery of guilt and hectoring demagoguery that had gotten him, his fellow-combatants, and his sympathizers into this terrible mess in the first place. Writing down his insane utterances and splicing them into my text, I am forced to confront the fact that Holger Meins's visions, his prophetic chanting, and his Hamletlike obsession with the ghosts of murdered Jewish father figures are a belated response to my grandfather's having lived in a country that was, indeed, teeming with ghosts.

Rudi Dutschke, who was four years old when the Luckenwalde policeman came to my grandfather, turned up thirty-four years later at the Dornhalden Cemetery in my hometown, Stuttgart, at the open grave of the dead prophet Holger Meins, with raised fist and a call to continue the struggle. (Standing behind him on the TV news clip: Otto Schily, now German Minister of the Interior.) Is it a coincidence that Dutschke baptized his son with the name of the prophet Hosea, one of the "minor prophets" of the Old Testament (Jeremiah, Isaiah, and Ezekiel being the "major" ones)? Rudi gave his son the name of a man who reminded his people that (wrote Max Weber) "before Israel set a king over itself, the god of the covenant had been the sole and direct ruler, who had had no need of such office-, tax- and forced-labor machinery comparable to that of the contemporary kings. He had revealed his will and intentions to seers and heroes of the past, and if the people abided by his commandments he had always helped them." (*Ancient Judaism,* trans. Hans H. Gert and Don Martindale.) Is it a coincidence that a famous film of Alain Tanner and John Berger is called *Jonah Who Will Be 25 in the Year 2000*? (For a time after the spring of 1977, I saw it more than any other.) Is it a coincidence that my son, with whom I traveled to Berlin in the spring of 2001 to get my grandfather's diaries, also bears the name of one of the "lesser" Old Testament prophets?

I don't know. One rarely does, about this kind of thing. It must have been in February or March 1978, a half-year after the "German autumn" and at the height of the hallucinatory prophesying about the true face of the German state. The Section ARG (American & English Literature/Literature of the Romance Languages/German Literature) of the MSB Spartakus met every Tuesday night at a commune in central Stuttgart. I remember the nineteenth-century, oil-colored, brown-gray apartment house as a rundown building on a very noisy access road. From the tram, I saw an ambulance parked on the sidewalk in front of the entrance, its blue light rotating silently. Young men in white came toward me in the otherwise empty stairwell, carrying the lifeless, cloth-covered, naked body of one of our comrades strapped to an aluminum stretcher.

For just a moment, I saw her wet, pitch-black hair and then her face, very fat and soft, as if she'd been in water for a long time. Indeed, when I reached the top of the stairs and walked through the open door, I learned that she had lost consciousness while in the bathtub, perhaps because of gasses that had leaked from the old boiler. Her head had slipped under the surface of the water and she had drowned. Carrying a submachine gun on a black shoulder-strap, a uniformed policeman stood on the landing and guarded the entrance. Holding onto one another by the hand, the girl's boyfriend and her former lover sat in our meeting room on a folding sleeping sofa that was covered in brown, wide-wale corduroy. The face of her former boyfriend was distorted, mask-like; he looked as if he wanted to cry but couldn't. I was one of the last to arrive. Several of us stood, others sat on the old chairs in a circle as if a meeting had already begun, smoking, staring blankly. Someone was talking to the two plainclothes policemen, who were standing there, alert, cold, and matter-of-fact, observing us, stopping any incipient conversation, and taking in the Marxist-Leninist library and the party posters on the wall. My girlfriend stood at the window and looked out at the yellow lights of the expressway. Standing behind her, I tried to put my arms around her; she turned around without looking at me and pushed me away.

The police were silent. We waited an hour. They seemed to want to be sure that no one else was coming. At nine o'clock, we were driven in two green police vans, one policeman in each, to the stationhouse in Dorotheenstrasse— a building in which the local Gestapo was headquartered from 1933 to 1945. Video cameras looked down from over the heavy metal door with the buzzer. We were taken for questioning into separate rooms outfitted with potted plants, typewriters, filing cabinets, high ceiling-lights, and wall calendars. In the five or six hours that followed, the trembling that had seized me in the police van became stronger: my body wouldn't stop shaking, my teeth chattered so uncontrollably that I couldn't speak for minutes at a time, and for a while the interrogation became difficult. The officer questioning me, an older man, permitted me an occasional cigarette and a glass of water. He asked only that I recount again and again the events of the previous day and the details of my returning to the commune, and he asked me about these repeatedly. He didn't ask even once about the political content of our weekly discussions. All he wanted to know was whether this girl had been killed.

Toward midnight, my trembling abated. If I'm remembering correctly, we were driven home in the two police vans at about three in the morning. The funeral took place two days later. I never again heard from the Stuttgart criminal police. Spring arrived. My doubts grew about what we were once again discussing every week in that apartment in the rundown house near the expressway, though I spoke of them to no one.

Early that summer, my grandmother died. My girlfriend and I passed through Lörrach as we were driving to France for our holiday. Although I did not know it then, this was the last time I would see my grandfather. In Paris, I experienced something strange. At noon, we had taken the elevator to the upper floors of the Samaritaine department store, where we ate steak, bread, and salad, and shared half a liter of red wine. Through somewhat greasy windowpanes, we looked out toward the river and the Pont Henri IV. I told my girlfriend about Hemingway, who had fished in the small park to the right of the statue in the 1920s. I felt like looking for fellow travelers. For a few moments, there was an invisible storm over the city.

That same afternoon, we stepped from the Jeu de Paume out onto one of the terraces that look over the Place de la Concorde, the Grand Palais, and the woods of the Champs-Elysées. Large clouds almost gave the sky the appearance of evening. I had seen the paintings in the museum behind me often before, but on this visit they changed. They radiated a generosity and an indifference toward everything political and moral that I had never noticed before. They depicted lovely, gentle women, dancing and lost in themselves or, dressed in new clothes, looking at the painter. Entirely free of the slightest trace of suspicion or criticism, they were beautiful. This, according to the rules that were in force at the time, should have made them the perfect picture of hell.

But on this late afternoon, I noticed that they did not look one bit hellish. My girlfriend sat next to me. The trees blew about in the first gusts of wind that sometimes precede rain. Suddenly, I was very far away. Reality was a deep chair in a high-ceilinged lobby in a large, unknown city, maybe in America. I sat in this chair and smoked. For the duration of a cigarette in the foyer of the Hotel Reality, reality existed once again. A week or two earlier, I had dreamt about a small girl who somehow belonged to me, maybe a younger sister, a childhood friend, or a girlfriend. The point of the dream was that this small girl was more carefree and richer than I. Although she belonged to me, she had, mysteriously, a completely different history. In the dream, this girl talked me out of making an overly ingenious philosophical-political interpretation. She predicted a future for me without the MSB Spartakus. She dismissed a moral-intellectual problem with good-natured and carefree laughter. Sitting on the edge of the rain-cloud darkened Place de la Concorde, I remembered this dream. At the same time, I was overcome with the feeling of happiness that such dreams sometimes leave behind and that returns when they're remembered. We remained on the balustrade of the terrace in front of the museum until it began to get dark on the square, as if over a flat, broad valley.

Leviné correctly said that we Communists are the dead on holiday, but also people of life and love.   —Rudi Dutschke

17 The Dead

It was easy to get the e-mail address of Rudi Dutschke's widow, and soon we were sending messages back and forth. I also called his nephew, who works in the Luckenwalde town administration. (When I mistook him for Rudi's brother, we could only laugh.) Finally, on an October afternoon in 2001, I did indeed call the oldest of the four brothers, Manfred Dutschke. He is a friendly, helpful, elderly gentleman who, though retired, holds a seat in both the district and town legislatures (as a Christian Democrat, if I understood him correctly) and who talked at length and with enthusiasm about his famous brother, the churches of Luckenwalde, my grandfather, and the 1940s.

Strangest of all, as I sat at my desk on this sunny autumn day, were the voices, beginning with Gretchen Dutschke's good-natured, girlishly spontaneous, somewhat naive-sounding sentences with the typical American mistakes in syntax and diction. Then the bright, youthful, strongly Berlin-accented voice of Dutschke's nephew over the telephone. And finally the measured, intelligent, civilized but down-to-earth manner of his brother, audibly shaped by his long-standing involvement in civic and church affairs. Nothing in their speech reminded me of the voice and manner of the Protestant West German prophet and revolutionary who had shaped the lives of this family, bequeathing them a legacy of love, admiration, doubt, sadness, pride, and sometimes shame.

Rudi Dutschke's voice, of which there are surprisingly few recordings, evokes not the late 1960s, but rather the 1920s. The oddly elongated vowels and the rolling *r* sound, like the pronunciation of a foreigner from the years before and after the war who learned German late but very well. When, after a long time, I heard it again six months ago, it reminded me of a Romanian-Jewish professor who had spent almost his entire life in New York. It is the voice of exile, a voice that has absorbed the coloration of dissidence without the speaker even being aware of it. Dutschke's voice sounds as if it had been recorded at a séance, as if he were speaking the language of the dead.

The strangely uncontrolled intrusion of undigested theories from the twenties as well as Dutschke's simple and almost childish syntax contribute to the impression that he is using a language not his own, as though it had been assigned to him by someone else, or as if he were a ventriloquist's dummy, or possessed. It is as if this man—at the time he was actually still very young—understood himself in a corporeal sense as a *medium* of forgotten theories, whose creators and original spokesmen were murdered in concentration camps or survived in exile during the years when he was a child in Luckenwalde. He is their heir. He is a messenger, maybe an angel. He is not of this earth. Rudi Dutschke's voice betrays something about the political *family romance* that was to give shape not only to his scanty and scattered written oeuvre (which, when looked at more closely and less piously, is not all that impressive) but above all to his charismatic life and political prophesying.

"A younger child," writes Sigmund Freud in his famous essay on the *family romance* of neurotics, "is very specially inclined to use imaginative stories such as these in order to rob those born before him of their prerogatives—in a way which reminds one of historical intrigues; and he often has no hesitation in attributing to his mother as many fictitious love-affairs as he himself has competitors. An interesting variant of the family romance may then appear, in which the hero and author returns to legitimacy himself while his brothers and sisters are eliminated by being bastardized." (In *The Freud Reader*, ed. Peter Gay.) In her memoirs, Rudi Dutschke's wife alludes in passing to a strange circumstance that her husband seems to have exploited early on and then for the rest of his life in order to develop the theme of this *family romance* in his own biography (a romance in which my entire generation played along for a while). "Like many others who were not entirely successful in repressing what they didn't want to confront," she writes, "Rudi had difficulties with his identity as a German. Sometimes he was resigned, and thought he'd have to give up thinking about the Nazi years. The sense of shame was indescribably deep. In order to distance himself from it, he imagined that he was a Jew whom the Dutschkes had hidden in their house. He based this fantasy on the fact that he was circumcised."

It is difficult to find a reasonable explanation for the information that Gretchen Dutschke conveys here. The most likely is that Rudi Dutschke was circumcised when he was a small child, or perhaps even an infant, to correct a phimosa (without much medical justification). Talking on the phone to Manfred Dutschke, I twice came close to asking him about his brother's circumcision, but I couldn't summon the nerve. In any case, the fate of Rudi Dutschke's foreskin at the time that he and my grandfather came to Luckenwalde from their different directions is not all that important. (And yet this autumn, I have read and thought a great deal about the fact that there was extended scholastic speculation about Jesus Christ's foreskin as the only part of the Savior's body that remained on earth after his Ascension, still on our planet, buried somewhere.)

What is certain is that Rudi Dutschke was as influenced by fantasies of sacrifice and redemption as by the fantasy that he had to embody and resurrect murdered Jewish thought and speech—not only academically and intellectually, but quite directly in his very self and in the reality of the German Federal Republic of the 1960s. As with many charismatic people, unconscious fantasies seem to have lodged just beneath the threshold of consciousness and thought for all of Rudi Dutschke's life, governing all that he said and did. That is the secret of his voice. And not only his American wife but also some survivors of the Jewish political and philosophical tradition that had been choked off and silenced at the time of Rudi's birth and Luckenwalde childhood seem to have shared and strengthened these fantasies. He sought their closeness—a very personal closeness—for his entire life. (The goal of Gretchen and Rudi Dutschke's honeymoon, for example, was a visit with Georg Lukács in Budapest.) "Rudi meant as much to the Blochs during this time as they did to him. For them he personified the principle of hope and also a fragment of a culture that had been destroyed in Europe long before, namely the subculture of the Jewish left. It was astonishing. Rudi had no exposure whatsoever to Judaism during his childhood in conservative, rural Germany, and until he was over twenty, he had never even met a Jew. His intensity, intellectual curiosity and openness seem to have come out of nowhere. Carola Bloch pondered the riddle of this exceptional man: 'I, who am not religious, find a similar riddle in Christ. He, the Son of Man, so humiliated, has always been loved by all kinds of different people. I, too, love him. He's my lodestar. But how is it possible that so many people in this corrupt world love and worship Christ? This is actually a consolation, a sign that the good is present in people, that they respond to the good. Ernst's optimism has its source in this belief in the good. And you, too, Rudi, have been thus graced.'"

It is a complicated, dreamlike, even contradictory fantasy of redemption whose contours become visible in these letters, journeys, friendships, suppositions, and facts: a secret Jewish principality in Luckenwalde; martyrdom and death; and above all, the ubiquitous feeling that with Rudi's peculiarly childish and moving life and death the Nazi experience was annulled. Once again, it was possible to sit at the wellspring of the 1920s.

The two memories that I have of Ernst Bloch (except for the largely aphoristic *Traces,* his books never left a strong impression on me) sometimes feel as if I have, in fact, imagined them—as do many of my other memories of the late 1960s and early 1970s. Then, too, we lived in a different country, one that is now invisible. And one evening in that country, in the lobby (narrow as a living room) of a basement theater in Tübingen, I stood next to or squeezed past Ernst Bloch on my way to the box office (to get tickets for Peter Weiss's play on the persecution and murder of Jean-

Paul Marat). I was seventeen, and happening to stand next to Bloch or squeeze past him, I recognized him. In retrospect, it seems to me that even then (probably 1969) he reminded me of three sentences from Hermann Hesse's novel *The Prodigy*, in which Hesse describes the famous Protestant boarding school he had attended (as had Hölderlin, Schelling, and Hegel) and where, as chance would have it, I was boarding at the time of this coincidental and anonymous meeting. Since then, whenever I hear of Ernst Bloch, I think of this passage, as if by reflex:

> That strange and ancient language of Jehovah, harsh yet mysteriously alive, loomed up difficult and baffling before the eyes of these students, striking in its amazing ramifications, delighting by its remarkably coloured and fragrant blossoms. Thousand-year old spirits peopled its branches, some fear-inspiring, some friendly, fantastically terrifying dragons, naïve and attractive legends, wrinkled, grave, desiccated gray-beards alongside handsome boys and quiet-eyed girls or war-like women. Words that had sounded distant and dreamy in the Lutheran Bible now became a thing of flesh and blood in the powerful original and took on a ponderously archaic but tough and sinister reality. (Trans. W. J. Strachan.)

I, too, was learning Hebrew at the time. (This was part of my training for employment by the Protestant Church of the State of Württemberg, an opportunity I was to decline shortly afterwards.) But the significance of the wrinkled, earnest old man's face that was among the "handsome boys and quiet-eyed girls or war-like women" in the lobby of the Tübingen basement theater on that evening in 1969 was different from that of the Hebrew language for Hesse's young hero; the life that sprouted from the gnarled old philosophy professor in 1969 was also antiquated and awkward, but differently, and it was tough and wondrous.

"That was Lenin, not Bukharin." I heard this sentence from Ernst Bloch's mouth as I was standing next to him or squeezing past him. He was speaking to a small group of university students or teaching assistants who were probably still basically kids themselves, though to a seventeen-year-old they seemed unreachably adult. "That was Lenin, not Bukharin." A tree that was brittle and dried-up and yet still secretly alive and exotic grew mysteriously before the eyes of the youths, its wondrous branching conspicuous and the blossoms surprising in their colors and smells. I thought of the interview in *Der Spiegel* with old Georg Lukács in Budapest—he who had been the goal of the Dutschkes's honeymoon—about which I remembered and still remember mainly the Kilim carpet with geometric patterns that hung on the wall behind the low sofa or bed that the philosopher was sitting on; and again one single sentence.

Georg Lukács, small and wrinkled, glancing up from that sofa that looked like something from a student's apartment, was quoted in *Der Spiegel* as saying, "Lenin was against it." He was talking about the unions' role in the Soviet state, if I'm remembering the interview correctly (if, indeed, it happened and was carried in *Der Spiegel* at all). At some point Trotsky had, as usual, probably been representing the most radical and hard-line position possible in a discussion with Lenin, while Lenin was still clinging to whatever meager remnants of the reality principle still survived in Russia in 1920. Thank God, those things that people in the Soviet Union in the early 1920s argued and shouted about are no longer of any interest whatsoever. But in 1969, it was still all about eternal truths, scary dragons, and naively sweet fairy tales. It seemed at the time that they had left the branches, hollows, and roots of *the stem of Jesse* behind—the Jewish-dissident, communist-surrealist, libertarian tradition of the 1920s—and joined our reality, right into the lobby of the Tübingen basement theater. Lenin and Bukharin spoke to us with the same immediacy as the murdered anarchists, reformers, feminists, and fighters of the 1920s. We were now they. We believed that we would carry their tradition forward. The dead spoke from us, and our voice became Romanian-Jewish—causing, for example, our Luckenwalde-bred leader to roll his *r*'s as if he were broadcasting from a historical newsreel.

In my next memory of Ernst Bloch, I'm carrying a raised red banner bearing the emblem of the MSB Spartakus. On a dramatically dark October or November day of muted colors, thousands of us are standing on a tree-lined road or square somewhere outside Tübingen's old town center. Very soon, people will start to give speeches, or they already have done so. The speeches have something to do with increasing state-funded scholarships (of which, in any case, I was not a beneficiary), or some other claim on the government that had been refashioned according to the sharply anti-monopolistic demands of *the masses* that would break *the System* according to Leninist principles. Dusk falls, but I am warm in my new leather jacket (a gift from my mother). Ernst Bloch's voice rings out from a tape recorder over the square or the road.

I was not even paying attention to the content of the philosopher's speech. It was as if he were participating in a film, but even he, if asked, would not have known exactly which film it was. (I have no idea how the Tübingen student association got the ninety-one-year old man to record this statement that presumably had little to do with our demands.) Be that as it may, as soon as his voice sounded, my new leather jacket and I found ourselves in another time, in a country saturated with ghosts. Goebbels, Hitler, and Göring were not yet in Berlin, victorious. In a coffeehouse, Walter Benjamin gets together with the owner of the voice that is resounding over the square in 1976 and asks his wife, Carola, whether she has ever noticed the sickly appearance of the marzipan pigs. Soon, my grandfather will stand under the lindens, in the light of the torches, under the waving hand of the wooden, almost mummified Hindenburg, and he will see roses flying through the searchlights, and his prewar hopes resurrected in Adolf Hitler. Soon, my comrades in the SA's cellars and improvised prisons will be beaten until they are sick or dead. (At this point, my grandfather has already passed Tenerife and its blossoms, and the steamer is heading to Portuguese Angola.) In my own era, I am fighting against Goebbels, the SA, and my grandfather. The expensive leather jacket that my mother bought according to my specifications at Lodenfrey in Munich keeps me warm. The red flag above me waves in the October wind.

But in the year of Ernst Bloch's death (less than a year after the demonstration in Tübingen), more than the times were in disarray. It was 1977. In September, I walked for entire afternoons with my new girlfriend in the hills, gardens, and vineyards of Stuttgart. One foggy-sunny autumn day followed the next. Over radio and TV, the news forced itself into our private little world. The Red Army Faction had kidnapped the president of the German employers' association, Hanns-Martin Schleyer, murdered his guards, and thrown my country into a national crisis. In my memory, the news, updated hourly—and the feeling that my life, too, had taken a turn and that there was no going back—will always be linked with a feeling of being in love that I thought would never end; with sunny afternoons under the plum trees of Uhlbach; with endless conversations on wobbly chairs in outdoor restaurants on the Rotenberg where we had stopped to snack on ham sandwiches, drink wine, and look out into the early dusk, while, in the valley below, the lights of the city began to go on.

I had many years afterwards—much more time than the events, the memberships, friendships, and unfolding circumstances themselves took—to think about the historical confusion that came over us in the decade after 1968. Thinking about it since then, it has become increasingly evident to me that the most fitting model for the mistaken identities and ghost-appearances that took us to the edge of madness was Shakespeare's *Hamlet*. It is a literary model and also a prototype of the nervous and swashbuckling heroism, the hysterical performances, historical false pregnancies, theatrical self-deceptions and misperceptions in which we were then trapped. And now, after writing this account of my grandfather, it also strikes me that this Hamlet prophecy of 1968—the transformation of every one of us into the characters of this tragedy—must have begun sometime between 1940 and 1945 in Luckenwalde.

My family, wearing Hitler Youth shirts, silk dresses with small floral prints, and scratchy socks, smiles heroically and with fake cheeriness into the camera. Marja is terribly homesick. It is likely that she will never return and see her mother again. She will probably freeze to death somewhere, or be killed between the German and Russian front lines. Or, once home, she will disappear into a gulag as a collaborator. Who knows whether her mother didn't starve long ago in Leningrad. Who knows what became of the other Russian girls in the Luckenwalde parsonage. *(Where Kyra disappeared when the Russians were standing at the gates, whether she went to the paymaster or to Russia, we never found out—we had our own problems.)* In the meantime, fathers disappear and then reappear as strangers. "Prisoners" come to the Dutschkes out of nowhere and "work the soil." One must not let oneself be touched by them. Jews, Communists, and disabled children suddenly vanish. Policemen become murderers, walk around town during their holidays as if lost, and can no longer sleep at night. Everyone keeps it all well under wraps. No one says anything. *Something is rotten in the state of Denmark.*

Children can see ghosts. They know what adults are dreaming of. And not only a Luckenwalde child by the name of Rudi Dutschke will have known instinctively that something was not right with the town, with the country, with the world. That the adults (maybe even *Herr Superintendant Wackwitz* of the large, beautiful old *Johanniskirche* who is so near to God; maybe even God himself) knew something terrible and dreamed about something they did not speak of. It was then that Rudi's (and our) theatrical identification with the victims began, the shamanistic play within a play through which my generation wanted to metamorphose into Jews and Communists. It was then that our anger must have been born, our historic dream life, our political sleepwalking. "For us he was king and father," said Rudi Dutschke in his eulogy at Ernst Bloch's funeral. From the unconscious depths that had motivated him his entire life, he was finally saying that his and our actions in the years from 1967 to 1977 presented the novel of a Luckenwalde childhood in the form of great baroque intellectual tragedy. For if Bloch and Lukács, Walter Benjamin, Leviné, Trotsky, and Karl Liebknecht were our kings and fathers, we were Danish princes. A murder about which all are silent took our king, our father from us. He finds no peace. His ghost appears at the palace gates by the sea and demands that we avenge his murder. But we cannot be sure whether he speaks the truth. Is our uncle, the new king, really a murderer? Is our mother his accomplice? Is the specter that appears at the gray, roaring ocean really a messenger from our father, or did he rise from hell to deceive us and cast our country and kingdom into catastrophe? "O my prophetic Soul!" cries Hamlet, little as he may trust his prophetic gifts. But as prophetically and poetically as he aimlessly wanders the palace, like the political clown Rainer Langhans in Berlin's streets—"the city at the front"—or the terrorist Andreas Baader in the Bonn Republic's conspiratorial apartments and high-security prisons (stabbing innocent people and driving his girlfriend to despair): he can't get to the bottom of it. Instead he stages political performance art. Actors are assigned to their parts.

> . . . I'll have these players
> Play something like the murder of my father
> Before mine uncle: I'll observe his looks;
> I'll tent him to the quick; if he but blench,
> I know my course. The spirit that I have seen
> May be the devil: and the devil hath power
> To assume a pleasing shape; yea, and perhaps,
> Out of my weakness and my melancholy,
> As he is very potent with such spirits,
> Abuses me to damn me: I'll have grounds

More relative than this: The play's the thing
Wherein I'll catch the conscience of the King.

If the political performances of our red decade followed a strategy, it was that we acted out the fights and murders of the 1920s and 1930s as demonstratively and provocatively as possible, confronting the conditions of a country that, for all we knew, was not ours. We wanted those in power to show their real faces. So we slipped into the roles of the murdered Jewish kings, published their books in pirated editions, wore leather jackets and the newsboy caps that we had seen on the yellowed black-and-white photos and that could have been like theirs, founded parties that bore the same names as theirs. Meanwhile, we observed the slightest twitching in the faces of the mighty, always ready for the moment when their masks would fall and they would revert to their true identities as Goebbels and Hitler. But this play within a play took a turn that was as paradoxical and convoluted as in any baroque drama. In response to the play's unmasking, the silence became thicker and finally impenetrable. The King reacts (very pale, he totters to his feet), but whether he is simply indignant at the accusation, or whether his swaying and pallor are proof of real guilt we cannot know, and we become increasingly melancholy and paralyzed. Our fictions, hunger strikes, self-stylizations, founding of parties, actions, murders, demonstrations, suicides, and fake battles become ever more absurd.

In the soulful autumn light of 1977, while in the real world the police were running their computer searches, while the photographs of the kidnapped president of the employer's association, forced to hold up the day's newspaper before the camera, were broadcast on TV and became daily more humiliating until at the end they were hardly more than a blur, while Palestinian terrorists were highjacking airplanes in Africa—while all this was happening, we were walking in the hills, enjoying endless discussions in the garden restaurants of Uhlbach and Obertürkheim, on the Rotenberg, between Esslingen and Stuttgart . . . and it became apparent not only to me that things could not go on like this. And at last it was cold and foggy, and everything having to do with suicides and funerals and surprise attacks by special police units ceased. It was the autumn of the year in which Ernst Bloch, Hanns-Martin Schleyer, Andreas Baader, and Gudrun Ensslin died. Even so, a year or two passed before I found my way back to reality.

For the length of a September night in 1979, two weeks after my girlfriend had left to study for a year in San Jose, California, I lost my mind. I walked on Stuttgart's Schlossstrasse toward the city center, the streetlights casting the fine shadows of robinia branches onto the large flagstones, when I suddenly lost a previously unquestioned and unconscious sense of my identity. I spent the rest of the evening and the night in a state of panic on a friend's couch. Trying in various ways to put this experience behind me, I made it through the autumn and winter. A new decade began. Neither my grandfather nor Rudi Dutschke was alive to experience it. Is it a coincidence that Andreas Wackwitz died on the night my girlfriend drove to the Stuttgart airport, where she walked in tears through the metal detector and disappeared from my life for four months?

When the news of Rudi Dutschke's death reached me on the day after Christmas, I was visiting my girlfriend in America. As I emerged with the other passengers from the ramp at JFK, she came toward me with open arms, wearing a brown woolen suit and high-heeled boots that I had never before seen on her. She looked a little like Annie Hall in Woody Allen's movie. In the course of this autumn, she had become a woman. The Soviet army had marched into Afghanistan, and for a week we walked together through the parks, streets, and museums of New York, as intimately as if we were once again in Stuttgart. We would never again be what we had been in 1977, nor would our relationship ever be the same. But in her arms and in the streets of New York, I knew again with certainty who I was, and I know today that this had to do with the fact that on the threshold of the 1980s my grandfather and Rudi Dutschke had both been buried—the one by me, the other by us all.

We come on the ship they call the Mayflower
We come on the ship that sailed the moon
                    —Paul Simon/Art Garfunkel

18 Shipwreck

THE SHIP

Autumn has arrived for the third time since I began this
manuscript. I sit at my window, look into the garden of
Kraków's Bernardine monastery, and reflect on the events
and lives that have occupied me for the past three years.
Since the sinking of the *Adolph Woermann* in the South Atlantic, my father and I—though we neither wanted nor
planned it—seem in our own ways to have done little else
than continue the life of my grandfather, as if his life were
not only something independent of the three of us, but perhaps greater and more important.

Dawn breaks. I have been jogging and am home having
breakfast. The puddles on the promenade along the Vistula
shone in the light of the street lamps as I was running down-
river in the dark. Now the clouds are passing my window,
and the wind that descends from the Carpathians into the
plains is blowing the bare branches. In Germany, it is already
snowing. I light a cigar, and again, as so often has happened
in the early mornings of the past three years, the images of

people and places I've gotten to know through my grandfather's notebooks gather around me. This is one of the last dawns that I will spend with them. I think of Friedrich Schleiermacher in the garden of the Anhalt parsonage and of the bees in the linden that was probably planted by his father and then, in 1925, struck by lightning—an event my father witnessed as a child. I think of Eva Mandzla, the seer of Seibersdorf, of her dream of the open Bible on Saint Urban's Day in a year deep in the eighteenth century. I think of the Luckenwalde policeman who is unable to sleep at night because he dreams of women and children in the Ukraine whom he had been ordered to shoot.

I think of the *Adolph Woermann* lying in the blackness of the South Atlantic and its captain, torpedoed on a prisoners' transport to Canada in 1940 by his own navy. The British crew had already abandoned the ship and its prisoners when Otto Burfeind assumed command of the sinking steamer. He managed to get many of his comrades into the remaining lifeboats—though not himself. I think of the cigar that my grandfather smoked in 1939 with Deputy Principal Lehfeld in the lifeboat of the *Adolph Woermann* while the huge ship was sinking behind them. I think about how I recently saw a reconstruction of this ship's command bridge when I was with my son and his friend in Munich's German Museum, and how the two boys could not understand why it preoccupied me for the entire afternoon that followed. (Not long ago I even dreamed of the wood-paneled pilot's cabin that the museum curators placed toward a painted and brightly lit panorama of the port of Hamburg, so that museum visitors, their hands on the wheel, could feel like Captain Burfeind as he was preparing to ship out to German Southwest.) I think of Johann Peter Hebel's story of unexpected reunion.

I think of Rudi Dutschke. I think of Richard Rorty and the clouds in Tokyo.

When I was at my father's house at Lake Constance two years ago, he gave me the camera that had returned from the war with the words "Wackwitz Windhuk" etched with a pocket knife onto the back of its black case in November 1939. And after he had been digging around for a while in the attic, he brought down a manuscript that he had written (he no longer remembered why) in our apartment on Stuttgart's Killesberg in the 1950s. On that afternoon at Lake Constance I read for the first time my father's eight typed pages about the sinking of the *Adolph Woermann*. One of the few literary pieces that he ever finished, strangely and probably quite unconsciously influenced by Arno Schmidt and Uwe Johnson, it struck me immediately as perfect in its way, the best thing of its kind he had ever written.

Then we sat in the garden and drank wine. The old man told me for the first time of his memories of Deputy Principal Lehfeld, who had returned from Sumatra and whose cigar box was the source of the smoke that he and my grandfather enjoyed on a lifeboat on the high seas while the *Adolph Woermann* sank, and who then went with my father to Canada as a prisoner of war. He told of the friendships among the twenty-year-old prisoners in the camp. Their mentor Lehfeld (under whose tutelage, in forests far from the sea, they were studying for their high school diplomas), fat and full of longing, in love with all of them, probably had gone to Sumatra because such longings had made him unemployable at home. Our story doesn't end here, though I'm leaving it. And Deputy Principal Lehfeld is, as we shall see, not the most unfitting of its characters to wave us goodbye from his invisible country, even though until now he has appeared only at this story's margins.

But now, at the very end, he steps forward. I have sometimes thought that my father probably described Deputy Principal Lehfeld so well and so precisely on those eight typed pages in order that both of us, as Germans living outside the country, might have a model, one who was less Protestant, dry, reactionary, and oppressive than our own father and grandfather. It was as if he needed Lehfeld to balance my grandfather in the lifeboat, so that we would be forever safe from capsizing. And the unusual and deeply respectful tolerance that Andreas Wackwitz and Captain Burfeind accorded their eccentric peer seems to me a much more beautiful message from the land of the dead than if a camera that survived the century had preserved a picture of my grandfather and Deputy Principal Lehfeld as they rocked and smoked on the waves of the South Atlantic.

Deputy Principal Werner Lehfeld: R.I.P.
by Gustav Wackwitz, 1956–57

Lehfeld came on board in Lobito. The ship was still docked at the pier. Later, we moved to the outer harbor. We waited, and only gradually did it dawn on us that the great war had begun. The bay was as still as lead. Later, when only the diesel tenders were going back and forth between the ships and Portuguese soil, it became difficult for Lehfeld to leave the ship or to struggle back up the rope ladder, gasping for breath like a walrus. The sweat on his bald head glistened like burned bacon grease, the wrinkles and stains on his Sumatra suit multiplied. He was always the last to leave the tender, because the sailors and the boiler men, the farmers with their open collars, and the colorfully dressed young women did not want to be waiting elbow to elbow down below while he was working his way up the ladder. When he reached the deck—his fat, trembling hands desperately clasping the wooden railing—the tender was already chugging over to the *Windhuk* or the *Wagogo*. As if drunk, Lehfeld shuffled to the salon at an angle, his long arms swinging loosely, his tie hanging off-center past his shapeless belly.

I couldn't stand him. No one really cared for him. Once when we were sitting by the *Windhuk*'s swimming pool, Sigrid Merker said, "When Dr. Lehfeld passes by, I'm afraid he'll fall over and squish me." She flew back to Southwest after the Polish campaign was over and the war was dragging on, and the English and French were unwilling to concede that they had lost. Her family had a farm in the north. Sigrid said good-bye to Lehfeld, whereupon he attempted a hippo-like bow and squawked, "Send a postcard! If we make it home, we probably won't be able to write you, and if we don't make it, you'll read about it in the newspaper."

That Lehfeld was on a German ship in a bleak South Atlantic harbor at the outbreak of war made no sense. He could have stayed in neutral Angola and founded more German private schools. It was said that he had also been in Java and the Celebes Islands. Now and then he spoke of his years in Chungking. It was rumored that he had tons of books, butterfly collections, East Asian masks, shadow-puppets, and his entire photographic studio, all sunk in the cargo hatch. "Do you know what tastes best?" he asked me, looking at the palm of his quivering hand. "The balls of your thumb." I just stared. "The balls of a young person's thumb," he said. "An old cannibal told me this. Some of them are still around." I thought: And now what? "He was a friendly old grandfather," he said. "When I left for Manila, he presented me with two especially lovely butterflies."

I laughed and he shuffled off, probably for a round of *Doppelkopp*. My father had asked him to tutor me in Latin conjugations, lest I forget the little that I had learned in school. But it seemed ridiculous, and I balked. Five, no six years later we were sitting together after all, dissecting Cicero.

One night in November 1939, the *Windhuk* and our *Adolph Woermann* left Lobito Bay. On the pier under the lights, a few Portuguese police waved their arms about, but the telegraph office was closed, and the British consul was not able to pass the news on to Cape Town until the next morning. We pushed our way around the spit of land, the Milky Way stretched over the sea as though it had been poured, Scorpio lay on the horizon. The *Windhuk* tore into the night, the green sea spraying as it passed, and we limped behind at thirteen knots, heading west. The escape was a success. We passengers, too, had been told nothing; Lehfeld had gone to Benguela on the same day and was barely able to make it back by train.

I can still see him as he stood at the railing with his protruding belly. Behind us, the after mast swayed among the stars, and Lehfeld was laughing. He gurgled and groaned, until his voice—he could not control it—became very high and asthmatic. People were standing in groups on the deck, their shoulders tense. Everything on board vibrated. We had reached the open sea and were on our way. The heavens were turning around us, shining green plankton was splashing high beneath us, the ship—a black, untamed mass—groaned and hissed. The tar smelled fresh again, and we were off: cowboys and Indians between Africa and Brazil. Cigarettes glowed in cupped hands.

Lehfeld gurgled. I despised him. I was alive, I hissed along with the gurgling of the ocean and dug my fingers into my upper arm, flexing my muscles. Renoldi stood next to us. Lehfeld giggled over to him: "All my laundry is still on land! An armful of shirts. The cackling in the laundry tomorrow! Just imagine it! The small black women! They'll all want to take at least one shirt home. But they're afraid of the boss. He'll want to take some, too, but he's afraid of our Consul General. And he—he's afraid as well!" He was seized by another attack of asthma. "And I'm rid of the shirts!"

I couldn't bear him. I went up to the forecastle and leaned over a chair toward the bow and screamed down into the glowing double cataract that the bow lifted out of the sea—finally! (Shirts! The Idiot!)

The ship was repainted. The Portuguese *Nyasa*, which had almost the same outline as our ship, had left Lobito the day before. After two days we were covered in beautiful war paint and had become the *Nyasa*. Without enough oil to get us to Santos, we used copra for fuel at night. Copra—we had two thousand sacks of it in the hold—lets off lots of black smoke, but at night that was not a problem. All the men worked. Every day I took my shift in the crow's nest. The ocean was like a landscape. I was surprised to see Lehfeld carrying copra down below. The old hippo.

At the latitude of Saint Helena, we came into the sights of an English freighter. It was faster than we were and had a cannon. Probably following instructions from Simonstown on the Cape, it stayed within range, and even at night we could not escape, as the weather remained clear and the other ship had its searchlight on us. We practiced the rescue drills, and our emergency luggage stood ready. The cruiser was sure to come the next morning. And it did, while I was eating my porridge.

On the last evening our *Doppelkopp* game never really got going, although Lehfeld and Wackwitz, Sr., pretended otherwise. Three thousand tons of vanadium ore, 180 meters of ship, steel and beautifully polished wood: down it went—5,000 meters! (Only the oranges in the crates on deck would be bobbing about in the water.) And then us, into the boats. The sea was friendly in spite of the old ladies who were always playing solitaire, in spite of the ten or twelve children, in spite of old Mr. Wiese, who could hardly crawl any more. The weather was clear. Captain Burfeind spoke with Mrs. Drews and took the pipe out of his mouth, stood for a while with fat Otto and finally signaled to the head steward, an oily, bloated ape, that he shouldn't sell Otto so much wine that evening, as he'd need his balance the next day. Laughing, he ran into Lehfeld at the door to the promenade deck. Lehfeld was much bigger than the captain. Gargantua and Volpone.

The English reappeared at our stern, playing around us like a puppy. The spotlight on their bridge had been turned on at full beam, chalky light and shadow cast the contours of our ship out of the night and the black swell of the ocean as if it were a stage set. Lehfeld stood in the doorframe enveloped by an aura like the sun in an eclipse. He and Burfeind greeted one another ceremoniously with a handshake. "How long will it last, *Herr Kapitän?*" "Until Christmas, or longer. What are you smoking there, *Docteur?*" "Dannemann. Care for one? They last longer." "Thank you. Smells good. I'll save it for tomorrow." "When everyone's off the ship?" "In which boat are you sitting, *Docteur?*" "If *I* sit in it . . . the boat that displaces the greatest amount of water." Burfeind nodded. I listened. They understood one another. "Maybe we'll end up in the same camp," said the Captain. "By the time we get back to Hamburg, you'll know how to play *Doppelkopp*," said Lehfeld. "*Herr Kapitän*," said the Second Officer, suddenly appearing. "Please . . ." "I'd better be off," said Burfeind. "See you at Philippi!" said Lehfeld. (Burfeind did not return to Hamburg. In June 1940, when a large British ship carrying prisoners of war was torpedoed northeast of Ireland and sank within twenty minutes, he quelled a panic that had broken out on deck and managed to get a few lifeboats into the water. He went down with the ship.)

The cruiser came for us the next day. We got into the boats, everything went well, the children hardly cried, a drunken sailor fell between the wall of the ship and the side of the lifeboat, a few women got seasick.

Initially our boat was the scene of some excitement. Lehfeld was missing. We had helped steer him and the two elderly ladies with whom he was playing solitaire into the lifeboat, and there was a bit of teetering. And then Lehfeld disappeared, the lifeboat was supposed to have been lowered, the petty officer cursed. Next we saw Lehfeld staggering over to the railing, dragging two mammoth suitcases, grunting and rasping and hissing to the petty officer—"Oh, *Doktor*," cried Miss Wunsen, "our suitcases!" "Suitcases!" moaned Miss Höderling, "oh *Doktor!*"

The two good ladies had indeed forgotten their suitcases. Lehfeld dragged them over, and the petty officer pulled them into the lifeboat, after which Lehfeld rolled himself into it. "Lower it!" screamed the petty officer. "Ugh!" groaned Lehfeld. "You idiot! Can't you wait until we're ready?" But the petty officer was busy, three or four oars pushed the boat from the side of the abandoned ship, and then it fell heavily into the swelling sea.

We lay for a time like ducks on the lee side of the English freighter. Thin sailors looked down on us from the deck,

smiling and calling *"Führer kaput"* but they above and we
below were quite comfortable with one another. The boats
went three to four meters up and down against the wall of
the ship. My father and Lehfeld were crouching together on
a bench, and a Chinese man was vomiting into the green
water behind them. Suddenly Lehfeld took a leather cigar
case out of his stained Sumatra suit and offered my father
a Dannemann. "Lehfeld," said my father, "I will never forget this." And the gentlemen lit the fat Brazils and smoked.
And then Lehfeld began to gurgle again, asthmatically. It
was grotesque. For a long time he could not speak. The face
of the ship's violinist sitting across from him became ever
greener. Lehfeld searched awkwardly in his pockets, pulled
out a toothbrush that he held in front of his nose and turned
lovingly back and forth. He was able to speak again: "Look!
I did it! *Omnia . . ."* he growled, *"Omnia—omnia sua se-
cum!* And a handkerchief!" He had left his suitcase on
board. "Oh, *Doktor!"* groaned Miss Höderling.

The cruiser picked us up. Everything went smoothly. My
youngest sister, looking downwards the whole way, was
hauled up in a wicker basket. By the time we got on deck,
she was in the arms of a young officer and eating chocolate.
"A charming young lady! Here you are, madam!" he
laughed and handed Anne over to our shaken mother. We
stood together on the afterdeck. When our ship didn't sink
quickly enough, the British shot at it until it caught fire, and
then it disappeared quickly. At the end, just look!—the
lovely South African oranges in the green Atlantic! The English crew cheered, and we broke into a three-fold *Sieg-Heil*
for *Führer* and fatherland. Then we were taken below deck.
The women and children stayed in the cabins of the commander and the British officers, who moved out immediately and slept with the crew in hammocks. Within half an

hour, we had received a letter from the commander saying that he greatly regretted not being able to provide us with better accommodations, but as we could probably see for ourselves—and, indeed, we saw it—his own men did not have it any better. This was the Royal Navy.

We sailed across the equator. In Freetown, we encountered another large cruiser and continued in convoy to England. At the latitude of Gibraltar, U-boats sunk two of the convoy's ships, but we made it safely to England.

In Plymouth, we said farewell to the women and children, who were sent across the Channel to Germany a few days later. My father was interned with me. I found the whole business irritating, like a shirt that doesn't fit. Then I saw Lehfeld. One couldn't miss him. He had a bad cold and was blowing his nose. As it had been a long time since he had lived in Germany, there was no one for him to send regards to. (He had gone to China in the 1920s after his fiancée had run off with his friend. But I learned this only many years later. In any case, when I was seventeen, it would have left me cold—in Plymouth, in the December dusk, in the port; seagulls screeching in the mist, the women trying not to cry. Black battleships lay in the port.)

But Lehfeld was blowing his nose like a trumpet at Jericho. He wobbled over to dark Gerda. She was standing next to tall Peter who worked for Lufthansa, and her hair brushed against his arm. He didn't know what to say either. Paralyzed as if under tons of deep sea. So Lehfeld came over to her. Clearing his throat, he sounded like the chain of an anchor: "Now look at him. Not at me—at him! Right. The beanpole. Stands there and doesn't want to leave. But he has to. Harrumph!!—Now, child, look at me. At me." She looked at him. "Just think," he cawed, "how lucky you are! At least it's not me you're having to part from. That wouldn't

hurt at all.—Harrumph! Wish I had another handkerchief!"
She gave him hers, although she could have used it herself.
The deep sea was lifted, they breathed and stretched their
legs, laughed a bit, and Lehfeld padded off.

Then for a while, I lost sight of him. Perhaps for five
months. We met again in a camp, and then we were separated again. Four years later, I saw him in Canada. He was
still very fat, but his face had aged. We lived together in a
small wooden hut, he, I, and thirty other men, among them
the small baron, and Paulus Heerwagen from Accra, Ivan
Konarsky from Tokoradi, old Timmermann, Dreeger from
Lagos, the ball of fire, the retarded man, Stinky Socks, whose
bunk was in the corner, and . . . Lehfeld. He was called *Ursus lavans*, the raccoon. With the passion of someone very
determined, he washed everything that wasn't clean. He also
forced others to do their washing and helped them. He rum-
bled and grunted, he gnashed his teeth and butted in with
his 550 pounds and the hot zeal of a hero. And in his vicinity, camp life smelled a little less sour than otherwise.

When he made fires in the winter, the coals would tum-
ble from the shovel because his hands were always trembling. Once in the course of a nap, he managed, tossing
about and groaning, to knock over a cup of milk on the
empty steel mattress-frame above him. The milk dripped
onto his bald head. Tiedemann was furious, Paulus disappeared stiffly into the washroom, and Stinky Socks slept on.
Lehfeld just lay there and laughed. Finally he was laughing
so hard that people came over and stood around him, until,
in the end we were all laughing.

In the camp, he founded a school, naturally. We were
twenty young people who, thanks to him, graduated from
high school in the Canadian forest. What was buried inside
us, he coaxed out. We had a few very good teachers—but

what would have become of me without Lehfeld? He ran with us, with Heinrich Prätorius, with Gerd Abt, and me, laps around the barbed wire; we played *Doppelkopp* and learned to tell Horace from Ovid, and not only by the meter of their verse. Young sailors arrived, and he would pore over dictionaries with them. We had better teachers than him, especially Isermeyer, with whom we dug into Goethe for half a year and acted *The Merchant of Venice*, twice through until dawn, very happy; and Hägele, the Swabian Simpleton (as I thought of him). We had wonderful teachers.

But it was Lehfeld we loved, the *Ursus*, the hippo, the homeliest colossus under the sun, the Knight of the Funny Figure, gnashing his teeth, quivering, Hercules in the Augean stables. And he loved us, as Socrates loved Alcibiades. And like all Germans living abroad, he loved Germany with a terrible, blind longing. The war burned out. It was horrible. Dresden. Berlin. We didn't believe the horror stories. Once, in England, at three in the morning, I heard Lehfeld's anguish. He couldn't suppress it entirely. One day he was ill. He lay in the infirmary, where I found him quite changed, with a voice like a child's. He didn't say much, and the doctor wouldn't let me stay long. But he said I should come back often. It was, as one calls it, a collapse. Nerves. It lasted a few weeks. He had also seen the first photos of Bergen-Belsen. He was kept in England after I was released. Thanks to him, I had an address in the Ruhr area where I was able to sit out the winter.

I met him once more, in the spring of 1947. Naturally, he had lost weight and had become quite wrinkled. In the morning we ate dry bread and drank *ersatz* coffee. He gnashed his teeth, and several times he called me an idiot. A year later, I received a brief note informing me that he had died in Mülheim. He had no possessions to pass on, and we have no picture of him. Heinrich Prätorius, who was at the funeral, visited me sometime afterwards. Gerd and I asked him what had happened. Heinrich said, "I think it was his anger at evil that killed Werner Lehfeld. That's the only way it makes sense." In the Latin of the Church, we say: *Requiescat in pace.*

Notes

The towns and villages of Silesia are known by both their Polish and German names, and both forms are used in *An Invisible Country:* Anhalt/Holdunów, Auschwitz/Oświęcim, Bielitz/Bielsko-Biała, Kozy/Seibersdorf, Laskowitz/Laskowice, Pless/Pszczyna, Primkenau/Przemkow.

1 Ghosts

3   The Dual Monarchy refers to the Austro-Hungarian Empire, which stretched across a large expanse of Central and Eastern Europe and included some of the area that is now southern Poland.

5   The areas of Silesia that belonged to Germany were divided into Lower Silesia in the northwest, and industrialized Upper Silesia—extending into southern Poland—in the southeast.

2 An Unexpected Reappearance

8   Windhoek (*Windhuk* in German) is the capital of present-day Namibia (formerly the German colony of Southwest Africa).

8   Johann Peter Hebel (1760–1826), German short story writer and poet.

8   The copper of Falun, in south-central Sweden, had been mined since the Middle Ages.

10   Southwest Africa was a German colony from 1884 to 1915. After World War I, it became a League of Nations mandate admin-

istered by South Africa, which maintained sovereignty over the territory through the 1980s.

12   "Calendar stories" was a term appropriated by Johann Peter Hebel for his tales. Originally, it was used to designate stories published in calendars or almanacs.

12   "Family romance" is a Freudian term that describes the fantasies a child has in which he imagines that his "true" parents are better (richer, more noble, more famous, etc.) than his actual parents, i.e., the ones who have raised him. Freud originally developed this notion in a short article entitled "The Family Romance of Neurotics," published in 1908.

3 Silence

17   The High Tatras are a mountain range straddling southern Poland and Slovakia.

19   Kaiser Wilhelm II (1859–1941), the last German emperor.

20   Friedrich von Erckert (1869–1908), a military leader in Germany's African colonies.

21   Dahlem is an area in western Berlin.

21   The Curonian Spit, a peninsula off the Baltic Sea, once belonged to Germany and is now part of Lithuania.

22   Murmansk, a Russian city on the Barents Sea, is the western terminus of the Northeast Passage.

23   Witold Gombrowicz (1904–1969), an eminent Polish writer who lived in Buenos Aires from 1938 to 1962.

25   The Day of Prayer and Repentance is a German Protestant holiday celebrated in November.

4 Chameleon Years

35   The Kapp Putsch was a four-day takeover of the government in Berlin by right-wing opponents of the new republic in March 1920. Wolfgang Kapp was designated Chancellor during the aborted rebellion.

36   Karl May (1842–1912), a hugely successful writer of German adventure novels and stories set in the American West and other exotic locales.

36   The outspokenly nationalist Hans Grimm (1875–1959) was Germany's best-known author of colonial fiction.

36   Togo (in west Africa) was a German protectorate from 1884 to 1914. Nauru, a Pacific island, was a German possession from 1888 until the First World War.

39   Friedrich Schleiermacher (1768–1834), a German philosopher and Protestant theologian with close ties to the German Romantic movement. He is regarded as a seminal figure in modern Protestant thought.

39   Brandenburg is the region of Germany that surrounds Berlin.

39   Rudi Dutschke (1940–1979) remains an enduring symbol of the tumultuous years in postwar Germany from the late 1960s through the 1970s. "Danny Le Rouge" refers to Daniel Cohn-Bendit (1945–), another figure from the rebellions of that era. He is now active in European politics as a member of the Green Party.

40   Kurfürstendamm is West Berlin's best-known thoroughfare.

5 Anomie

45   Wilhelm Busch (1832–1908), a popular German artist and writer known for his biting, sometimes cruel humor, most famously in *Max and Moritz* (1865). His *Bilder zur Jobsiade*, humorously depicting a life of relentless failure and well-deserved bad luck, was first published in 1872.

46   The Kaiserstuhl denotes a hilly area near the Rhine in southwestern Germany.

6 Invented Story

49   Joseph Freiherr von Eichendorff (1788–1857), a writer whose poetry to this day epitomizes German romanticism.

50   *Sturm und Drang* refers to the German literary movement of the 1770s and 1780s that signaled a rebellion against the restraint and decorum of the previous decades.

50   Johann Wolfgang von Goethe (1749–1832) and Friedrich Schiller (1759–1805) were identified with the *Sturm und Drang* movement in their early works, though later they exemplified the ideals of German classicism.

50   The Illuminati, closely related to the Freemasons, enjoyed about ten years of existence, from ca. 1776 until the late 1780s.

51   "Schinderhannes," or Johann Wilhelm Bückler (1783–1803); the "Bavarian Hiesel" is the name given to Matthias Klostermaier (1736–1771).

56 The Thirty Years' War was fought from 1618 to 1648.

56 The reign of Frederick the Great (Frederick II) (1712–1786), king of Prussia, began in 1740.

57 Thuringia and Coethen-Anhalt are regions in central Germany.

58 Karl Barth (1886–1968), an influential Swiss Protestant theologian.

58 *Bewusstseinsphilosophie* translates as "philosophy of consciousness" and is used to designate Johann Gottlieb Fichte's premise that the objective world is constituted by the subject's own consciousness and reflection, and therefore open to active mental, political, social, and spiritual change.

58 Friedrich Hölderlin (1770–1843), a great poet; and Georg Wilhelm Friedrich Hegel (1770–1831), an influential philosopher.

59 Johann Kaspar Lavater (1741–1801), Swiss theologian.

59 Johann Kaspar Hirzel (1725–1803), Swiss educator, doctor, and politician devoted to the ideals of the Enlightenment.

59 Like Friedrich von Schiller, Jakob Lenz (1751–1792) was a poet and dramatist. Johann Gottfried von Herder (1744–1803) was a philosopher and critic.

60 The Peace of Hubertusburg (1763) concluded the Seven Years' War between Austria and Prussia, leaving Silesia under Prussian control.

62 The Breslau Board for War and Domain was an administrative agency of the Silesian government.

7 Four Wars

69 *Skat* and *Doppelkopp* are popular German card games.

72 Robert Musil's *The Man without Qualities* is one of the great modernist novels of the twentieth century. It was never completed.

72 The Herero are a Bantu people in southern Africa.

72 Patrice Lumumba (1925–1961).

72 Dag Hammarskjöld (1905–1961) was killed in a plane crash in Africa.

72 Nikita Khrushchev (1894–1971).

86 Ernst Jünger (1895–1998), German writer, was best known for his aesthetically heightened renderings of war and violence.

87 Max Beckmann (1884–1950), German painter.

88   The Spartacus party (1916–1818) was the socialist precursor of the German Communist Party.

8 In the Emperor's Palace

93   Gebhard Leberecht von Blücher (1742–1819), a Prussian military leader during the Napoleonic Wars.

94   Caspar David Friedrich (1774–1840), a German painter, known for his landscapes suffused with religious symbols.

98   *Treu* means "faithful" (corresponding to "Fido").

98   The *Gartenlaube* was a magazine that epitomized German middle-class values in the second half of the nineteenth century.

99   Franz von Lenbach (1836–1904).

9 An Island in the South Pacific

106   The full quotation (from Horace's *Odes*) reads "Dulce et decorum est pro patria mori": it is sweet and right to die for your country. It was a byword in the early days of the First World War and provided the title for Wilfred Owen's famous poem.

10 An Invisible Country

118   Paul Celan (1920–1970), born in Bukowina (now in Romania), was probably the greatest poet writing in German in the years after World War II.

119   Wojciech Korfanty (1873–1939).

120   Adalbert Stifter (1805–1868, Austria), Theodor Storm (1817–1888, Germany), and Gottfried Keller (1819–1890, Switzerland) were three of the nineteenth century's greatest writers of German fiction.

11 Five Professors, Dreams of Jürgen Habermas

125   Lars Gustafsson (1936–), a Swedish writer who teaches at the University of Texas in Austin.

127   Jürgen Habermas (1929–).

128   Heinrich Böll (1917–1985), Nobel Prize-winning novelist; Peter Brückner (1922–1982), psychologist and activist; and Walter Jens (1923–), writer and critic, were/are prominent left-liberal intellectuals.

128   *Der Spiegel* is Germany's major newsweekly.

128   Botho Strauss (1944–).

129 Marcel Reich-Ranicki (1920–), Polish-born and Jewish, is Germany's best-known contemporary book reviewer.

132 The German Second Republic refers to the present-day Federal Republic of Germany, founded in 1949.

133 Eckhard Henscheid (1941–), a German novelist, strongly influenced by Italo Svevo.

137 Joseph Roth (1894–1939), a major Austrian novelist.

141 *Powstancy* is a Polish word designating the participants and organizers of an uprising.

143 The philosophy of Johann Gottlieb Fichte (1762–1814) was a wellspring for German romanticism, as well as for German nationalist thinking. His *Addresses to the German Nation* (1808) concerns German identity and German education and is associated with the beginnings of nineteenth-century German nationalism.

144 Immanuel Kant (1724–1804).

144 Friedrich von Schelling (1775–1854).

145 Peter Handke (1942–), Austrian author.

146 Jósef Piłsudski (1867–1935), Polish general and left-leaning, authoritarian politician.

146 Mikhail Tukhachevsky (1893–1937), Soviet general.

146 White Poland refers here to Polish supporters of Czarist Russia.

151 Henryk Jordan (1842–1907).

151 Rahel Varnhagen (1771–1833) and her Berlin salon played an important role in German literary life of the early nineteenth century.

152 Karl Kraus (1874–1936), Austrian writer famous for his excoriating wit.

153 Arthur Schopenhauer (1788–1860).

12 Abandoned Rooms

158 Gustav Frenssen (1863–1945), a popular German novelist whose *Peter Moor's Journey to Southwest Africa* (1907) depicted the Herero uprising against the Germans (1903–1907) from an aggressively racist viewpoint.

159 Gustav Freytag (1816–1895), novelist and playwright, popular in his day, now seldom read.

159 Arno Schmidt (1914–1979), major German writer (e.g., *KAFF auch Mare Crisium*, 1960, and *Zettels Traum*, 1970).

160 Cuxhafen is the last German town passed by ships that sail from Hamburg to the North Sea.

160 *Weizenbier*, a light, wheat-based beer.

160 Pannonia, a southeastern European province of ancient Rome.

161 "The time of Marcus Aurelius" refers to the second century C.E.

161 Sorbs are a Slavic people, also known as Wends, who live in eastern Germany.

161 The chronicle of Thietmar von Merseburg (975–1018) remains an important source for the history of the early Middle Ages.

162 Biedermeier alludes to a style popular in the first half of the nineteenth century. It represents straightforward simplicity and solid hominess.

13 The Jacaranda of Madeira

169 Kurt von Schleicher (1882–1934), Hitler's immediate predecessor as German chancellor.

169 Paul von Hindenburg (1847–1934).

169 The SA ("stormtroopers") grew out of the Nazi Party, whereas the Stahlhelm ("steel helmets"), also a para-military force, had been founded as an organization of World War I veterans.

170 Alfred Hugenberg (1865–1951), industrialist, press and media baron, and far-right politician, was Minister for the Economy, Agriculture, and Food in Hitler's first cabinet.

170 Franz Seldte (1882–1947), founder and leader of the paramilitary, anti-Weimar *Stahlhelm*, was Hitler's Minister of Labor.

170 "Lo, how a rose e'er blooming" is a popular German Christmas hymn.

172 David Lloyd George (1863–1945) led the British government during the second half of the First World War and was instrumental in shaping the Treaty of Versailles.

173 Walther Rathenau (1867–1922).

173 Ernst von Salomon (1902–1972).

173 Max Weber (1864–1920), eminent German sociologist.

173 After the First World War, the Saar region became an autonomous region under French administration.

174 Grimm's "Kaempffer, ein junger Deutscher" was published in his collection, *Das Deutsche Südwester-Buch* in 1929.

175 Yasushi Inoue (1907–1991).

177 *L'Education Sentimentale* (1869), a novel by Gustave Flaubert.

14 Tale of the Snake

178 Eduard Mörike (1804–1875).

178 On November 8, 1939, Georg Elser (1903–1945) planted a time-bomb set to assassinate Hitler. Several people were killed, but Hitler had left the hall shortly before the bomb went off.

178 Charles George Gordon (1833–1885), Governor of Sudan, was killed two days before the arrival of British relief forces that ended the ten-month siege of Khartoum.

182 "Unheard-of event" was a term devised by Goethe for his famous definition of the novella.

183 *Heart of Darkness* was first published in 1902.

183 Samuel Maherero (ca. 1854–1923), Paramount Chief of the Herero from 1894 until his death in exile, and leader of the 1904 uprising.

15 Murder

187 Thomas Müntzer (1489–1525), a Protestant reformer whose radicalism secured him an exalted status in the pantheon of the German Democratic Republic.

187 The Lada automobile was first manufactured in the Soviet Union in 1967.

187 The church of the Cistercian Zinna monastery was built in the twelfth century.

188 *Lebensraum* (literally "space for living") refers to Germany's perceived need to expand its territory for eventual German settlement, especially into Poland.

190 *People without Space* (1926) was Hans Grimm's best-known work.

190 Sebastian Haffner (1907–1999).

193 *The Magic Mountain* was first published in 1924.

195 Paavo Nurmi (1897–1973), a great Finnish runner who won nine Olympic gold medals in the 1920s.

195 MSB Spartakus (Marxistischer Studentenbund Spartakus) was one of the most active and prominent of the radical student

organizations in Germany in the 1970s. The national organization was dissolved in 1990, though some local chapters still exist.

195 Brandenburg is a region in eastern Germany.

196 The first *Baedeker* guides were published in 1827.

197 Hans Frank (1900–1946), Governor General of German-occupied Poland.

201 Bethel von Bodelschwingh is a charitable clinic with close ties to the Lutheran Church. It was founded in 1867.

205 Margrit Schiller (1948–), a radical active in the 1970s.

205 Ulrike Meinhof (1934–1976), captured in 1972, committed suicide in prison in 1976.

16 Minor Prophets

207 The Pythia was a Delphic priestess, known for her trance-like prophetic states.

207 "Death-wing" was the expression used to describe a floor of a prison on which only a single prisoner was held.

207 Gudrun Ensslin (1940–1977), a leader of the Red Army Faction until her capture in 1972. She killed herself in Stammheim prison on the same night as Andreas Baader and Jan-Carl Raspe.

207 Holger Meins (1941–1974).

207 Jan-Carl Raspe (1944–1977).

208 RAF is the acronym for the *Rote Armee Fraktion,* or Red Army Faction, the "official" name of the group also known as the Baader-Meinhof Group or Gang. It came into existence in the late 1960s and had more or less disappeared by 1973, though it was not officially disbanded until 1998.

209 Heiner Müller (1929–1995) and Volker Braun (1939–) were among the best-known writers of the German Democratic Republic.

210 Otto Schily (1932–), a lawyer for RAF activists in the 1970s. Later he entered mainstream German politics, first in the Green Party, and then as a Social Democrat.

211 The "German autumn" alludes to six terrible weeks in September and October 1977, beginning with the kidnapping and eventual murder of Hanns-Martin Schleyer, the president of the national employers' association, and concluding with the triple suicide of Baader, Ensslin, and Raspe in Stammheim prison.

213   The Jeu de Paume is a museum in central Paris, now housing contemporary art but known until 1987 for its collection of French Impressionist paintings.

17 The Dead

215   Chicago-born Gretchen Dutschke (1942–), Rudi Dutschke's widow and biographer.

218   Georg Lukács (1885–1971), a Hungarian Marxist philosopher and critic.

219   Carola Bloch (1905–1994), wife of the Marxist philosopher Ernst Bloch (see below).

219   Ernst Bloch (1885–1977), German Marxist philosopher. Having fled the Nazis, he left the United States after the war for the German Democratic Republic, but in 1961, he and his wife moved to the German Federal Republic.

219   Peter Weiss's *The Persecution and Assassination of Jean-Paul Marat as Performed by the Inmates of the Asylum of Charenton under the Direction of the Marquis de Sade* was first performed in Berlin in 1964.

220   Hermann Hesse (1877–1962).

221   Vladimir Lenin (1870–1924); Nikolai Bukharin (1888–1938), Russian Communist theoretician.

222   The expressions "stem of Jesse" and "root of Jesse" appear in Isaiah, Chapter 11.

222   Tübingen is a university town in southern Germany.

223   Walter Benjamin (1892–1940), German philosopher.

223   Lodenfrey is a venerable Munich clothing store.

226   Walter Benjamin, Eugen Leviné (1883–1919), Leon Trotsky (1879–1940), and Karl Liebknecht (1871–1919) were all Marxists of Jewish origin. Leviné, Trotsky, and Liebknecht were murdered. Benjamin, fearing that he would be captured, killed himself while fleeing the Nazis.

226   Rainer Langhans (1940–).

18 Shipwreck

232   Uwe Johnson (1934–1984).

242   Bergen-Belsen was a concentration camp near Hanover.

STEPHAN WACKWITZ is the director of the Goethe-Institute in Bratislava, Slovakia, and holds a Ph.D. in German literature. He is the author of two novels and an essay collection. *An Invisible Country* is his first book to appear in English.

WENDY LESSER is the founding editor of *The Threepenny Review* and the author of six books of nonfiction.

STEPHEN LEHMANN is a translator and the co-author of a recently published biography of the pianist Rudolf Serkin.